THE CHURCH AT THE CROSSROADS

THE CHURCH AT THE CROSSROADS

S. Vasanthakumar

Christian Institute for the Study of Religion and Society (CISRS)

&

Christian World Imprints™

First Published in 2018 by

Christian Institute for the Study of Religion and Society (CISRS)
Rev. Dr. Vincent Rajkumar, Director, CISRS
73, Miller's Road, Benson Town
Bangalore 560046 / Karnataka
cisrsblr@gmail.com
Phone: 080 23332981, 09980036926

&

Christian World Imprints™
Christian Publishing & Books from India
H-12 Bali Nagar, New Delhi-110015
info@christianworldimprints.com
www.ChristianWorldImprints.com
Phone: +91 11 25465925

ISBN: 978-93-5148-264-2 (HB) ISBN: 978-93-5148-265-9 (PB)

Cataloging in Publication Data--DK
Courtesy: D.K. Agencies (P) Ltd. <docinfo@dkagencies.com>

Vasanthakumar, S., author.
The church at the crossroads / S. Vasanthakumar.
pages cm
ISBN 9789351482642 (HB)
ISBN 9789351482659 (PB)

1. Church of South India--History. 2. Church of South India--Missions. 3. India, South--Church history. 4. Church and social problems--India, South. 5. Christianity and other religions--Hinduism. 6. Hinduism--Relations--Christianity. I. Christian Institute for the Study of Religion and Society, Bangalore, publisher. II. Title.

LCC BX7066.V37 2018 | DDC 287.94 23

Dedicated to the fond memories of
BISHOP KENNETH EDWARD GILL
Bishop of Karnataka Central Diocese: 1972-1980

A Spiritual giant, Visionary leader,
Administrator *par excellence,*
Compassionate friend,
And above all, a Spiritual mentor for all
Young pastors, including me.

Contents

Moderator's Forward

I am immensely delighted to find that a meticulous reflection on 'the Life, Ministry and Mission of the Church of South India' by Most Rev. S. Vasanthakumar entitled as 'The Church at the crossroads' is being published by him. This book is valuable and unique because this book incorporates his immense ministerial experience, enormous knowledge of CSI and substantial expressions as a minister as well as administrator of the church. Bishop Vasanthakumar is a dear friend of mine and God has blessed him with a sharp intellect and he along with his wife Rev. Nirmala Vasanthakumar contributed very much to the Church of South India in its ministerial journey. He is a person vested with a historic mission.

Bishop Vasanthakumar was an able administrator of CSI as deputy moderator and moderator in the Church of South India in its difficult times. His exalted vision for the CSI Church enabled him to create many historical movements in the Church. Bishop Vasanthakumar's life and vision, thoughts and writings are inspirational not only for the CSI Church but also to the wider Christian Communities in India. As he acknowledges in his books in all humility, he was not a learned or trained historian or theologian, but his unending quest and search to find the true ministerial and missiological facts made him to produce all his initiatives during his tenure as a church leader. By explaining the church as a community or communitarian characteristics of the Church, he pushes it further and throw light on the missional nature of the Church.

There is an insatiable urge in him to present the historical journey of CSI church in India in all its authenticity and diversity. He was always focused in his ecumenical mind and vision and never allowed anything to distract him from his vision of the church. The whole life of Bishop Vasanthakumar was committed to the faith journey of the church in all its dimensions and explains it to the public in a clear and meaningful way. He was successful in making intelligible observations from the perspective of a bishop/minister. It is this intellectual underpinning, he gave to the readers and all that implies that characterizes his writings. The readers can easily make a co-travel with the Church of South India, during his period by listening series of minute events which is quite unaware to many of us.

Bishop Vasanthakumar in his very inspiring book named as 'The Church at the crossroads' speaks of the primary role of the Church as reflecting Christ to people around us. The first chapter of this book invites each one of us to make clear observations on our 'inheritance' (history of the church) in its richness and fullness. The deep rooted Hinduism in this soil is not a monolithic religion rather it is a collection of diverse beliefs and practices. To attain the ultimate goal of life ***moksha*** or ***self-realization*** one has to opt any one of the three margas-***Gnana Marga, Bhakti Marga*** or ***Karma Marga***. It is in this context and different religious and philosophical background, Christianity started its journey in this land. The journey starts from the St. Thomas Traditions to Catholic tradition to Protestant Missionary movements which is mentioned in the second chapter 'heritage'. This book provides enormous life experiences, struggles, attempts and engagements, service and success of the Christian church in this life journey in its qualitative terms and it should not be quantitative. The reformation reformed the whole concept of faith and practice prevailed in 500 years back. The missionary conferences and the derivation of the comity principle paved the way to the reformed practical thinking in mission and ministry. The church in the local areas developed in association and in fellowship with the other religions like Hinduism and other ideologies. This chapter also deals with the heritage which deals with collective tradition or collective past of the Church.

The major allegation against the Christian missionaries in India was they are 'hand in glow' with the East India Company and the ruling class (Government Officials). The third chapter clearly explains the crux of early missionary work and its varied dimensions. He narrates the development of this missionary work and its spiritual formation in an ascending order. The missionary work of the church is the participation in God's mission, ***Missio Dei*** since our God is a missionary God who not only sent prophets and committed people but His own son Jesus the Christ. Missionary functions in this country develop from personal salvation, human compassion (charity oriented), social transformation and upliftment of the downtrodden people upto financial emancipation of the common people. This narration ignores all the previous allegations about the Christian missionary work, like soap-soup-salvation.

The criticisms of Christian involvement in the socio-political as well as religious sphere of this country are an inevitable task to sharpen our thoughts and deeds and redefine our commitments. Bishop Vasantha's analysis and evaluations of the challenges of Christian Mission in this country are done by the perspectives of the criticisms from within-from various Christian ideologies and philosophies, the various Christian communities and from Indian Christian Theologians and from the Hindu Communities-Hindu organizations, militant Hindu forces and also from different Dalit movements within the country. This self evaluation is very much needed in a period like today for self correction and further meaningful engagement for a better world.

Asia, within Asia, India is the cradle of Spirituality and spiritual thoughts. This spirituality is not related to any of the religions rather relational with the Supreme Being, God. This chapter attempts to show that Christian Spirituality is in tandem with the Indian Spirituality and not in opposition. Both the spiritualities begin from individual and ends with the Divine. When we find true spirituality it will encourage us to move to the other dimensions of spirituality, spirituality of service and spirituality of engagement etc.. Spirituality of service will lead us to community building process. Indian social structure is basically premised on caste system and we need to find out ways and means to surpass this social evil only through making Christ communities. Early Christian missionaries showed us the way in which Christian communities formed and participated in the mission of God (***Missio Dei***) and we need to perceive similar experiences to establish a borderless church.

The last three chapters thoroughly deal with the Church of South India-its organizational structure and functions, administrative measures and leaderships, property management and resource mobilization, its mission and vision. Being a person who travelled the nook and corner of the various dioceses of this great church, Bishop Vasantha narrates the historical developments and moves which he witnessed very closely. There is spiritual presence in his writing when he talks about the church with all its vulnerability, diversities, deficiencies and richness. The chapter 'CSI-A Democratic Church' is a self critic assessment of the structural as well as functional aspects of the church while 'CSI-A Mission Focused Church' critically evaluates the missiological foundations, models and the agenda of the CSI church with respect to this matter. The Concluding chapter replicates his conceptual framework and visional attitude of a church in the phase of new challenges. The golden thread that runs through his writing is the necessity of being a true spiritual church, the fundamental conceptions that we had during the formation of the united church. Surely this writing will definitely have a seminal influence on the future generations in helping them to know more about the development of Christianity and Church of South India.

Bishop Vasanthakumar is a person who contributed significantly to the church and society in different parts of the world where he got exposures. The strength of the present day church is the active involvement of the laymen who can contribute immensely to the development of the church. Though CSI dreams of the emergence of such a category, unfortunately the category of such laymen is decreasing nowadays. Bishop Vasanthakumar always upholds the Christian perspective of giving and not considering what we get back from any engagement.

I offer my congratulations to the author Bishop Vasanthakumar. May this book help the readers know about CSI more clearly, to love this church more dearly and to walk with CSI more nearly for establishing the Kingdom of God in this part of the world. My heartfelt wishes and prayers.

Kottayam
01. 09. 2017

Most. Rev. Thomas K. Oommen
CSI Moderator &
Bishop in Madhya Kerala Diocese

Preface

The inspiration to write a book on 'the Life, Ministry and Mission of the Church of South India', (CSI in brief) came to me under strange circumstances. It was a decade ago, when I was the Deputy Moderator of the Church, in one of the CSI Synod meetings we were discussing the different ways of celebrating the 'Diamond Jubilee' of the CSI which was to take place the following year, i.e. 2007, in a befitting manner. Many programmes were chalked out, one such being reflecting on the life, ministry and mission of the Church. A suggestion was made that the work should be entrusted to a well-known theologian of the Church teaching in a theological college. I opposed the idea of entrusting the work to a theological teacher and insisted that it should be done by a Church worker, who has experience at the grass-roots level. I elaborated my position with the following arguments. A theologian reflects from the perspective of 'normative principles' based on the Scripture and the resources available in the library. In this process, a theologian might question the relevance of the Church. A social scientist reflects adopting 'operational principles' as a starting point, based on the data available through surveys, census and other such material. A social scientist in his/her conclusion refrains from passing judgement but only records the findings. On the other hand, a Church worker's only strength is his/her experience in the day-to-day working of the Church. A Church worker, therefore, begins the reflection from the stand point of 'the Church as it is'. The existential reality of the Church is the starting point for a Church worker, which would lead to an 'action-reflection' process in the minds of the people concerned.

Listening to my arguments, the then General Secretary threw a challenge at me to take up the task personally. The challenge came to me so suddenly that for a few minutes I did not know how to react. It was the Bishops who were present at the meeting who goaded me to accept the challenge. I accepted the challenge on condition that the Bishops would help me as Consultants. Thus, began my journey to reflect on the life, ministry and mission of the Church.

The first approach I had, was to prepare small write-ups on various aspects of the Church and present it to the Bishop's Council, which the then Moderator of the CSI, Bishop Sugandhar was kind enough to convene whenever I made the request. The discussions were elaborate, insights thought provoking and concerns expressed genuine. The one aspect that emerged very strongly during these deliberations was the rich variety of beliefs and practices prevailing in the Church, even though we are a united Church. To illustrate the point: the CSI unequivocally affirms its faith in the Trinity. However, some believers emphasize the transcendent nature of God and so approach reverently. Others see the centrality of Jesus Christ in Salvation History and in their own personal struggles and aspirations. Some others would depend on the empowerment of the Holy Spirit in their helpless and hopeless situations. The Church has no hesitation in accepting all these positions of the believers. Another illustration: The CSI has accepted representative form of government based on democratic principles, but never thought of imposing uniformity in governance. Based on the former practice of earlier denominational churches, it has allowed each Diocese to formulate its own constitutions, subject to the same being not 'at variance with the provisions of the CSI Constitution'. As a result, some Dioceses have a four year term, some three and some two years for their Diocesan Council. Again in some Dioceses, the Treasurer of the Diocesan Council is elected by the Diocesan Council and in some others the Treasurer is appointed by the Executive Committee on the recommendation of the Bishop and in other Dioceses a Presbyter is appointed as the Treasurer while in others only lay people hold the office of the Treasurer. I remain grateful to the Bishops for bringing home to me afresh the rich variety of faith and practice prevailing in the Church. The lesson that I learnt was that 'unity in diversity' is at the heart of the Church's life. This experiment of consultative process had to be stopped when I stepped down from the post of Deputy Moderator.

The Church of South India is often described as a 'litigant church'. To a great extent this description is true. I was elected as Moderator of the

Church of South India in January 2010, in a miraculous way, in the midst of Stay Orders from the Court and the vacating of the same by a higher Court. Thereafter, from day one till the day I demitted my office two years later, it was a constant battle against court cases. The cases were both civil and criminal in nature, against individuals as well as the corporate bodies. The cases were not just limited to election disputes, some of them were for non-compliance of the statutory rules under Company Laws, Income Tax Laws and Foreign Remittance Acts. The cases were filed in different courts throughout the geographical jurisdiction of the Church. Others were filed before statutory authorities. Some were taken to the High Courts and the Supreme Court. In all these cases, the interesting factor is that the Church was never a plaintiff but always a defendant. Initially the complaints were filed by some members of the Church before statutory authorities which ultimately ended up in litigation. There were times when Officers of the Synod had to seek refuge in remote areas to avoid being arrested – and this for no fault of theirs, until such time relief is sought from the appropriate Courts. This prompted me to think of the reasons for such litigations in the Church, which will be analyzed in later chapters. To say the least, I have experienced the ugly side of the Church.

The third experience which I would like to narrate here is equally impressive. The then Mysore Diocese of the Church of South India, while accepting a new constitution for the Diocese, introduced a new chapter called 'City Mission', based on the initiative taken by the Madras Diocese in this regard. The purpose was to identify Christians living in the newly formed layouts in and around Bangalore and help them to form worshipping centres and later to be developed as full-fledged congregations so that they become effective witnesses to the Lord in those areas. Under the leadership of the Bishop, the Diocesan Executive Committee appointed the then Rev. W V. Karl, who later became the Bishop of Karnataka Northern Diocese, as the first Director. As a result of his hard and sincere work a number of congregations were newly formed in the suburban areas. The Karnataka Central Diocese continued with the tradition under the new title 'Urban Church Extension'. Kothanur CSI Congregation is a result of this effort. It started as a 'house group' in the home of a congregation member in the year 1997 and was recognized as a congregation by the Diocese in the year 1999. A piece of land was purchased for both the Parsonage and the Church in the year 2002. The Church building was constructed and dedicated in the year 2006. The Church which began with a few families worshipping in the home of one of its members has now grown to 350 families with a membership of more than 1000 on its roll. Worship Services are conducted in Kannada, Tamil, English and Hindi. Its membership comprises of an interesting blend of people speaking different languages drawn from the four Southern States of our country and some from States in the North India as well.

When I laid down my office as Bishop of Karnataka Central Diocese in the year 2012, I became a member of this congregation. The first thing I did was to inform the congregation members that I would not accept any form of leadership role including preaching and conducting Worship Services. Initially, the congregation members were not happy with my decision, for they hold me in highest esteem, not only as the Bishop of the Church, but also as one who helped them in recognizing the congregation, posting a Presbyter for pastoral care, helping them to acquire land for the construction of Church and Parsonage, completing the Church building in 2006 and Parsonage a few years later. But, they gradually began to respect my decision. The purpose of taking this decision was to study beliefs and practices and behavioral pattern of congregation members, not from the perspective of a leader, but purely from the point of view as an ordinary member of the Church. Thus, I became a participant cum observer in all the activities of the Church. This has paid rich dividends. I could observe the congregation from an entirely different perspective, a 'view from below'. I began to see things which I did not not fathom as a leader.

I observed three basic characteristics of the congregation which of course is not alien to other congregations. Firstly, it is a *spiritually oriented community*. People come to the Church for spiritual nourishment. It is not just a social gathering but a community looking for spiritual empowerment. Hence, the church building becomes a holy place and the altar represents the presence of God; the Pastor becomes a representative of God channeling the grace of God to the faithful; prayers help the people to concentrate on God; preaching from the Word of God motivates them to new possibilities in their life; and the Holy Communion deepens relationship of individuals with God and fellow believers by way of receiving and sharing the grace of God. This in a nutshell is the starting point of a spiritual journey of the congregation.

Secondly, it is a *participatory community*. The spiritual journey is not a one-way street – from God to the Pastor and to the members of the congregation. It takes place among the members also. The number of activities that take place are indicative of the efforts of the members in strengthening their spiritual life with one another. Children taking part in

Sunday School and Worship Services; Youth leading 'Praise and Worship' for the whole congregation; Women offering their voluntary service in various activities including teaching in Sunday School; Choir leading the worship through music and singing; regular meeting of a group to pray for various concerns; Bible Study groups meeting in different homes every week; Men's Fellowship members visiting the sick and comforting them through prayers and above all the congregation members expressing solidarity with the members of a bereaved family by their physical presence and prayers. These are some of the activities in which members of the congregation actively participate and offer their services willingly and voluntarily. All these programmes take place with or without the assistance of the Pastor. In short the members share their spiritual values with one another. I note that while participating in all these activities parochial considerations like language, status, gender and caste have never been a hindrance. They are together as a community of the faithful around the Table. Therefore, it is a participatory community.

Thirdly, it is a *community looking beyond itself.* The goal of spiritual empowerment is not for self-aggrandizement, as otherwise it will end up as a self-centred community. The congregation is aware of this fact. Thus, many individuals are involved in supporting mission activities through various organizations – such Mission agencies are in abundance in India. But the mission activities initiated by the congregation have attracted my attention. The first one is 'Bagalur Mission', a village on the outskirts of Bangalore North, located at a distance of about 10 kilometers from our Church. The congregation has not only placed an Evangelist there, but has also started a Pre-school for the children, conduct Sunday Worship, organize Sunday School and most importantly the medical personnel from the congregation visit the place and conduct medical camps regularly. All these programmes are conducted for the benefit of the poor in the village, irrespective of caste. The second mission activity of the congregation is the support extended to the transgender community through a mission worker. The interesting part is to bring the members of the transgender community to participate in the worship service and allow them to share their experience with the congregation members along with a brief presentation on the ministry extended to them by the missionary. The third mission activity is teachers conducting coaching classes for poor children from the larger community to prepare them to face the examinations confidently in order to obtain School Leaving Certificate. The result has been a resounding success for the last several years and many of the children have returned to thank the teachers. These illustrations prove that this congregation is ready and willing to share their spiritual gifts with the less privileged in order to empower them in their own context.

This is not a perfect community, for at the time of election or at the time of finding suitable life partners parochial considerations like language, region and caste may raise its ugly head. But, the congregation has the willingness to overcome parochial considerations and move ahead in forming themselves into a model community with spirituality as the basis and service to society as the focus. Such a community can truly become 'a basic ecclesial community' as the Latin American Theologians would describe – a community grounded in faith, growing together by nurturing one another and serving the society around it, without expecting any reward. For me, this is the most beautiful experience of the life of the Church.

A note about the book: Even though the challenge to write my reflections on the Church came to me a decade ago, I was not in a hurry to complete the task; because first of all I wanted this to be a spiritual exercise for myself evaluating my own faith and actions of the past in the light of my study and reflections. I wanted to understand the true meaning of spirituality. I wanted to discern the dynamics that operate in Church and Society and their inter-connectedness. There was no compulsion whatsoever, either internal or external to complete the task undertaken. However, the recent diagnosis by the Doctors that I am suffering from Chronic Lymphocytic Leukemia (CLL) and the subsequent treatment schedule prompted me to complete the unfinished task. In this new situation I have realized that I was not alone. The compassionate treatment given by the doctors and nurses, the loving care and support extended by members of my family – both immediate and extended, the sympathetic understanding exhibited by my friends, the assurance of prayers by a vast number of believers all over the Diocese and outside, above all the constant prayerful support extended by the worshipping community that I belong to, have all played their part in instilling new hope in me. In particular, I must mention the three public testimonies presented by three individual members of the congregation:

Janet, a young house-wife is suffering from breast cancer and has been under treatment for the last several months. When she was able to lift her left hand she decided to come to church to play the violin during the church service as her way of expressing her gratitude to God for bestowing health on her.

Joseph, who met with a nasty accident while travelling to his home town in his car and as a result, he had to be hospitalized for more than three months. Then one day he came to Church on crutches and gave a testimony declaring that Jesus protected him even in the midst of such a nasty accident.

Dr. Veena, a professor of Dentistry who had to undergo a complicated double valve replacement surgery. She literally went through the experience of death on the operation table and she was assured of health by a voice from above. She recovered totally even to the amazement of the doctors who were treating her. She gave a testimony stating that Jesus, her Lord gave her a new life.

In the face of the strong faith exhibited by these three people my own faith appeared to be fragile. My faith in God's healing power was re-inforced tremendously by their testimony. I realized that it is the people of God who are the reservoirs of faith and not the Bishop. I was also convinced that preaching, teaching and healing cannot be compartmentalized. Together they form a wholistic mission. Therefore, in appreciation of unwavering spirituality of the ordinary congregation members who practice their spirituality in their day to day struggles in life, I decided to complete this unfinished task pending in my life.

The intent of the book is to provide assistance to the members of the congregation in their search for spirituality in day to day life situations. Hence, simple language is used bereft of theological jargons, technical phrases, while cross references are minimal. However, an academic may find the inter-disciplinary approach used in the book interesting. Further, I am conscious that experiences are subjective. They vary from person to person, depending on the context in which one finds himself/herself. The experiences provide valuable insights to change the course of history. They may also lead one to be bitter about the unjust treatment meted out to him/her. They may also prompt one to glorify his/her achievements in the midst of difficult circumstances. Hence, I have used my experiences, very sparingly, however, whatever appears in the following pages is based on experiences. I offer these reflections to the faithful members of the Church with a hope that it will help them in their spiritual journey.

Though the book bears my name, in actual fact, it is the outcome of the contribution of many people in various ways. The journey began with the acceptance of a challenge posed by the then General Secretary, Mrs. Pauline Sathya Murthy and prompted by the CSI Bishops during the period 2005 – 2007 to accept the challenge. The desire to write was nurtured by the enthusiastic participation in the discussions and preparatory papers presented at the Bishops' Council convened by the then Moderator, Bishop B. P. Sugandhar. But for this initial push, the flame would have been extinguished long back. Hence, I owe my thanks to the then General Secretary, Moderator and the Bishops for having fired this desire of writing my reflections on the Church.

Two of the Bishops continue to encourage me even after my retirement and theirs. Bishop V. Devasahayam would enquire about the progress over the telephone. Whenever he was in Bangalore, he would make it a point to visit me and impress upon me the need to complete the work. He even initiated a discussion on finding a suitable Publisher for me. The role of Bishop P. J. Lawrence is even greater. He would never miss an opportunity to encourage me either through personal visits or over the overseas telephone calls. But for the generous financial assistance extended by Bishop Lawrence and Mrs. Shanthi Lawrence, this book would never have seen the light of day. I am deeply grateful to Bishop V. Devasahayam, Bishop P. J. Lawrence and Mrs. Shanthi Lawrence.

CSI Kothanur Church of which I am a member for the last 5 years and in which I have participated as a 'participant cum observer' has given me a new perspective of the Church itself. The members' enthusiastic participation in the Church activities without being prompted by the leaders and their willingness to look beyond themselves has brought home to me the depth of their spirituality, particularly their care, concern and solidarity expressed through prayers for me when I was under treatment made me feel that it is possible to build 'a basic ecclesial community' at the congregation level. In short, this congregation has taught me a life-time lesson of 'viewing life from below' as a cardinal principle of spirituality. To this congregation I owe my gratefulness for having introduced 'course correction' in my thinking.

The conducive atmosphere and the constant encouragement given by my family members is invaluable. My wife, Nirmala, being a Church worker herself was a great support for me. She would enter into discussion with me on various issues, particularly on issues affecting women and children. My son, Amar, and daughter-in-law Preethi provided all moral support needed for my work. My daughter, Arpana and son-in-law Rajiv, downloaded important articles from the internet and ordered books which are not easily available in bookstores. Our helper, Mrs. Veniamma kept my library spick and span every day. My driver, John Christopher, willingly took me to meet different people. Above all, I enjoyed the probing questions

– such as, 'If your book is based on experience, why do you read all these books? Or if you are writing to the congregation members why don't you write in Kannada instead of English?' – posed by my grandchildren, Varun and Vivan. I cannot forget to mention that the prayers offered daily by my mother, Kanakamma for me, her other children and their families have been a great spiritual strength for me. To all of them, I remain grateful.

Mrs. Jessie Shiri who has been a friend of Nirmala and myself from our student days at United Theological College has been a great blessing for me. She would borrow books for me from the UTC Library whenever I needed them. I am thankful to her. My special thanks to Mrs. Patricia Job who has painstakingly deciphered my manuscript, typed the draft, introduced corrections and prepared the manuscripts for publication. Apart from this she also gave comments on the flow of thought, contents, missing points etc. I am extremely grateful to her.

I express my grateful thanks to Dr. A. Ebenezer, my good friend from school days, who later became the Principal of Bishop Cotton Boys' School, Bangalore. Having undergone a surgical procedure for throat cancer himself thirteen years ago, he understood the inner turmoil of a person suffering from such life-threatening disease. He used to visit me regularly and encourage me to face the challenge courageously. He even came forward to share the cost of publication expenses.

When the draft manuscript was ready I gave them to different people for their comments – Bishop Devasahayam from the perspective of a theologian, Bishop Lawrence from the perspective of ministry, Rev Nirmala Vasanthakumar from the perspective of women, Mr. Prashanth Solomon from the perspective of a layman, and Mr. Richard Nathaniel on the presentation of the book. Some of their comments are incorporated in the final manuscript and I am indebted to all of them. In particular, Prof. Richard has meticulously and patiently gone through the book, sentence by sentence, correcting grammatical and punctuation errors and made suggestions to rephrase sentences for greater effect, my sincere thanks to him. However, some errors may have inadvertently crept in, for which I am solely responsible.

While my grandson Vivan was graduating from El Santos Pre School and Child Care, I noticed an art work which was used as a backdrop of the stage which was very creative. On enquiry I was told it was the work of none other than the Director of El Santos, Mr. Jerine Santo. When I approached him with a request to design a cover page for my book, he readily agreed and produced it as his contribution to the Church. I am deeply grateful to him for capturing my vision for the Church rooted in the soil.

While we were discussing the various options for publication of this book, Rev. Vincent Rajkumar, Director of Christian Institute for the Study of Religion and Society (CISRS) offered to co-publish along with Christian World Imprints publishers. I am deeply indebted for their creative, prompt and excellent work in the art work and printing work.

Finally, I am ever grateful to the Most Rev. Thomas Oomen, Moderator of the Church of South India for having agreed to write the Foreword to my book.

S. Vasanthakumar

Introduction

'Reflection on the Church' is a complex process. Firstly, it has to take into account the faith of the Church. This faith is given - either handed down from the past or formulated from time to time or both. Faith is central to Christianity. It demands individual believer to shift the center from oneself to God and in His salvific actions in and through the Cross and Resurrection of Jesus Christ. It calls on the believer to rely on God's continuing empowerment through the Holy Spirit. It requires a believer to cast oneself entirely on the goodness and mercy of God, without seeking scientific explanation for the same.

Secondly, reflection has to be mindful of 'beliefs and practices' of individual believers. This is largely influenced by the socio-economic-cultural and political conditions prevailing in and around the life of believers. For instance, the beliefs and practices of a believer living in a free society is different from a believer living in a totalitarian regime, where the State regulates every realm of life including religious beliefs and practices. So, the socio-economic-cultural and political factors that influence the life of the Church need to be analysed carefully.

Thirdly, the Church is not just a collection of individual believers. It is a community of faith. The believers gather together to form an organized religion and adopt a suitable structure to govern themselves. Broadly speaking, three types of structures have been adopted in the Church. They are: 'monolithic', 'democratic' and 'autonomous'. These structures are adopted with good intentions that they would enhance the quality of life among its adherents. But sometimes, the structure itself can become a hindrance to further the quality of life and in such cases conflict arises which can destroy the very essence of community life. Hence, the structure that the community of believers adopt for themselves needs to be analyzed thoroughly. Since the focus of this reflection is only the Church of South India, the structure adopted for the governance of this Church will be analyzed in the following pages.

Fourthly, the adage that 'the Church is the only club that exists for its non-members', which is universally accepted, is also true in the case of the CSI for the mandate comes from the Lord Himself, as found in the New Testament texts such as Matthew 28:19 and 20; Luke 4: 18 and 19 and Luke Chapters 9 and 10. The Constitution of the CSI which did not have a Chapter on 'Mission of the Church', in the earlier editions, filled the vacuum by incorporating the same in its 2003 edition after discussing the same in the CSI Synod in January 1999 and duly ratified by the Dioceses in 2002. The new Constitution proclaims in the beginning of Chapter III that 'the Church exists for mission and by mission' and commits itself to 'carry on the mission of God in the world'. In the body of the Chapter the CSI has accepted the 'wholistic mission' as its cardinal principle for the existence of the Church. The beliefs and practices and the structure of the Church need to be examined sincerely and their course corrected if the Church truly wants to be effective in its mission.

Fifthly, the community of faithful or 'the people of God', as the New Testament describes do not live in isolation. They live and work in the midst of people of other faiths and interact with people of other faiths in their day-to-day activities. The beliefs and practices of the neighbours, therefore, make an impact on the lives of the believers either positively or negatively just as believers' live and do the same things in the lives of neighbours who do not share the same faith. In the long run, these influences end up as 'traditions' or 'culture' which would be followed without much difficulty. Similarly the Church as an organized body cannot be oblivious of the existence of other religions. The Church has to examine concepts, beliefs and practices prevailing in other religions, in the light of their own precepts and practices and arrive at a conclusion whether some of them could be adopted or rejected for the benefit of the common life of the Church. While this principle applies to the attitude of the Church towards all religions, the predominant religion in the geographical area of the CSI, being Hinduism, only the influences of Hinduism on the Church and reaction of Hinduism towards the Church are discussed in the subsequent pages.

Sixthly, the Church has a history, either denominational history or in the case of the CSI, the history of the United Church. Past events, activities, development and experiences transmitted in a written form for the benefit of future generations are described as history. Knowing the past is important to understand the present and plan for the future. History is more than just the narration of dates, events and important personalities. It also reflects the underlying struggle and aspiration of groups, movements and communities. As in other denominations, the CSI is also blessed to have historical documents, which the present generation can use to understand the Church's history. But, on a closer look one detects that the available historical records portray two distinct types of writing. The first, historical records penned by missionaries that can be described as, 'history of missionary movements'. For they describe the activities of the missionaries rather than the communities they served. The second, historical records written by Indian Christian leaders. In the initial stages all the academics, including the historians were from the 'upper castes', for education was made available to the oppressed section of society only through the efforts of the missionaries and therefore, the emergence of leaders from those communities took considerable time. The Christian leaders from the upper castes had nothing but contempt towards Christian communities coming out of 'lower caste' groups. As a result they did not even hesitate to describe Christians from lower caste groups as 'rice Christians'. Hence, the historical records that we have with regard to Christian communities are either 'missionary history' or interpretative history by the upper caste Christians, the history of the communities were not their primary concern.

The history of Christian communities in India is buried in oral tradition. One has to dig deep into these oral traditions to discover some skeletons of their history based on the indications given by the people of the community themselves in passing on their history from generation to generation orally. To buttress the point, I would like to narrate two incidents from my childhood days. I used to spend my holidays in my grandfather's village. Every evening my grandfather used to tell stories and particularly of the spreading of the Gospel in the villages of Mysore. As a child, dedicated to God, I understand that my grandfather used to visit the temple in the 'Male Mahadeswara' (Temple of Mahadeswara in the hills). On one such visit, my grandfather who was a young man at that time found a leaflet containing 'the Lord's Prayer'. The very first words in the leaflet 'Our Father' attracted his attention, and began to wonder who is this 'Our Father' and not just 'my father'. Thus, began his search for 'our father'. He went from village to village in search of this inclusive god, which led him to my native village, where he met a Christian named Sunandappa who had returned from the tea estates of Ceylon. He was married to a local girl and lived there. He taught my grandfather about this 'Our Father'. He was so touched by the story of the Cross of Jesus that prompted him to walk all the way to Mysore to invite the Methodist Missionary to come to his village and start a congregation by conducting Baptism and Worship Service, which they did in the year 1923. He, himself along with his children and a few family members were baptized, one of them being my mother who was 3 years old at that time. My grandfather was named 'Dharmappa' – a person searching for truth and my mother 'Kanaka' – pure gold. My grandfather offered his own house to conduct Worship Service. The Worship Services used to be vehemently opposed by Orthodox Hindus accusing missionaries of converting people by inducements. But, my grandfather withstood all the onslaughts and thus began a worshipping community in that village. This finds a passing remark as 'baptism in Kirugunda' which had 'disturbed the orthodox Hindus' by Bishop N. C. Sargant in his book *From Mission to Church in Karnataka* (pages 14 and 15). Other historians did not even consider it worth mentioning the motivation of the people of this village to accept Christianity as their religion. To my knowledge, in all the villages in the entire Mysore District which includes the present District of Chamarajanagar where people accepted Christ as their Saviour and not a single person received any monetary benefits or agricultural lands or houses from Missionaries. All were small land holding farmers and continue to be so even today.

The second incident that I would like to recall is again from my own family history. While on the one hand Christianity was fast becoming a village movement, simultaneously, a cry for freedom from Colonial rulers was also gaining momentum under the charismatic leadership of Mahatma Gandhi. He went to every nook and cranny of every State throughout India. He visited a place called 'Badanavalu' in Mysore District. My father, as a young man attended this meeting walking all the way covering about 25 kilometers. He was inspired by the speech of Mahatma Gandhi and came back to the village determined to start a 'Cottage industry' by learning to weave khadi. He further taught the family members to weave and supplied the material to Holdsworth Memorial Mission Hospital to be used as bed sheets. Though, his profession was agriculture and sericulture, he took up weaving not only as an income generating project for the family but also, to demonstrate his commitment for 'swaraj' as envisaged by Mahatma Gandhi. His faith in Christ did not alienate him from his avowed commitment to patriotism. He was considered as the leader of the community not only by the Christian community but also by the people of other faiths as well, till his last breath.

The purpose of narrating the above incidents is not to enlist my background but it is to draw some lessons for us today. I am sure such stories are found in every family and group that has accepted Christianity. Firstly, the available history of the Church in India is a history of the missionary societies and not of the families and groups who have accepted Christ as their Saviour. In the missionary history, the families and groups were nameless people counted only as numbers in their 'sheepfold'. Secondly, the educated 'upper caste' Christians looked at them with disdain and condemned them as 'rice Christians'. Thirdly, the authentic stories of family and groups, who accepted Christ remain buried in the forgotten pages of history. They have to be 'resurrected' to become truly authentic. They are transmitted only through the medium of 'oral tradition' from generation to generation. But, there are two problems in this process. The memory fades away in due course of time and further, in transmitting there is a possibility of myths being mixed up with the true story. So, to get at the real story of the Christian community one not only has to dig deeper and look beyond the annals of history but also, has to 'demythologize' the contents. This is a herculean task and only the affected people can undertake such a venture. A ray of hope is that from 1970's onwards leaders emerging from oppressed communities are now beginning to realize their responsibilities and are making attempts to take the believers to their roots, through their writing.

Keeping the above concerns in sight, the chapters are organized as follows:

The first Chapter is entitled 'Inheritance'. Inheritance is what is passed on from the previous generation to the present generation. A person inherits a property left behind by his/her predecessors. He or she does not need to work towards acquiring such a property. It comes to them by virtue of belonging to that family of ancestors. It is not just the assets but even liabilities are also passed on from generation to generation. The three distinct phases at which Christianity entered into India are St. Thomas tradition, which is supposed to have begun in the First Century itself; Jesuit Mission of the Roman Catholic Church in the 16th century and the Protestant Missionary Societies in the 17th and 18th and 19th centuries. Whatever the denominational package it may have come in, Christianity, had to deal with people with a civilization of 5000 years, having their own beliefs, customs and practices. While interacting with the people of other faiths and particularly of Hinduism which is a majority religion of the locals, the Church has inherited certain qualities. This chapter explores the qualities that the Church has inherited which have affected the life and mission of the Church both positively and negatively.

The second Chapter under the title 'Heritage' explores the common heritage that the Church has received from the Missionary movements. While 'inheritance' and 'heritage' can be used interchangeably, 'inheritance' traces its origin to personal history, whereas 'heritage' traces its history to the collective past. The past needs to be celebrated as well as critiqued for the benefit of the future. The heritage that the church received from the missionary movements is enormous and only a few essential qualities are highlighted in this chapter.

When the Gospel confronts human beings in their own context, it produces 'response'. All responses may not be the same. They differ from person to person and group to group as described in the Parable of the Sower found in Mark Chapter 4. The scope of the Gospel, methodologies that were used, motivation of the people in accepting the Gospel, and various types of responses are identified in Chapter 3, which goes with the caption 'Spiritual Formation'.

Religion operates both in private life as well as in corporate life. It is both voluntary as well as institutionalized. It has vertical and also horizontal dimension attached to it. It is here and now as well as beyond history. While individual and groups may respond in one particular way, the 'reaction' of the organized religions, when confronted with each other would be totally different. Some of the 'reactions' in response to the impact of the Gospel, both from within and also from outside the Church are elaborated in Chapter 4. This Chapter is entitled 'Religious, Cultural and Social Resurgence'.

Usually when one talks of spirituality, it is always referred to individual spirituality and very rarely to community spirituality. In Chapter 5 an attempt is made to explain the true meaning of spirituality as it relates to community. In the light of this understanding the salient features of the early Christian communities are also explained.

The effort of the Union Negotiators in working towards a United Church, as well as, a National Church, with a deep commitment to Mission of God is the subject matter in Chapter 6. It is entitled 'The Pilgrim Church'.

The CSI has tried to integrate spiritual with the secular by adopting democratic principles of governance. The challenges involved in a democratically administered church with spiritual concern as a main focus is discussed in Chapter 7.

The Church can forget its missionary call only at its peril. What it means to remain as a mission focused Church is discussed in Chapter 8, taking three Biblical modules as pointers in the right direction. The mission practices in the Church are also discussed in this Chapter.

In the final chapter, a few suggestions are given, as possible ways of remaining on the way of the Cross in order to continue our pilgrim journey in thc mission of God.

I have used my experience and observation as well as my vision for the Church as a basis for reflection. It is both subjective as well as objective in its presentation - subjective in terms of reflection, but objective when it depicts the realities of the Church.

I do hope that both these aspects would help the readers to reflect for themselves on the Ministry and Mission of the Church.

Chapter 1

Inheritance

India is considered as a land of spirituality. The quest for spirituality is ancient. It dates back to 2000 B.C. This ancient history is a religious and cultural history. Civilization in India emerged in a cultural setting. Culture, in turn was intertwined with religion. The discovery of artefacts at Mohenjandaro and Harappa in the Indus Valley and the excavations of stone cuttings at Lauriya and Taxila are instances of cultural heritage of ancient India. The art and culture depict religious beliefs and practices of ancient people. Therefore, religion and culture are inter-related in ancient India. It's main goal is to search for an authentic spirituality. In this search, ancient India has produced spiritual giants called '*Rishis*' who conquered the desires of the world by renouncing everything that could be described as 'worldly'. It has produced thousands of wandering saints called 'sadhus' to transmit the spiritual values to ordinary people through their preaching and teaching. It produced eminent scholars to articulate their faith in a systematic manner. It has also kindled the desires in ordinary men and women to discover truth from within their own tradition. Therefore, the quest for authentic spirituality stems from religion, which in later years is described as 'Hinduism'.

But, Hinduism is a complex phenomenon. It has certain distinctive features unlike other religions. Firstly, it does not have a founder, like in Christianity, Islam, Buddhism, Jainism and Sikhism. So, when there are conflicting views on issues one cannot take refuge in the founder to defend one's own position or interpretation. Secondly, the Hindu scriptures primarily are *Rig Veda, Sama Veda, Yaju Veda and Atharva Veda. Brahmanas* describing sacrificial rituals and *Upanishads* portraying the hidden religious thoughts emerged during the period 2000 B.C. to 1000 A.D but, none of them has attained the status of 'canonical scriptures' as in the case of the Old Testament and the New Testament for Christians. The different interpretations may emerge from the Scriptures but not necessarily dependent on them. Thirdly, there is no central organization in Hinduism which legislates its faith and doctrines, beliefs and practices, rules and regulations as well as conduct and behavior of all its adherents. Each sect and more so each individual can explore and follow one's own spiritual path depending on the spiritual status that he or she occupies.

Despite all these distinct features Hinduism has held a sway over its adherents during the course of its religious history. It is because it does not insist on right doctrine, right knowledge and right conduct. It allows freedom to individuals, groups and sects to explore true meaning of their faith in their own contexts. It never considers others' beliefs and practices as 'apostate', but only as 'a way of life', within the corridors of Hindu faith. 'It is a way of life,' is the description a majority of Hindus give concerning their faith. For this reason, Hinduism is often described as '*Sanatana Dharma*'. The root word for 'Sanatana' comes from the Sanskrit words *'Anadi'* and *'Anantha'* which means that which does not have a beginning or that which does not have any end. It is more like the concept of 'Alpha' and 'Omega' of the Christian Church. Therefore, 'Sanatana' means eternal and everlasting, perennial without the beginning or the end. The word 'Dharma' is also derived from the Sanskrit root word *'Dhri'*, which means holding together. Almost all the scholars are of the opinion that the word *'Dharma'* cannot be adequately be translated into any other language, without losing its essence. It denotes divine law, passed on from generation to generation; one who follows Dharma is a seeker of divine wisdom; follower of justice and righteousness; eternal principles; fulfilling one's own duties faithfully and sincerely.

Sanatana Dharma, therefore, has two dimensional meanings attached to it. The first one is divine nature of the Dharma, it is God who created and Dharma is not founded by human beings; it pervades all human nature but never confined to one particular doctrine. It is transcendent but makes abode in the hearts of people; it includes all shades of opinion and never sits in judgement over the other. The second being the human side of Dharma, in order to reach the highest goals of Sanatana Dharma, one has to make conscious efforts. Every individual has to find appropriate methodology in pursuing that goal. Individual spiritual exercise is of paramount importance in seeking such goals. It is not the doctrine that matters but the approach that counts. It includes all experiences as valid and never rejects any of it, as irrelevant. Through these spiritual exercises one reaches the goal of Sanatana Dharma. Sanatana Dharma, therefore is rightly described as 'a way of life'. But the way of life, to a large extent is conditioned by the 'view of life'. Hence, it is necessary to unravel the 'view of life' in Hinduism in order to understand the 'way of life'.

As mentioned earlier, Hinduism is a complex phenomenon. It pervades all aspects of human life. Both the view of life and way of life are enshrined in Hinduism. For the benefit of a common person, the four different aspects of Hinduism to the extent that they make impact on Christianity are described hereunder:

1. Philosophical Hinduism

One of the main questions being asked in the arena of spirituality is in regard to origin, nature and destiny of human beings. In order to systematically answer this vexed question, a number of philosophical systems have arisen during the course of history. Of these three philosophical systems – all originating from the South, have occupied prime importance among all Hindu traditions.

The first one is *Advaita* philosophy, propounded by Sri Shankarachary. Shankara was born in Kaladi in the northern part of present day Kerala, became a Sanyasin and a religious teacher at a very young age. He travelled all over India and established four *Mutts* (religious schools) one in Sringeri in Karnataka, the second at Puri in Orissa, the third at Dwaraka in Gujarat and the fourth at Badrinath in the Himalayas. The system that he has expounded has come to be known as *Advaita* – a non - dualistic philosophy developed in the 7th Century. The core principles elucidated in this system are:

- Brahman, the supreme cosmic spirit alone is true and ultimate reality. He is infinite, changeless, omnipresent, omnipotent and omniscient.
- The universe, material objects and individuals are all illusory – *Maya.*
- The spirit of the human-beings is identical with supreme being but entrapped in the life cycle of Karma.

- *Moksha* or salvation is attained when a person transcends the conditions of time and space and through meditation realizes the absolute unity with the ultimate reality.

The second system is called *Visishtadvaita* (qualified non-dualism) philosophy. The prominent person who expounded this system was Ramanujacharya, a religious teacher at *srirangam* in Tamil Nadu during the early part of the 12th Century. The following are the essential tenets of his philosophy:

- There are three ultimate realities, namely, God, Soul and Matter.
- God is independent reality, whereas soul and matter are dependent on God. They are characteristically similar but distinct ontologically. Hence, it is *Visista* or special.
- Moksha can be attained by way of self-surrender through *Bhakti* – an enjoyment of bliss in the presence of God.

The third system, developed towards the end of the 12th Century and is called *Dvaita* philosophy (dualism). This is the contribution of Madhvacharya who lived in Udupi in Karnataka State. According to him:

- There are three ultimate realities, namely God, Soul and Matter. They are fundamentally different from one another.
- God is independent whereas soul and matter are dependent on God. This distinction between God, soul and matter are absolute and un-quantified.
- *Moksha* or salvation is attained through bhakti, a deep attachment through bhakti, a deep attachment or self-surrender to a personal God.

a. Three Philosophical Schools

It is clear from the above description that the view of life, as viewed from the perspective of the three philosophies differ from each other. However, one can see a common thread running through all the above systems. They are: the source of life is God; the universe and the individual are dependent on God; Atman – the individual soul is caught up in the life-cycle of karma. The highest goal of every individual is to attain Moksha. While for Shankaracharya the ultimate goal for every individual is to attain identity with the ultimate reality, for Ramanujacharya it is to be in the presence of this ultimate reality and for Madhavacharya it is to live in the domain of the same ultimate reality. Therefore, quest for authentic spirituality is the essence of human life. In order to attain such a goal, Hinduism has given three paths, namely *Gnana Marga, Bhakti Marga and Karma Marga.* While these paths are distinct from one another, they are not mutually exclusive.

Gnana Marga (Path of knowledge)

This path has been expounded by Shankaracharya. According to him, the spirit of a human being is released from the life cycle of karma only through the knowledge that the ultimate reality, the universe and the individual spirit are one. This can be achieved only when *Avidya* (ignorance) is eradicated and true knowledge is acquired. And the true knowledge is attained when the individual self sees the ultimate reality within and around and reaches the stage to say '*Aham Brahmasmi*' (I am Brahman). This path is called Gnana Marga or the path of knowledge. Gnana Marga places emphasis on the systematic study of the scriptures and constant contemplation in order to reach the goal. This marga appeals to the intellect of human beings.

Bhakti Marga (Path of devotion)

Knowing the true nature of God and individual self identifying with ultimate reality was not an easy path for all. It was in this context that Ramanujacharya placed emphasis on the Bhakti Marga, which was also accepted by Madhvacharya. Bhakti Marga is a spiritual quest to experience the ultimate reality rather than the knowledge of ultimate reality. Ramanjacharya, based on the experience of mystics and poets of that time, worked out a system which appealed to the heart rather than the mind. This path leads one to experience and enjoy bliss in the presence of God, who is personal and not distant. It is through complete surrender to God one can achieve Moksha.

Karma Marga (Path of action)

From ancient times, Karma has been associated with the doctrine of transmigration of souls. Every human being is necessarily involved in work. Such actions by humans produce good karma and bad karma. These actions result in *Samsara* – a process of cyclical births and re-births. *Dwijas* – twice born, are those who performed good works in their previous births, and those who are presently at the lower rung of the social structure are those who performed bad works in their previous births. In order to escape this cycle of births and rebirths, one has to perform good works without expecting any rewards. Therefore, doing one's duty sincerely without expecting any reward leads one to a state of bliss which is Moksha.

However, the present day scholars, following Dr. S. Radhakrishna – a great philosopher and statesman – are interpreting Karma Marga as actions taken in this life, would have their impact in the next life. This Marga places emphasis on ethical living in the day to day life of an individual.

b. Spirituality for Self-Realization

According to ancient Hindu Scriptures, there are four stages of human life, which every male member of the twice born communities has to undergo in order to attain Moksha. This spiritual journey commences at the cradle and terminates at death. The first stage is *Brahmachari* or student life. In this stage a student is constantly under the guidance of a spiritual teacher, who not only teaches him scriptures but also ethical values of leading a life of purity. Therefore, the student has to lead a disciplined life, abstain from all sensual pleasures, learn to have purity of thought and be obedient to his spiritual teacher. This is the foundation of life for the student. Humility, purity of thought, celibate and simple life without any attachment to worldly pleasures, disciplined life, cleanliness are some of the marks of this stage in life. While there may be some people who remained *brahmacharis* and then became *sanyasins* later in their life; all the other *brahmacharis* have to go through the other three stages to obtain Moksha.

The second stage is *Grihasta* or married life. This stage of life permits a person to enjoy sexual pleasure by marrying, producing children, earn money in order to support his family and children, teach children spiritual values and lead a happy life, follow all rituals and practices as prescribed in the Scriptures. It is a combination of spirituality, economics, ethics and sensual pleasure that is involved in this stage of a human life. A pertinent point to note is that even today, at any Hindu marriage ceremony conducted by a priest there is a ritual called 'Kashi Yathra' (journey to the Holy Shrine in the Himalayas) wherein the bridegroom with a simple traditional attire holding an umbrella in one hand to protect him from sunshine and rain and a pot containing water in the other hand to cleanse himself and declares that he is pursuing the path of *Sanyasin*, a life of detachment from the world. Then the father of the bride goes to him and pleads with him to come back by assuring that he would give his daughter in marriage so that he can enjoy the pleasures of life.

The third stage is *Vanaprastha* (life of a recluse in the forest). After having a settled life with wife and children and enjoying the pleasures of life, it is now time for a man to retire from family life, give up all responsibilities and focus his attention on spiritual matters. Since, living in a family set-up is a distraction for him to concentrate on spiritual matters, he goes to the forest and leads a life of a recluse. He undertakes spiritual journeys to pilgrim centres. He leads a frugal life in the forest surviving on produce available in the forest.

The fourth stage is *Sanyasa* (Renounced life). This stage requires that a man should renounce the world completely and devote himself entirely to spiritual matters. Nothing that happens in his family or in the world matters any more. He has conquered worldly desires and has no attachment to this world. He is the one who is in a position to attain *Moksha* – self-realization that God is in him and he is in God. Therefore, the ultimate aim of every human being is to attain moksha, a stage where an individual identifies totally with the ultimate reality. This is described here as 'spirituality for self-realisation'. Such a person is called *Jivan Mukta*, one who has been liberated while still alive.

c. Spirituality for Service

Attaining Moksha is an individual goal. It is achieved by renouncing the world. But, what about one's duty to maintain order and stability in the world? Is it not the duty of every individual to contribute towards maintaining order and stability in society? Later Scriptures try to answer this question. The epics and classics such as *Ramayana, Mahabharata and Bhagavad Gita* written around the period of 400 B.C. and 600 A.D. represent this trend. *Ramayana* describes the story of Rama. He was considered as an ideal King with divine qualities. His rule over his subjects was exemplary where the voice of the individual was heard, needs of every person met and justice extended to all. Therefore, his kingdom had been described as *Ramarajya* (Kingdom of God) even by Mahatma Gandhi, in later years. His obedience to his father was such that he agreed to go on exile for fourteen years sacrificing his claim over the throne as the eldest son. He even banished his wife Sita, because her chastity was questioned by his subjects, even though he himself was convinced that Sita was blameless. This was because of the expectation of the subjects that the king should be above reproach. The well-being of his subjects was uppermost in his mind and his own suffering secondary. He demonstrated that social order and the welfare of his people are the essential and primary duties of a king. Performing one's own assigned duty sincerely for the well-being of the people and maintaining harmonious relationship in society is a spiritual task which is described as *Dharma.*

Mahabharata is the story of two related clans – Kauravas and Pandavas – trying to control the reigns of the kingdom which ends up in an epic battle. *Bhagavad Gita* which has occupied the pre-eminent position among Hindus today, is the advice given by Krishna to Arjuna to fight the battle in Kurukshetra as it constitutes his religious Dharma. It is now being referred to as 'Raj Dharma' – duty of ruling class to establish a harmonious society by fighting for justice. Two incidents are normally quoted by many scholars to support their view of Raj Dharma. The first one is Arjuna's dilemma at the battlefield. Realising that he had to fight against his own relatives and friends, Arjuna, a great warrior and one of the Pandava brothers – expresses his reluctance to fight to his charioteer, Krishna. Krishna, in turn convinces him to fight stating that renunciation of the world is not the only method of achieving Moksha, but doing one's duty diligently is also a necessary step, not only to maintain social order but also to be liberated from a cycle of rebirth. The second incident is after the battle was won and the kingdom restored to the Pandavas. Yudhishtara realizing the gravity of pain inflicted in the battle wanted to abdicate his responsibility as King and take up the life of a Sanyasa. He was then counseled by his brother, including Arjuna and his wife, Draupadi, not to undertake such a venture and continue his duties as king for the benefit of the people in his kingdom.

Effectively, therefore, there are two trends in Hindu Spirituality. One is *spirituality for self-realisation* and the other *spirituality for service* by performing one's own duty without expecting any reward for the same. The goal of the first one is to attain Moksha and the goal of the second is Dharma. The first goal is attained through a rigorous disciplined life at the end of the present life. The second is achieved in this life itself but through dedicated and appropriate action. The first one places emphasis on the Gnana Marga and Bhakti Marga in general to achieve the desired goal, whereas the second one lays its emphasis on Karma Marga. The first one is individual attainment, whereas the second one focuses on an individual's responsibility towards society.

2. Practical Hinduism

It is amazing to note that beliefs and practices, rituals and rites, signs and symbols used in Hinduism vary vastly from region to region, caste to caste, language to language and even sect to sect. Practical Hinduism begins with the very nature of God : There is a god for creation, another for preservation and third one for destruction. There are gods from the celestial world, ethereal space, animal kingdom or even from human species. There are male gods as well as female gods. Some gods have pleasant features whereas, some others have fierce look. In all the temples the presiding deity is installed in the *sanctum sanctorum* surrounded by thousands of other gods placed all around the temple; whereas in the slums and poor colonies a small statue is installed inside a temporary stone structure of 3" × 3" size which is worshipped equally enthusiastically by the residents.

Worship is always individual centric. A person may worship in ancient temples assisted by the designated priest or by himself or herself at the roadside temple without the assistance of any priest, or even at home where most of the middle class families have a room designated exclusively for pooja (worship). Worship is always a simple affair – no liturgy, exposition of scripture and repeating of mantras. The three important elements of any worship is to have *Darshan* (a glimpse) of the Lord, followed by prostrating (lying flat on the ground with head, body and feet touching the ground) before the Lord. Secondly, the devotees offering to god coconut, fruit and flowers. Thirdly, to receive *prasadam* (holy water) in recognition of becoming a recipient of God's grace.

In addition to the above, people undertake annual or occasional journey to the Holy Shrines built on mountains or on the banks of rivers. The rough terrain, restricted food habits and lifestyle and exposure to the vagaries of nature does not dampen their spirit. Their only goal is to have darshan of the Lord and in this process, the suffering that they undergo is a penance which is cleansed by their dipping in the holy river before having a glimpse of the Lord.

In everyday life, all important decisions are taken based on auspicious or inauspicious time calculated astrologically. Match making in marriages is based on 'Jathakas' (their time of birth and the star attached to it). Even at death each sect or group has different religious ceremony. Some sects cremate the body while others bury. Therefore, the entire life of a Hindu is religion based. Religion encompasses the entire life of a Hindu.

3. Social Structure in Hinduism

Individuals for a meaningful life have to necessarily interact with other individuals. This process of socialization ends up creating social systems in a given society. Each society formulates its own social systems and rules and regulations. While the social systems deal with social structures and social processes, religion deals with beliefs and practices concerning sacred values. Religious beliefs and practices though individual in nature they ultimately become group activities. In the end, religion and social systems interact with each other, influencing one another.

India has one of the unique and distinctive social systems in the whole world which goes by the name 'caste system'. This is a rigid hierarchically ordered system. A person is born into a caste and therefore cannot change the caste into which he or she is born. Here the theory of Karma comes into play. A person who has done good deeds in the past life enters the womb of a high caste woman. Such birth is called 'Dwijas' – twice born - those whose deeds were bad in their previous life would enter the womb of a low caste woman and will be born as a 'chandala' – an outcaste in their present life. A number of theories have been propounded to explain the origin and development of caste system in India. Only a few theories are mentioned in the following paragraphs. They are:

- *Religious Institution*

  The ancient scripture Rig Veda talks of the evolution of man. According to this hymn, *Brahmin* came out of the mouth of Brahman, *Kshatriya* from his arms, *Vaisya* from his thighs and *Sudra* from his feet. The first three castes are twice born and the fourth only once born. Later scriptures such as the *Upanishads and Manusmiriti* confirm this caste system in one way or the other. In view of the above, caste system in Hinduism is a religious institution emerging from the scriptures themselves.

- *Historical Evolution*

  According to this view, Aryans when they entered India had to encounter the original inhabitants. The Aryans who had better skills in warfare overpowered the local inhabitants and pushed them out of the plains. Some fled to mountainous areas and some to the South in order to survive and maintain their own traditional systems. That is why they are being called 'Adivasis' (original inhabitants) or 'Adidravidas' (original Dravidians). While some others integrated into the Aryan society creating a mixed set of caste system. In this process the systems namely, Vedic tradition of Varna system and the local tradition of 'Jati' system merged to form the existing caste system.

- *Ethnological Amalgamation*

  This theory deals with the migration of different racial groups into India at different points in history speaking various languages, entering from the North West and North East and integrating themselves with the local people and creating a social system called caste system.

- *Functional Division*

  Primitive society adopted a 'barter system' wherein each group specialized in certain occupations. Since they did not have a fiscal administrative system, they followed a system of exchanging their products with others and in return receive their products. This also created stability in the society defining definite roles for each community. In due course of time, the system began to determine the social standing of a particular group depending on the occupation that they were involved in. Thus, a practical arrangement turned into a system called caste system.

The theories mentioned above are only illustrative in nature and not exhaustive. They only point out the complex nature of the origin and function of the caste system in India. However, caste system has become a rigid social institution because it is organized hierarchically empowering only the higher castes on the top rungs of the ladder with power and positions leaving the people on the lower rungs as lower castes and committed to a lifetime of servitude. It is restrictive in nature allowing only the privileged higher castes with access to religious, educational and economic institutions; whereas, such opportunities are not available to the people of the lower castes. It is discriminative in that it oppresses the people on the lower rung of the ladder denying facilities in the social and public arena.

Traditionally, caste system operated on the principles of 'purity' and 'pollution'. Vedic systems describe the first three groups, namely, Brahmins, Kshatriyas and Vaisyas as twice born and hence they are pure; whereas, the Sudras who are born only once are impure. With the integration of Jati system into the Vedic system, if that is to be believed, a fifth caste, was created, which is outside the Vedic system of caste structure. This fifth caste is being described by various names such as 'Untouchables', 'Depressed Classes', 'Exterior Castes' and lately as 'Dalits'. The description of these very names indicate that they are outside the caste system – oppressed, marginalized – having no benefits and privileges available to them'.

The principles of purity and pollution operated mainly at three levels, namely, 'purity of race' which safeguards the progeny through a carefully arranged endogamous marriage system, 'Purity of culture' – which determines the status of the community in relation to other communities by way of rituals and practices, customs and traditions and 'Purity of habits' – which relate to dietary habits, cleanliness, living conditions etc. Though, one can observe that these principles are losing their grip in modern India; mainly, due to the urbanization process, but, they are still predominant in the minds of many including the educated. Therefore, caste system continues to be a mindset rather than an openly acknowledged oppressive system.

4. Cultural Hinduism

The Dictionary meaning of culture covers a wide range of human activities. It covers beliefs and values, ideas and knowledge, which result in social action. It depicts the shared values of a group or groups. It is concerned with traditions and behavioral patterns of a particular group of people at a given time. It finds its expression in music, art, dress, mannerisms and social pursuits. Therefore, it is difficult to define what culture is for a group of people at a given time. However, culture is a group activity. Individuals simply follow the culture of the group.

In India, culture has been handed down from ancient times because civilization is ancient. But, Indian civilization is intrinsically linked with religion. Hence, culture cannot be discussed without reference to religion. Religious beliefs and practices, values and ideas found their expression through a cultural medium of arts, music, drama and literature. Temple was the centre of cultural activities. The images crafted in stone, the pictures carved in wood found in the temples are examples of artistic expression of religious beliefs in ancient India. Temple was not only a place of worship, but also a place for social gathering; where religious beliefs were communicated through dance, drama and discourses to the concerned group. The musical instruments were specifically designed to be used in the temple. Scriptures have been handed down in literary form. So, the temple was the centre of cultural activities. This culture comes from Vedic tradition which is otherwise known as Brahmanical culture.

But, this Brahmanical culture was exclusive and not inclusive. It was not available to the vast majority of people of the lower castes. They were excluded from the temple culture. In order to perpetuate their own beliefs and practices, the low caste people devised their own medium of communication. That was the oral tradition. They passed on their culture by way of an oral tradition. This was and continues to be a powerful medium for dispossessed people. Rather than elaborating this concept, let me give two examples to highlight the significance of this tradition. Professor U. R. Anantha Murthy, one of the greatest writers in Kannada and a Gnanapeeth Award winner, describes how the masses have been carriers of culture in India. In his Kappen Memorial lecture entitled *'Indian Culture – An end of century view'* , describes how the Ramayana has been passed on in folk culture. When Sita had to go to the forest, Rama out of deep concern for safety and love for her, suggests that Sita need not go to the forest to experience the harsh realities of the forest. His persuasion did not convince her to stay back but rather she resolutely states. 'I am your wife and I have to come'. Further she says 'I know Sita goes to the forest in every Ramayana – How can you deny it to me'. Professor Anantha Murthy concludes that it is this oral tradition in their vernacular language which has been an effective instrument of passing on culture by the masses who are illiterate and dispossessed.

The second example is from my childhood days. I remember attending a Dalit wedding in my village when I was around 10 years old. The wedding ceremony was conducted with the usual traditional Hindu rites. But the differences were glaring, which remains in my mind even to this day, even though nobody prompted me to remember those differences. A group of Dalit women went in a procession to fetch water from the village tank to sanctify the Mantap with holy water, where the marriage ceremony was to be conducted. On the way back, one elderly lady began to behave strangely stating that she was possessed by the goddess. People around her did not ridicule her but instead, attended to her tenderly as if she was truly carrying the goddess on her head. The second difference was, there was no official priest, but an elderly gentleman officiated as a priest and in Kannada, pointing out to the bride and the groom that the people gathered together along with the sun and the moon and the universe were witnesses of the marriage. The third difference was a group of illiterate women singing a folk song which recalled the presence of Siva, their god in the wedding. The gist of the folk song is this: 'All praises to god Siva// He has arrived from the magnificent mountain// He is now present in this humble abode// To bless this wretched couple// to start a life of hope//. I did not understand the meaning then, neither did I put in efforts to preserve the event in my mind. It is only now after reflection I realize the importance of oral culture in India. Through this incident, I have learnt many lessons. They are: Importance of oral tradition; God's identification with the wretched of the earth; priesthood of all believers and the participation of women in social activities which are also spiritual in substance.

During the course of history, Vedic culture and oral tradition further diversified to form a multi-cultural context based on language, region, caste, beliefs and practices, customs and traditions. So, today, India portrays a rich diversity of cultural heritage and not a homogeneous culture as some would imagine.

The question that has been asked by many scholars is that what is it that binds all sections of Hindu society together inspite of their diverse culture, religious beliefs and practices and sociological differences? They try to answer this question from within Hinduism itself. They note that Hinduism has certain inherent qualities which promote unity in diversity. The first quality is tolerant nature of Hinduism. Hinduism is known for its tolerance. It tolerates different shades of opinions and beliefs. It allows innumerable ways for expressing one's own faith in practical life. It can accommodate even contradictory issues within itself. For example, belief in *Ahimsa* – non-violence, co-existed with the practice of animal sacrifice; traditionally the women who have been given highest status in life, even to the extent of worshipping them as goddesses, but also bans women from temple entry because they are considered impure. Tolerance is based on the principle 'live and let live' and this principle of tolerance has been handed down to the present generation from ancient days. The second inherent quality is accommodative nature of Hinduism. This quality operates on the principle of 'give and take'. The barter system that was prevailing in the primitive society is an example to demonstrate that the people involved in different occupations, exchanged their products with each other and established a fairly stable and harmonious social life. The third inherent quality found in Hinduism is the nature of assimilation. This quality operates on the premise that two different systems functioning independently can come together to form a synthesis for a common good. It operates on the principle of merger – two organisations coming together to form one organization for a common goal. The very fact that two different systems such as varna system of the Aryans and Jati system of of the Dravidians came together to form what is now known as caste system is an example in this direction. The fourth inherent quality found in Hinduism is the quality of absorption. This quality operates on the principle 'survival of the fittest'. When substances specially, in science come together they not only merge together but, the dominant substance takes control and weaker substances get dissolved in the process. This is also true of human nature. The dominant group always takes control of the weaker group by using money power, muscle power or political power, either through persuasive methods or through coercive force. Saffronisation of education is an example in this context. When Hindi was made compulsory subject in all schools in the 1960's and 70's to promote it as a national language, the Southern states, vehemently opposed the same stating that it is an imposition on their culture. Ultimately, the effort had to be abandoned. Now we see that through the official government machinery meant for promoting higher education, namely, 'Human Resource Development Ministry' at the Centre Sanskrit has been made a compulsory subject in all the Universities. This attempt has not created any ripple in the South now. Therefore, slowly and steadily saffronisation of education under the guise of cultural education is taking over the diverse nature of the earlier educational system.

The intrinsic values of Hinduism namely, quest for authentic spirituality, freedom to practice religion according the one's own understanding and ability, being part of a social system and promoting cultural diversity are ingrained in every Indian, be they from the higher caste or the lower caste, vegetarians or non-vegetarians, educated or uneducated, rich or poor. Those values have been passed on from one generation to another. Therefore, they are values inherited by every Indian, whatever their religious persuasions may be. Sometimes, these values are demonstrated openly and many other times remain dormant; erupting only at crucial points in their lives. We also need to be aware that Hindu fundamentalists have denied this legacy for Christians on the ground that they have changed their religious affiliation. Even, among the Christians the situation is ambiguous. The high-caste Christians use Indian spirituality with the sole aim of preserving their communitarian isolation from the rest. The educated Christians tend to use Indian spirituality to promote their individualism, whereas, vast number of village Christians are caught up between inheritance from Indian spirituality and heritage from the Western Christianity. However, the tension between quest for self-realization and the need for spirituality for service remain unresolved which is the subject matter of the subsequent chapter.

What are the specific qualities that we, as Indian Christians have inherited from the Vedic religious tradition which is deeply embedded in our innermost beings? I can identify three intrinsic qualities: Firstly, the quest for authentic spirituality. This search is ancient and it is ingrained in all Indians, be they from high caste or low caste; vegetarians or non-vegetarians; rich or poor and educated or uneducated. This quest for spirituality has been handed down from generation to generation and therefore cannot be erased if one follows alternate ways of spirituality. For, Vedic religious tradition itself has demonstrated that alternate spirituality is possible, if we compare the three philosophical schools mentioned above. Of course, Hindu Fundamentalists would deny this legacy for Christians on the ground that we have changed our religious affiliation. But, I am sure even they cannot accuse us as non-spiritual. Quest for spirituality is at the core of every Indian's life. This quest has resulted in two types of spirituality, namely – Spirituality for self-realization. This is individual search which ends only with the self-identifying with the ultimate reality or the self in fellowship with the ultimate reality or the self being in the domain of the ultimate reality, depending on the philosophical persuasion that one follows. This process of self-realization, demands one to renounce the world. As against this spirituality which calls for renouncing the world, there is another spirituality that requires the individual to do his/her duty sincerely. This spirituality is called spirituality for service; which indirectly affirms the world. Both these types of spirituality can be found in Christianity and particularly the former at the time of death by categorizing the world as 'Maya' or 'unreal' and the true life is beyond this world.

The second quality that we as Indian Christians have inherited is the approach that needs to be adopted in pursuit of spiritual goals. Vedic religious tradition stipulates Gnana Marga, Bhakti Marga and Karma Marga to achieve these goals. These Margas need no elaboration for they are part of Christian Spirituality as well.

The third quality that we as Indian Christians have inherited is cultural values. Qualities of tolerance, accommodation, assimilation and absorption are not alien to the Christian Church in India. They can be observed at every stage of a Christian's life.

Chapter 2

Heritage

'Study and Reflection' during the course of a decade has made a tremendous impact in my personal life. Some perceptions, views, presuppositions that I took for granted in earlier years got changed drastically while some others got reinforced. One view that got reinforced was my conviction that Indian Christianity is an end product of the confluence between Indian spirituality and Western spirituality. I remember as a young boy reacting angrily when a lady missionary kicked an idol lying on the ground to demonstrate that it has no life in it. My protest to the lady missionary was 'what others consider as holy, let us not call it profane'. On the other hand, an incident that happened in my college life has not only remained fresh in my memory but also changed the course of my entire life. For my college studies, I had to stay in a general hostel for economic reasons which accommodated students of all religions. Worship in the morning and evening was compulsory for all students but purely general in nature and never sectarian. However, at the end of the worship service Hindu students used to bow down before the idol placed in the chapel. One evening, prompted by the instigation of one of the students, the Warden who was from the RSS background noticed through the window that I was not bowing before the idol like others. He then called me to his office room and gave me an ultimatum that either I bow before the idol or quit the hostel within 24 hours. This was when I was a final year student of the undergraduate course. He knew that for the sake of my education I would fall in line with his dictates. When I discussed this tricky situation with my father, back in my village, he expressed his inability to support my education any further and advised me to discontinue my studies. It was then my father's younger brother, a bachelor, who argued with my father saying that under no circumstances my studies should be discontinued, even if it meant that a portion of the property which he was entitled to as a member of the joint family be sold. So, I continued my studies by renting out a room right in front of the hostel to demonstrate to the Warden that my studies were not curtailed for not obliging to follow the forceful imposition of his faith on me. It was this incident which was the principle reason for me to enter Christian ministry rather than pursuing a career in science being a science graduate. Rootedness in one's own faith is the basis for one's own search for spirituality.

Let us come back to the point that I started with, that is, Indian Christianity is an end product of the confluence between Indian spirituality and Western spirituality. Let me illustrate it by way of an example, with a proviso, that examples are used only to make a point but stressed further they become erroneous. During the summer vacation the boys from our village used to organize a trip to places of interest. We used to go on our cycles carrying snacks and eatables packed by our respective mothers. One such place we frequently visited was 'Sangama' – the confluence between the Cauvery and Kabini rivers, at about 12 kms from my village near a town called T. Narasipura. Because the two rivers come together it is named as 'Sangama' and it is also considered sacred by Hindus. What fascinated me was the scene at the point of confluence itself. The clear waters from the Cauvery River and the muddy waters of the Kabini River did not merge with one another instantly. They ran parallel as if they were not affected by the merger. We used to walk on the river bed observing this unusual phenomenon of maintaining their individual identity in spite of merging with one another. After covering a long distance, we used to observe that the two gradually merged with one another to an extent where it was difficult to distinguish between the waters of the Cauvery and that of Kabini. The same principle is valid with regard to Indian Christianity as well. When the two streams of spirituality, namely Indian and Western, confront each other, forming a confluence they may appear to run parallel retaining their original characteristics but, gradually, definitely, merge with one another forming a new entity called Indian Christianity which is different from the

Christianity practiced elsewhere. Otherwise, how can we explain some of the specific practices prevailing in the Indian Churches? A few practices are mentioned here only to highlight this point. The practice in village and semi-urban Churches of leaving behind one's footwear before entering the Church premises. Is it because of the Hindu understanding of 'sacred' and 'profane' and the profane needs to be left behind before entering the holy sanctuary or is it due to the scriptural injunction given to Moses to leave his sandals behind 'for the place on which you are standing is holy ground' (Ex. 3:5)?. Again, the practice of separate seating arrangements for male and female inside the Church premises -is it due to cultural segregation as found in Hinduism or is it coming from the Old Testament wherein, there was a separate women's court as distinct from men? Further, covering of the head by female members inside the Church – is it due to cultural practice prevailing in India indicating that women are inferior to men or is it due to the instructions given by Paul that 'women ought to have a veil on her head…' – is it proper for a woman to pray to God with her head uncovered?' (I Cor. 11:10-12). Consequently does it mean that those city congregations wherein, these practices are not in vogue are more spiritual than village Christians or does it indicate that they are more westernized? We need not attempt at answering these questions for our concern is not about the 'form' or the 'content' but rather our focus is on the 'essence' and the 'effect'.

For this purpose, we need to understand the contributions of Western Christianity into the process of spiritual formation of Indians. But, first we need to place Western Christianity in its own context before we discuss their contributions. This context and contributions of those who came to India from the West have been described under the caption 'Heritage' in this chapter. The words 'Inheritance' and 'Heritage' are used interchangeably. However, 'inheritance' refers mainly to the individual right to succession from one's own ancestors, whereas, 'heritage' is normally referred to the past treasures handed down to the present day society collectively. For example, a building may be designated as a 'heritage building' for its historical importance, aesthetic value, architectural beauty or depiction of art and culture of the past. Such building is considered as prized possession by the entire society and not just by a few individuals. Christian Church in India has received 'faith' from western Christianity. It is the prized possession of the entire Church in India. Hence, it can be described without hesitation whatsoever as 'heritage' from the past.

Christianity came to India through various sources at different points in history. The three main sources are: The St. Thomas tradition, which is believed to have started in the very first century by St. Thomas, the disciple of Jesus Christ. This Church, later developed its association with the Church of the East, which is now described as 'Orthodox Churches'. The second stream is Roman Catholic Church, which began with the arrival of St. Francis Xavier to Goa in the 16th Century. The third stream began with the arrival of the Protestant missionaries in the 18th Century. Since, our main purpose is to reflect on the 'life, ministry and mission of the Church of South India', we will concentrate only on Protestant Missions and particularly of those who came to South India. Even though, the subject is particular in nature, I am sure, the implications are universal and therefore, some common threads can be identified.

The name 'Protestant' was used for the first time in 1529 in Germany. Martin Luther's teachings were spreading rapidly throughout Germany. He defended his teachings at the Diet of Worms in 1521 (Diet was the Parliament of the Empire) by stating 'Here stand I. I can do no other. God help me.' German Princes supported Luther and as a result in 1526 at the Diet at Speyer the Princes decided to order ecclesiastical affairs in their respective states – according to their own conscience. But in 1529, at the second Diet held at the same place, the above permission was withdrawn. The Princes 'protested' against that decision. Hence from that time the name 'Protestant' was given to the new movement. But Germany was not the only place where protest was taking place. It was taking place in Switzerland through the teaching of Ulrich Zwingli and in the French speaking city of Geneva through the teachings of John Calvin, born and studied in Paris. Similarly, the Church in England protested against the official Church. So the protest movements spread throughout Europe. The protest was mainly against the official interpretation of some of the key doctrines in Christianity and the practices prevailing in the Church. The two basic principles on which the protests were organized were

(a) *Sola Scriptura* – Scripture alone. The Bible contains all truths necessary for salvation. Hence, all the Christian doctrine and practices should emerge from Scripture alone.

(b) *Individualism* - Each individual can read the Bible for himself/herself and decide what the true Christian doctrine is. Using these two principles, the main purpose of the Reformation was to 'reform' the Church. By the time the Protestant Missionaries arrived in India during the 18th century, many denominations had

> come into being all over Europe based on their interpretations of the doctrines and the Church order as found in the Bible.

Two other developments need to be mentioned here. During the 17th and early part of the 18th century, two powerful movements swept across Europe. The first one was a philosophical movement called 'Enlightenment'. This movement stressed on the importance of reason in understanding the nature of God, human beings and the universe. This movement gave scope to critically analyze the existing ideas and social conditions. Interest in studying the classical languages was kindled when it was applied to religion, study of the Bible in its original language, namely Old Testament in Hebrew and the New Testament in Greek was emphasized. Scientific methodology was developed to study the Bible. So, for this movement faith is authentic only when it can stand the scrutiny of reasoning and critical scholarship. At the same time, another movement called 'Pietistic' movement caught the imagination of many. This movement stressed on the need for personal experience of Christ as the norm for authentic Christian life. The movement emphasized that mere intellectual assent is not enough but, a personal encounter with the personal God is the primary requisite for an individual; which should result in change of life style devoid of worldly pleasures and temptations.

The primary concern of the reformation period is to 'reform' – reform in the doctrines and reform in the prevailing conditions of society. So, reform in both faith and practice was the main aim of reformation period. The primary focus of the Enlightenment philosophy is to build one's own faith on the foundation of rationalistic principles and not just on tradition. Enlightenment philosophy, encouraged ascent through intellectual and scientific enquiry and not just by blind faith in tradition. The basic aim of Pietistic movement was to encourage individuals to have personal encounter with Christ, in other words, to have the 'conversion' experience before motivating others to undergo the same. Therefore, the basic aim of the pietistic movement was 'mission through self - surrender.' These concerns ended up in the formation of Missionary Societies.

These Missionary Societies were formed within their own denominational structures as they were committed to the denominational understanding of doctrines and Church order. However, all the Missionary Societies were voluntary organisations and not imposed by the organized denominational bodies. Only those who subscribed to the general principles of the society, became members and supported its missionary work through their voluntary contributions. Therefore, the Protestant

Missionary movement in India needs to be assessed on the basis of the above principles. Missionaries were representatives, sent by the respective Missionary societies to execute their 'Agenda'. Agenda, being to motivate people to have personal encounter with Christ and to bring reforms in the social conditions prevailing in society. Missionaries, at least in the initial stages of the movement, were those who were fired by the love of Christ, motivated by the Biblical call to evangelize the world and backed by a community of like-minded believers back home. They landed in India to explore the unexplored, to sacrifice their lives if needed, in order to implement the Agenda of the parent organizations.

A cursory glance at the historical data available for the period would reveal that they had to face hostile environment, physical ailments and social alienation. But, they willingly accepted those hardships. Some have even lost their lives for the sake of the Gospel. For these reasons, the missionaries should be distinguished from the colonists of that time, because the motive of these two sets of people were entirely different. While, the motive of the missionaries was to share their spiritual values with the local people through their sacrifices, the motive of the colonists were to gain profit through trade and control of the local people and establishments. Arnold Toynbee in his book '*Christianity among the religions of the world*' states that '... the attitude of the governments towards missionaries has been watchful and suspicious'. (p. 50). J. N. Farquhar in his book '*Modern Religious Movements in India*' states categorically that 'the government vehemently opposed Missions.' (p. 10) He goes on to list three policies of the Government in support of his argument:

- Policy of Government to take under their control the management and patronage of a large number of Hindu temples, paying salaries of the temple officials, supporting financially for the festivals and sacrifices etc.
- They refused to allow missionaries to settle in their territory.
- They refused to employ native Christians in any capacity.

J. N. Farquhar concludes by saying that the policy of religious neutrality was introduced only after the Crown took responsibility of the Government when the rule of the East India Company came to an end after the Sepoy Mutiny in 1857. We read from history the humiliating treatment meted out to the very first Lutheran Missionary Ziegenbalg and Henry Plutschau by the then Commandant J. C. Hassius, when they arrived at Tranquebar. In spite of the fact, that these missionaries were sent by the King of Denmark, they were made to wait from morning till evening to grant permission to enter. Further, Zeigenbalg was kept in solitary confinement for four months and released only after public outcry. (C. B. Firth: *An Introduction to India Church History*. P. 131-134). William Carey and his team were not allowed to settle down in Calcutta, a British Colony had to be shifted to Serampore outside Calcutta, a Danish settlement for them to begin their missionary work. (J. N. Farquhar p.10)

The policy of East India Company opposing the religious activities of missionaries in India, was changed in 1813, when the Company's Charter came up for renewal in the British Parliament. Under the influence of prominent leaders like Wilberforce and Claudius Buchanan the Charter of 1813 included a provision that 'sufficient facilities should be afforded by law to persons desirous of going to and remain in India for the purpose of accomplishing those benevolent designs', i.e. the introduction among the Indians of 'useful knowledge and moral improvement' (C. B. Firth, p. 158) making way for many Missionary Societies to enter India. This provision was further relaxed in 1833, which allowed Missionary Societies from the continent of Europe and USA to enter India. Thus, Missionary Societies from all over Europe and America began their Missionary work in India after 1833.

One important point to be noted here is that the different denominations under which the above Missionary Societies were formed, were at loggerheads with each other back home on the basis of their differences in doctrines and Church order. But, when they came to India, they had to devise some acceptable strategies in order to carry on their Missionary work without much hindrance. They are :

a. Co-operation

There seems to be some unwritten understanding among the missionaries who arrived in India, may be, because of the hostile attitude of the then Government towards the Missionary enterprise. Further, in a strange environment they needed to consult and comfort one another. Whatever the reasons might have been, there are evidences to show that the missionaries co-operated with one another and even at times relied on one another. The very first missionaries of the Lutheran Mission were sent by the King of Denmark, but were from Germany and later was financially supported by the SPCK of the Church of England, prompting the Church historian C. B. Firth to make the following comments:

It was a curious three cornered arrangement. The Board in Denmark administered, most of the candidates (not all) came from the University of Halle in Germany; and additional help in money and materials was provided by the Anglican SPCK in England.' (P. 134-135)

Alexander Duff, a missionary from Scotland was encouraged by William Carey of the Baptist Missionary Society, to open a School which later became a College with English as the medium of instruction and Bible as one of the core subjects. Alexander Duff in turn invited several missionaries to give a course of lectures on Christianity to a group of firebrand students at his house (P. 182 & 183).

W. T. Ringeltaube, who on his second voyage to India, came as an LMS missionary to Kanyakumari District, stayed in Tranquebar for some time and later made Palayamkottai, an 'English Mission' Centre, as his headquarters.

b. Missionary Conferences

Missionaries began to realize the need for formal consultation among the missionary societies. Co-operation between individual missionaries was good, but not sufficient. Policies would affect the relationships and relationships in turn would determine the outcome of missionary work. The first missionary conference seems to have taken place when representatives of six missions met at Calcutta, in the year 1855. This was a Conference of Missionaries of a particular province. Having realized the importance of such a consultation, the Missionaries began to organize decennial conferences from 1872 onwards at an all India level. The purpose was to share with one another the work being done in their respective fields; consult one another on policy matters and clear misunderstandings and difficulties that might have arisen in due course. Missionaries from different societies would present papers followed by discussions and arrive at possible decisions and resolutions for further guidance, without affecting their individual autonomous status. This exercise paved way for better understanding and co-operation among the Missionary Societies to the extent, in later years they could think of 'Union Institutions' managed by two or three or even a group of missionary societies. For example, Madras Christian College which was originally started by the Free Church of Scotland Mission – became a joint venture along with CMS and Wesleyan Methodist Missionary Society in 1887. Similarly, a medical school started by Dr. Ida S Scudder of the American Arcot Mission, later became a full-fledged Christian Medical College with the co-operation of all the major missionary societies in 1945. Most of the theological Colleges in India became Union Institutions.

c. Comity Principle

One outcome of the Missionary Conference was the acceptance of the principle called 'comity'. This principle recognized the territories occupied by different Missions as 'Mission fields' of those respective Missionary Societies. It further prevented other societies, establishing their missions in those territories. This unwritten understanding that was existing earlier, became an acceptable formula for all the Missionary Societies in a missionary conference held in Madras in 1902. The exception, being larger towns where different Missions had established their head-quarters, and where already more than one mission was in existence. The Conference also established a mechanism, wherein disputes between Missions regarding territorial issues could be sorted out. The consequence of the decision was that Christians living in a particular territory became Christians of a particular denomination; not because they wanted to, but because a particular denomination worked in that area. However, the 'comity' principle has minimized the conflict between Missionary Societies.

Another development in Indian history needs to be taken into consideration. After the Sepoy Mutiny in 1857, the governance came directly under the Crown. The British adopted a policy of 'neutrality' in terms of its relationship with religions. This decision might have been due to impact of policy of 'Separation of Church and State' prevailing in the West, at that time. The debate on separation of Church and State began in America, when the Baptists raised their apprehensions that the then official Church of Virginia, namely, Anglican Church might dominate the religions in America, through the instrumentality of the State. In reply, Thomas Jefferson assured them that the first amendment was to protect the religious liberty of all and not to infringe on their rights and used the phrase 'wall of separation between the Church and the State'. The idea behind it is that the church must stay out of the business of the State and likewise the State cannot interfere in the activities of the Church. However, in practice a strict and complete separation is impossible. The American President takes oath of office on the Bible. The words 'In God we Trust' is engraved on the walls of the legislature. The Supreme Court wall is adorned with the carvings of the Ten Commandments. In the European continent, Church of England is regarded as the official Church of the United Kingdom, Lutheran Church in Germany and Scandinavian countries and Roman Catholic Church in Italy and Portugal. But, the spirit of the debate, namely, the Church and the State have different roles to play in society has remained deeply rooted in the public understanding. Recognizing that

Hinduism is not a homogenous faith as it differs from sect to sect and caste to caste; as well as the prevalence of number of denominational and confessional churches in India, the Crown declared 'neutrality' towards all religions in its policy. It is worth noting the words used in the policy.

'Firmly relying ourselves in the truth of Christianity and acknowledging with gratitude the solace of religion, we disclaim alike the right and desire to impose our convictions on any of our subjects' (C. B. Firth, p.189). This policy resulted in the Government neither promoting nor assisting any religion or religious activities. However, it changed drastically the relationship between the Government and the Missionary Societies from the earlier attitude of opposition to that of peaceful co-existence. J. W. Kaye in his book, *'Christianity in India: An Historical Narrative* (p. 485-496) elaborates as to what this principle of neutrality meant. The gist of it is:

- No inclination towards a 'bolder Christian policy'.
- No financial support for Christian missions in India.
- No exclusive Bible teaching in Government sponsored educational institutions.
- Public processions of all religions are allowed, for the abolition of such religious processions might be construed as persecution or suppression of religious freedom.
- Public holidays of the Government offices on all national religious festivals to continue.
- Liberal support of the State patronage - to Christian converts was denied. Instead, converted Christians could have access to Government employment on the same criterion, like any other religious persons. This historical description would destroy all notions that the British rulers and Missionary movements were hand-in-glove in promoting evangelisation of India.

  Further the British government was actively involved in promoting reforms in the prevailing social conditions. J. N. Farquhar (pp 17-18) lists these reforms under three groups:
- Prohibiting customs, in the name of religion, that demean human dignity such as 'Sati' and human sacrifices.
- Treating every human being as equal before law. For instance, permitting Indians to take up government services irrespective of their religious and caste affiliation.
- Reforms in the area of education and in particular introduction of English as medium of instruction in the higher education.

As mentioned earlier, the Agenda for all the Missionary Societies was 'reform and mission'. In as much as Government was involved in 'reforms' the missionary societies felt obliged to co-operate with the government as 'reform' was also on their agenda. So, the era of co-operation between the government and missionary societies began, as far as the process of reforms was concerned, leaving 'missions' in the exclusive domain of the Societies. However, co-operation with the government also meant that the Missionary societies fall in line with government policies. In particular, the educational policies of the government altered the very basic understanding of mission itself in due course of time. The educational enterprise which was an integral part of mission became 'secular' subject under the influence of government policies.

The methodology used by missionaries in implementing the agenda of 'mission and reform' was precisely the methodology used by our Lord, that is, preaching (Mark 1:38; Luke 4:18ff, 9 & 10) teaching (Mark 1:21; Matt.5:1ff) and healing (Mark 1:29 ff, 40 ff; 2:1ff). All these three instruments were an integral part of the mission and not isolated units independent of each other. But, the early missionaries had a stupendous task of making the Gospel relevant to Indian conditions. They could not compromise on their Christian faith, and particularly on the salvific power of Jesus Christ. On the other hand, India was not a 'faithless' nation. It was deeply rooted in their own spirituality based on their religious beliefs and practices. Therefore, it fell on the shoulders of missionaries to be alert to the 'context' in which the Gospel was preached. In their attempt to devise ways and means of making the Gospel relevant to Indian conditions, they had to necessarily adopt creative and innovative methods. Further, the reform that had taken place in the West was within their own faith community, namely, Christianity. In India, they had to deal with another religion namely, Hinduism. But, they were not the missionaries of Hinduism. Reforms should take place from within and not enforced from outside. So, they had to modify their Agenda from 'reform' to 'transform'. How the missionaries implemented their Agenda of 'mission' and 'transform' and how people responded to this agenda is the subject matter of the next chapter.

Let us recapitulate what has been mentioned above. The early missionaries were the products of the Reformation period of the 16th Century. There, the concern was to 'reform' based on the Biblical teachings. Secondly, they were also influenced by the Enlightenment Philosophy of the 17th & 18th Centuries. There, the primary concern was that the 'faith' should be able to withstand the scientific and rational scrutiny. Thirdly, they were motivated by the Pietistic tradition of the early 18th Century. This tradition, emphasized on the personal encounter with Christ. With this background the missionaries came to India with an Agenda to involve themselves in 'mission' and to 'reform'. But, when they came to India, they met with opposition from the government of that day. As a result, the missionaries from different denominational background learnt to co-operate with one another. They further devised a principle of comity to demarcate their respective areas of operation. They also met regularly in missionary conferences, which enhanced their understanding and co-operation in the areas of missions. With the Crown taking over the governance of India, the relationship between the government and missionary societies improved. However, the mission remained in the exclusive domain of the missionary societies. They adopted the Biblical methodology of 'preaching, teaching and healing' as their sole method of implementing the agenda of mission.

In conclusion, we need to acknowledge that the Church in India is a recipient of spirituality from two streams, namely, Indian spirituality as 'Inheritance' and from Western spirituality as 'Heritage'. The heritage that the Church in India has received from the West is enormous. It is spirituality in context. It calls for individual commitment to Christ. But, it does not end there. The true commitment to Christ should result in 'transform' – transforming individuals to lead a value oriented life but also transforming the social conditions prevailing in society.

Missionaries' contribution to Indian Church is normally acknowledged in terms of material legacy, such as Church building that they have constructed; institutions that they have started; properties that they have left behind and the administrative system that they have passed down. These are true and valuable. But, we need to understand their contribution from the perspective of spiritual heritage that they have passed on to the Indian Churches. This heritage can be identified in three areas.

Firstly, Missionaries presented an alternate world view – a world view in which God is at the centre of human history. According to this view, it is God who created the world, the earth and its inhabitants. When God created the world, he called it 'good'. In other words, the world as God's creation was real and good. It is God who created human beings as the crown of His creation giving them freedom and creative power to be used for the benefit of the whole of humankind. It is the greedy, selfish and rebellious nature of human beings which alienated and continues to alienate human beings from God and human beings from among themselves. As a result, the deeper fellowship that existed between God and human beings and between human beings themselves was broken and the gulf widens.

God who considers the world as 'good' does not disown the world. His Mission is to restore the broken fellowship, and therefore takes different initiatives at different phases of history to reconcile the world unto Him. Finally, He sends His own Son to bridge the gap between Him and the human beings. Jesus sacrificed himself on the Cross in order to help human beings to come closer to God.

God continues to act in history, even after the earthly mission of His Son. He has now chosen His Church, the faithful people, who have responded to His call to continue His mission of bringing people closer to Him. Therefore, the world view presented by the Missionaries is an alternate world view, because it recognizes that God is at the centre of human history. God the Creator, Sustainer and Reconciler which is different from human-beings being at the centre of history.

Secondly, Missionaries have left behind a heritage of wholistic spirituality. They emphasize on individual spirituality. It is the personal encounter with Christ which is the foundation for true spirituality. But, this individual spirituality has to be nurtured and nourished in the context of the worshipping community. Individuals need to learn, care and share his/her experience with the community of the faithful. This individual as well as community spirituality is not for self-aggrandizement, but to be used as spirituality for others. That is, it should lead the individuals and the community of faithful to be involved in God's mission by becoming God's agents or ambassadors in the world to promote God's Mission of reconciling the world unto Him. Therefore, the Missionaries have left behind a heritage of wholistic spirituality for the Church consisting of individual spirituality, community spirituality and spirituality for engagement.

Thirdly, the Missionaries have left behind a heritage of unified system of approach to spirituality. Encounter with Christ is possible only when a person surrenders himself/herself to Christ. It is not based on individual merit, status or possessions. It is purely on 'leap of faith' that one can surrender to Christ – to realize one's utter unworthiness and casting oneself entirely on the mercy of Christ. This is Bhakti Marga. 'Leap of faith' is not a blind faith. God has revealed Himself in the Scriptures. The redemptive acts of Jesus Christ are described in the Scriptures, and the same have been made available to every believer in the language he/she understands. It is therefore, the duty of every believer to read and understand the Bible, which is a testimony for God's involvement in history. This is Gnana Marga. Every believer and every faith community is also called upon 'to lead a life worthy of calling'. That is, our faith affects our life style, our ethical life. Faith must result in actions, actions worthy before God, actions based on Scriptural principles and actions which would promote peace, harmony and justice in Church and Society. In other words, actions without expecting any reward for good work. This is Karma Marga. The missionaries, therefore, have left behind a heritage of unified approach of Bhakti Marga, Gnana Marga and Karma Marga for the Indian Church.

It is to be noted here, that the heritage, that we have received from Missionaries does not negate the inheritance that we have been bestowed with by Vedic religious traditions. Rather, heritage is a natural progression of the inheritance from individual to the collective.

Chapter 3

Spiritual Formation

The parable of the sower narrated by our Lord and recorded in the Gospel of St. Mark 4:1ff is illustrative of the mission work. This parable mentions three instruments necessary for mission. They are: the sower, the seed and the land on which the seed is sown. They represent the Messenger, the Message and the Context. All the three are equally important to realize mission. If this parable is read along with the plant analogy used by St. Paul in 1 Cor. 3:5 ff, it adds further dimension to the above instruments. They are: God's servants, the plants and God Himself. This means the messengers and those who receive the message and the author of mission itself, namely, God has to be taken together for effective mission. Therefore, God, messengers, message, context and the recipients of the message are integrally related to one another.

In other words, God is the author of mission and mission flows from the heart of God in the form of message – the Good News. God uses his servants as carriers of this Good news. But, this message has to be made relevant to the context in which people dwell. Those who respond to this message become recipients of God's grace, i.e., they become people of God; enjoying the fellowship of God and thereby, mission is achieved. Mission is the end result of the concerted and co-operative efforts of all the instruments mentioned above. The messenger needs to be deeply committed to God's mission. Then the message, namely, the seed or the Gospel needs to be of good quality and unadulterated. The land has to be prepared, i.e., the context in which the mission is to be implemented needs to be taken seriously, in order that the seed may grow as plant, without hindrance. Finally, people need to respond appropriately to the message only then God's mission becomes effective. The lesson that we need to draw from the above parable as well as the plant analogy is that mission belongs to God and not to any human being or the Church. The believers and the Church have been given the privilege of participating in God's mission. Each generation, must make efforts to find effective ways and means to communicate God's mission to the people around based on the prevailing context giving them an opportunity to respond appropriately and become recipients of God's grace.

Let me illustrate this point from my personal experience. Coming from an agricultural family, I used to help in our fields during the summer vacation. Before the monsoon sets in, summer was the time to get the lands ready for sowing. The fields would be ploughed not once, but three or four times and manure would be spread evenly across the fields. The sowing would take place the day after the rains has soaked the fields. When the plants begin to grow, the weeds which would also sprout up would be removed. At the time of flowering, there is a danger of insects attacking the plants and hence appropriate insecticide had to be sprayed. After all the strenuous work, there would be a time of waiting before the harvest. While the fields are harvested the entire family would celebrate the event in the fields itself by sharing a meal among themselves and sharing their food with the passersby. The celebration would be a joyous one. My father would ask me to join the family even when I was studying in college in Mysore. The celebration would indicate that 'mission accomplished' metaphorically speaking. Sadly, the fields that yielded sufficient grains and pulses for the entire joint family to be fed for the whole year are now lying barren because the younger generations have moved to the cities in search of greener pastures and those who have stayed back are old and cannot work long, tiring hours in the blazing sun. Further, due to the change in climatic conditions the monsoon rains are scanty and irregular.

In this chapter, I will be discussing the methodology used by the early missionaries to India, to implement the Mission Agenda and the response it generated from the people concerned, leaving the analysis of the present day situation in the Church to later chapters in the book. This is described under three different captions which can be categorized both as chronological as well as existential.

1. Spiritual Formation and Personal Salvation

Passion for Christ, rational thinking and primacy of individuals were some of the motivating factors for the early missionaries. When they entered India they discovered that religion was at the core of the lives of Hindus. Therefore, religion and particularly Hinduism became the context in which to implement their mission.

The missionaries arrived at the conclusion that superstitious beliefs and practices found even among the then educated class can be removed only by way of a proper and systematic biblical teaching. Further, they realized that education was imparted using Sanskrit as the medium of instruction. Against this practice, the missionaries introduced English as the medium of instruction which was also a means of spreading rational thinking and knowledge. The very first experiment in introducing English education in Calcutta by Alexander Duff, a missionary sent by Church of Scotland who arrived in Calcutta in 1830, was successful. It is said that at the end of the first year, in a public '*viva voce*' the boys demonstrated their grip over all the School subjects, including English Grammar and also on the teachings of the Bible. This experiment was reported in the newspapers and therefore, became a central part of discussion in all the educational endeavors. All the missionary societies being inspired by Duff's experiment adopted the same method in their mission work and started High Schools, and in some cases Colleges all over India.

In this connection, let me take a leaf out of the pages of history from my own Alma Mater – Hardwicke High School in Mysore, as recorded in the *Centenary Souvenir* edited by Rev. H. A. Crump, a Methodist Missionary to Mysore. The Methodist Missionary Society led by Rev. Hodson started a vernacular school for boys and girls separately in Mysore in the year 1839. They also began an English Medium School in 1840. The English Medium School attracted many 'respectable Indians in the city, who with a complete knowledge of the system of teaching sent their sons for instruction' (p. 2). The School opened daily with prayer and the first lesson every morning was a Scripture portion. The then Maharaja having enquired about the progress of the School had volunteered to pay all the expenses of the English School which worked out to be Rs. 177/- per month. Rev. Hodson, while appreciating the generosity of the Maharaja, categorically stated that he would accept the patronage provided that 'the Bible would be read in the School as usual, and that no alteration in teaching Christian truth would be made.' The Maharaja responded by saying 'The missionaries must teach what they think proper'. However, he laid a 'conscience clause', that 'if any boy should conscientiously objects to the reading of the Scripture, he might not be compelled to do so nor expelled from the School for refusing.' Rev. Hodson agreed and allowed such students to skip the morning prayers and catechism classes.

A second incident is also noteworthy. By 1852 the missionary strength in Mysore depleted to a large extent leaving only one missionary Rev. E. J. Hardey to manage the entire burden of the mission work. Even he was returning to England. At that time, a petition was sent to the Home Board signed by three thousand three hundred Hindus urging them to continue the English School. The following words are illuminating, 'You, gentlemen, having in many places established Chief Colleges for the peoples' children, and having taught them wisdom, you have acquired fame and honour; therefore, upon us and upon our children, look favourably, and in this place having established a College, cause our children to be taught by an English gentleman'. (p. 5) In response to this, friends contributed Rs. 2,000/- leaving Rev. Hardey to raise an equal amount when he returned to India. For this purpose Rev. Hardey constituted a committee consisting of highly placed dignitaries in Mysore. When a meeting was convened, a merchant offered to pay Rs. 4,000/- if the Bible was excluded from the syllabus. As his demand was not accepted, he left the meeting. But at the end of the meeting they were able to raise Rs. 1,600/-. When the School was re-opened it had 160 boys on the roll.

From the above description, we can arrive at the following inferences:

- Early missionaries adopted teaching as a method of propagating the Gospel.
- High Schools and Colleges were the preferred settings for imparting education.
- English was the medium of instruction.
- Bible teaching was the core subject along with other subjects to be taught.
- Spiritual formation in line with biblical teaching and rational thinking were the main goals of teaching.
- Lectures, discourses, debates and discussions, questions and answers were the methods used in teaching.

Through these methods the early missionaries in particular Alexander Duff hoped superstitious beliefs and practices of Hinduism would be demolished and positive knowledge of Christian faith would take its place. It is true that a few individuals did respond to the call of the Gospel, but majority of the students received 'Christian' education happily but did not feel obliged to leave the Hindu fold and become members of the Christian Church. The education imparted in Christian schools and colleges did attract a number of students for its discipline and rational content. It was a different form of following *Gnana Marga* which they were used to. Further, English education gave students access to world religions which made them look deeper into their own religious treasures. As a result, some of them turned out to become reformers of their own religion in due course of time.

Concentration of higher education also produced an unintended results. We know that the education imparted in the ancient days was a religious education and it was available only to the people of high caste. The low caste people could not even dream of going near the educational centres, which were the temples, leave alone getting educated. Consequently, only those who were already educated could continue their higher studies. So, when Christian missionaries started English education in High Schools and Colleges, it naturally benefitted the high caste students. The caste wise figure of students given in the report of my Alma Mater for the year 1855-1856 mentioned above demonstrates this truth. Out of the total students of 156, Brahmins were 95 and the rest from different Vedic religious sects, except for 10 Muslims and only three from the Pariah community. I am sure the trend would be the same in all the early Christian higher educational institutions throughout India. I am also certain that the same trend continues even today in all the prestigious educational institutions managed by the Church irrespective of their denominational affiliations. Further, those who accepted Christ and became Christians occupied leadership positions in the church and its Institutions as the time passed by. Thus, the leadership of the church and its institutions rested solely in the hands of the missionaries and Christians from the upper caste.

But, the education imparted through Christian Educational Institutions has made and continues to make impact throughout India, for the curiosity it arouses among the students; creativity in thinking; desire for search for deeper meaning in life; motivation for leading a disciplined life; broader outlook of the universe it provides and the quality of educational methodology.

As far as the spiritual formation was concerned, as mentioned earlier, Bible teaching was the main method of imparting spiritual knowledge. Schools and Colleges began the day with devotions consisting of songs, prayers and Bible reading, exposition of the Biblical text were the norms, rather than exceptions. Designated period of Bible classes for deeper exploration of the concepts, lectures, debates, discourses and interactive sessions were introduced and exchange of ideas were encouraged. Through this process the students were made to rationally think and follow the path that they were convinced of by their study and research. Even though most of these activities were done in a corporate setting, it ultimately resulted in search for personal salvation. This was the aim of the spirituality found in the Pietism of the West. But, it also coincided with the self-realization of the Indian spirituality. Therefore, the spiritual formation leading to personal salvation was the foundation for higher education imparted in and through Christian higher educational institutions.

2. Spiritual Formation and Human Compassion

History of India narrates affliction of a number of plagues like malaria and cholera as well as severe famines, periodically. One such appalling famine was during the period from 1876 to 1879, particularly severe in South India. It is a well-known fact that missionaries even though not trained particularly in the field of health care, with their limited knowledge of basic prevention of such diseases in their personal lives, plunged into saving the dying lives and alleviating the distress of hapless and hopeless people, left to care for themselves literally on the streets. It is reported that in the process many missionaries contracted the same diseases, for they were contagious and lost their lives. Many missionaries led a frugal life, for they sacrificed all their earning in meeting the demands of the testing time, for the sake of suffering people. All this, they took upon themselves, inspite of their inadequacies in the unexpected and unfortunate situation that they found themselves in. The context was dramatically changed from that of religion to human condition in distress. From the intellectual and rational discussions and debates on religious concepts, the missionaries had to make pedagogical shift in their approach to mission. It was a mission to the suffering humanity. Their faith was put to the test. In meeting such a gigantic task, they could not rely on any human beings nor on any human organisations. They had to depend solely on the faithfulness of the Lord in whom they had put their trust. They realized that Jesus was not only preaching and teaching; he was also involved deeply in compassionate ministry to the sick and the dying. They reminded themselves of the compassionate acts of Jesus. They were very humane and touching the hearts of the affected people. When a leper, an untouchable of the time came to him, Jesus was 'moved with pity, stretched out his hand and *touched him* and said to him, "I will; be clean" (Mk. 1:41). When a deaf man was brought to him in the region of Decapolis, Jesus '*put his fingers into his ears* and after spitting *touched* his tongue ... and opened his ears, released his tongue'. (Mk. 7:31ff) Again when a blind man came to him in Bethsaida, Jesus 'took the blind man by the hand ... spit on his eyes, *laid his hands on him* and opened his eyes'. (Mk. 8:22ff) Jesus *touched* the hand of Peter's mother-in-law, and the fever left her. (Matt.8:14ff) Jesus *looked with compassion* on a widow in the town of Nain, who had lost her only son and consoled her saying, 'Do not weep' (Lk. 7:11ff). Jesus invites himself as a guest into the house of Zacchaeus, a tax collector, who was considered a sinner and therefore marginalized from society, and declares, 'Today salvation has come to this house, since he is also a son of Abraham'. (Lk. 19:1ff)Jesus went to the home of Martha and Mary, whose brother Lazarus had died. He could understand their agony and feelings and in turn he himself '*wept*' – the shortest but most powerful verse in the Bible.

So, the missionaries girded themselves for the impending task of caring for the sick and dying and the vulnerable section of society, solely moved by the love of Christ, which compelled them to action. In that mission, they were not 'seeking their own advantage but that of many, that they may be saved', as St. Paul described his own ministry (I Cor. 10:33). It was a selfless and sacrificial love which motivated them to be involved in the mission of human compassion. The methodology that they have used in their mission, was also the same methodology that they adopted to teach the High School and University students, i.e., the Biblical methodology of preaching, teaching and healing. The only difference was the strategy of using those Biblical tools. For a sick person rational arguments would not bring wholeness; for a hungry person philosophy would not give relief from hunger; for a person literally lying on the street mere preaching that 'God loves you', would not mean anything. It had to be a demonstration of God's care and concern for such people through human compassionate acts, as found in the teachings of Jesus in St. Matthew 25:31ff. That was exactly what the missionaries did in situations like plague and famine. They identified three key concerns through which they could serve the afflicted. They are: Rescue, Relief and Rehabilitation, for it was not a temporary relief that the missionaries were looking for, but rather a sustainable model that could exist for a long period of time. Under the rescue operation, the people dying on the roads were brought to a central place, where they could be given shelter, care and constant supervision. They established orphanages under the programme for relief. The affected were provided with their daily necessities such as food, clothing and medicines. But, the long term programme was rehabilitation. It was the intention of the missionaries that these afflicted people should start a life of their own, and carve out a future for themselves. For this purpose, the missionaries taught them skills such as carpentry, tailoring, smithy etc. depending on the aptitude of a person so that he or she can use those to progress in life. Afterwards, these people were even given a piece of land on which they could build their homes and lead an independent life. It was not only a practical help but the missionaries provided counseling to make them strong mentally. They taught the Scriptures by way of telling them compassionate stories from the Bible; as they firmly believed that spiritual formation was the basis of all acts of love and compassion. Starting of dispensaries, hospitals, medical colleges and allied medical courses in later times, is to be considered as a result of this compassionate ministry of the missionaries. Further, introduction of skill oriented courses needs to be treated as attempts at empowering the marginalized to lead a dignified and decent life.

We do not have any statistics to prove how many people became recipients of such acts of love throughout India, or how many became 'Christians' or continued as Christians, even after a lapse of time. For, none of the church historians has found it worthy to do research on the impact of such acts of love and compassion on the growth of Christianity in India. The only parallel that we can draw in modern times is the compassionate ministry the missionaries of charity started under the leadership of Nobel Laureate Mother Theresa in Kolkata. I consider that it is truly inhuman to describe such acts of love and mercy as 'inducement for conversion'. But, let us remember that any act of love performed for the benefit of others without expecting any reward is also a spiritual principle in Hinduism as described in Chapter I.

3. Spiritual Formation and Social Transformation

One of the most intriguing and inexplicable movements that has not only changed the course of history of Protestant Christianity in India, but also challenged the very basis on which missionaries built up their mission was a phenomenon which is popularly described as 'Mass Movements'.

Missionaries failed to understand the importance of such movements. Theologians could not explain the phenomenon through rational theological principles. Church historians could not find any parallel to it in the history of Christianity throughout the world. Sociologists concluded that the motivation for these movements was to 'improve their social status, sense of personal dignity, self-respect, as well as for freedom from bondage to oppressive land owners'. (Sundaraj Manickam, *The Social Setting of Christian conversion in South India*, p.106) However, they all conclude saying that 'there was a definite note of perplexity and uncertainty in the missionary response to this movement'. (John C. Webster; *The Dalit Christians – A History*, p.50) It is my firm conviction that the Missionaries, Theologians, Church Historians and Sociologists failed to explain this phenomenon properly, because their starting point of inquiry and investigation was wrong and hence arrived at the conclusion wrongly. However, before we begin discussion on the subject we need to explain a couple of terms in their original context to assess their impact on the growth of the Church.

a. Mass Movement

The term 'mass movement' was first used and popularized by Dr. J. Waskom Pickett, who was commissioned by the National Christian Council, under the guidance of Bishop V. S. Azariah, Bishop of Dornakal Diocese, in his book entitled '*Christian Mass Movements in India*'. He, however, was not comfortable in using the term 'Mass Movements' to describe movement of the people from low castes, because 'nowhere in India have the people turned to Christ *en masse*'. Further, the term meant different things to different people. It meant 'hasty baptism' for some, to others it meant reception of 'outcastes' or 'untouchables' into the Church; to some others, it meant a 'nominal confession of Christianity'; it also meant to some that it was caste movements to Christianity without affecting their caste divisions in their new found religion. Hence, Dr. Pickett advocates the term 'group movement' instead of 'Mass movement' (p. 21-22). However, for convenience sake, he continued to use the word 'Mass Movement' throughout the body of the book. The apt term would probably be 'family movement' because it was a movement of the family, rather than the whole caste group, which accepted Christ.

b. Dalit

The word 'Dalit' was first used by Jyotirao Phule, a social reformer of the 19th century from Maharashtra. He was considered as 'Mahatma' of the oppressed. He was not a well-educated person but a great thinker. He realized that caste system in Hinduism inflicted enormous harm to the very dignity of human beings. He revolted against 'the tyranny of caste system'. He, even started a Primary School for the oppressed in Poona in 1851, which was a novelty at that time. He made efforts to unite all the castes outside the Vedic religious system, under one banner. In order to propagate such a view he used the term 'Dalit' which is a Sanskrit word. Scholars agree on the root meaning of the term 'Dalit'. James Massey has brought out the different shades of the meaning of Dalit in his essay entitled 'Historical Roots' (p. 6) (See James Massey: *Indigenous People: Dalits*).

Dalits, the plural of dalit, in Sanskrit is both a noun and an adjective. As a noun, dalit can be used for all three genders, masculine, feminine and neuter. It has been derived from the root *dal* which means to crack, open, split, etc. When used as a noun or adjective, it means burst, split, broken or torn asunder, downtrodden, scattered, crushed, destroyed, etc.'

Originally, therefore, the term Dalit did not refer to caste or group of castes from the lowest rungs of caste structure. Dalit was not intended to be a status in the caste system but an oppressive condition that a group of people suffer from. The word accommodated people, groups and communities suffering from oppressive conditions, heaped on them through social-economic-cultural and religious hegemonic system. All those who suffered from such oppressive system were called Dalits. It was for this reason that the term 'Dalit' was generally accepted by the people who had experienced such horrific conditions to describe their conditions. It is this aspect of new understanding of the condition of suffering people by Jyothirao Phule which made Dr. Babasaheb Ambedkar to appreciate him by saying, 'The greatest Sudra of Modern India who made the lower classes among the Hindus conscious of their slavery to the higher classes'. (James Massey, p. 34) According to this understanding, historically Dalits were those, who were excluded from temple worship or those who had been denied the services of the priestly class in performing their religious rituals and ceremonies. Dalits were those, who did not have access to public utilities such as roads and wells. Dalits were those who were denied of opportunities for education. Dalits were those, whose culture was not recognized by the heirarchical religious system. Dalits were those, who were deprived of even basic necessities of life and whose survival depended solely on the whimsical mercy extended by the oppressors. Therefore, the term describes the condition of people or communities, who were historically discriminated in religious beliefs and practices, segregated socially from public participation, denied access to education, culturally alienated and economically deprived. Any community, which feels that they were not part of this historical process of oppressive system, is free to exclude themselves from such description, except to mention that they are either 'camaflouging' their historical conditions or making efforts to 'up-grade' themselves into higher standing in caste structure, through a process of 'Sanskritisation' which will be discussed later. However, the term 'Dalit' is used in this book to indicate the condition of untold sufferings of a large section of communities in India under the oppressive caste system.

c. Distinctive Features of Mass Movements

The two categories of missions mentioned above, namely, missions to the educated and missions to the vulnerable were the products of missionary initiative. Missionaries, depending on the context of the constituency that they were serving adopted strategies suitable to that context. Some have responded positively to such initiatives and others partially. But, when we come to the study of the mass movements, the whole process was completely different from the established patterns, leaving even the committed missionaries confused. It is therefore, necessary to look into the distinctive features of these mass movements, in order to understand the import of those movements. Two of the experiences that I had at the helm of the Church prompted me to look afresh for reasons and motivations that led to these movements. The results were entirely different from what was generally recorded in the pages of Church history books and articles. These experiences are important milestones in reshaping my understanding of 'spirituality' itself, hence, I take liberty to mention them here.

The first one was in Vellore Diocese of the Church of South India. Bishop Y William of the Vellore Diocese invited me to participate in the 'Ponnai Anaicut Festival' (festival on the bank of the River Ponnai) conducted annually for three days. People from the Northern Districts of Tamil Nadu and the Southern Districts of Karnataka and Andhra Pradesh gather together to celebrate their spirituality through dance, drama, music, prayer cells, preaching and sharing testimonies. All those who gathered at this festival were poor people, coming as families and groups of families and friends, in whatever means of transportation that they could afford. They cooked their own food and shared in fellowship meals and participated leisurely in different programmes conducted not only by the organisers but also different groups and congregations. At the end of the day, they slept on the river bed under the open sky. There was a sea of humanity amounting to several thousands and even over a lakh of people. The most important thing that I noticed, was that they looked happy and contented. Their living conditions did not seem to bother them. It appeared to me that they came to be one with God in the midst of their daily human struggles. The legend says that a missionary on his journey lost himself in the wilderness and he could not figure out where he was. Wandering without food and water and totally exhausted he rested on a stone fearful of being attacked by the wild beasts. But, when he got up the next morning to his surprise he saw a river nearby. In thankfulness to God, he remained there and built a small church, using the stones and mud and sand available there. That place gradually came to be recognized as a Pilgrim Centre and people flock there to have their spiritual encounter with the Lord. This experience made me think whether the spirituality that we talk about is confined only to a set pattern of dogmas, rituals and practices or spirituality can be even in the realm of emotions, or crude beliefs. Could this be described as a 'leap of faith' for these poor people. I even reflected on these issues by way of an article in the 'South India Churchman', the official magazine of the Church of South India.

The second experience is in Nandyal Diocese. The Rt. Rev. Dr. P. J. Lawrence, the Diocesan Bishop invited me to be the Chief Guest at Tirunala (Holy Celebration) which is normally held on the 1st and 2nd December, every year, in a place called Kalasapadu, a remote part of the Diocese. This is a low lying area and there is a stream passing by. A church has been in existence in this place for more than a century. The legend says that on one occasion when it rained, there was a flash flood destroying everything that came in its way. The people near the church rushed into the church building to save themselves from the fury of the floods. When the floods abated, those who were inside the church realized that everything else except the church building had been destroyed. Only God saved them through that church building.

Today, it has become a pilgrim centre. Thousands of people visit this place annually. On the day that I was to visit this place there was a heavy downpour. We had to get down from our car and cover the distance walking through the slushy and muddy road. When we reached the place it was still raining. A huge crowd had gathered around the makeshift stage. Some under the protection of umbrellas and majority of them braved the downpour without any protection. When I asked the Bishop what they were waiting for he replied that they were waiting to hear the message from the chief guest. I felt humbled by their eager expectation. I began preaching to them in the form of story-telling which was translated into Telugu by one of the organisers. The first thing that I did was to ask the volunteer who was trying to hold the umbrella for me to remove the same and I began to preach in the pouring rain. This gesture on my part was deeply appreciated by the crowd by way of applause and loud cheering. They listened to my preaching with rapt attention bursting out into cheers and applauses now and then, whenever the message touched their hearts. At the end, I told them that I had learnt more about their spirituality than sharing my thoughts on spirituality. This experience again raised questions within my own mind as to the stereotype way we describe spirituality in the church. I learnt that there are a variety of ways that people express their spirituality and the Church needs to be sensitive to this aspect.

With these experiences at the back of my mind, I began to re-read the historical records of mass movements. I looked beyond what has been recorded. The results were astounding and they are presented here as distinctive features of mass movements.

i. Mass Movements were First and Foremost Movements in Search of Spiritual Experience

It is a human tendency to attribute spirituality to those who are able to articulate their faith in public discourses, debates and discussions. It is specifically applicable to people who follow religious traditions, practice rituals and go on pilgrimages regularly. Spirituality is also seen in charity works for the benefit of lesser mortals. In effect, spirituality has come to be associated with the high and mighty, rich and powerful, educated and influential. Very rarely, human society attributes spirituality to the poor and marginalized, oppressed and downtrodden section of society. For, they are not able to articulate their faith, neither can they demonstrate their faith through regular religious practices nor can they involve in acts of charity because they have nothing to give. But, the reality is that even though these people are crushed from every side, not just existentially but historically as well, they have kept their flickering hope burning deep down in their hearts. That flickering hope is their eternal trust that God will deliver them from all afflictions one day. It is this unwavering trust in God which motivates them to follow a new path whenever an opportunity presents itself. Remember, when Israelites were crushed under the atrocities of Pharaoh in Egypt, they did not appeal to any human agency, but cried unto the Lord to such an extent that the Lord had to raise up Moses as a leader of the community saying, 'I have surely seen the affliction of my people who are in Egypt, and have given heed to their cry because of their task masters, for I am aware of their sufferings' (Ex.3:7) Again in the struggles of Black people over and against the dominance of the White supremacists, the Black people sang what has come to be known as 'Negro Spirituals', 'We shall overcome some day'. In the words of James H. Cone, one of the prominent Black Theologians, 'the art of survival' was due to 'Grace of God. We call it grace because we know it to be an unearned gift from him who is the 'giver of every good and perfect gift' (*God of the Oppressed,* p. 2).

Similarly in India, mass movements are the 'irruption of the oppressed communities' in search of spiritual quest. It made a sudden appearance in some cases and gradual influx in others. It might have started in some parts of India, but, spread to many communities throughout India acquiring national character in the process. There is no history of charismatic personalities like Moses and Martin Luther King Jr. who led the Israelites and Afro-Americans respectively. But, God raised many Moses and Martin Luther Kings from among different communities. It is they, who took initiative in search of spiritual quest. They were not looking for economic gains or status in life. They were looking for spiritual experiences. As the Scriptures say, 'They craved to seek ye first the Kingdom of God and His righteousness'. (Mat. 6:33)

Narrative I

Vedamanickam, a Sambavan by caste, which is one of the castes of the Adi Dravida community was a resident of Mailady in the then Travancore District, but now in Kanyakumari District. He was a religious person and desired to seek illumination and peace in the presence of the Lord. Knowing that he would not be allowed to enter the precincts of the temple, yet, he along with his nephew, undertook the pilgrimage to Chidambaram so that he could be as near the temple as possible. At the outer courtyard of the temple, he dreamt that an old man was rebuking him for undertaking a fruitless journey and asking him to go back to his native place. On his way back he went and stayed with his relatives in Tanjore who had become Christians by then. They shared the Christian gospel with him and subsequently he and his nephew were baptized. After returning to his native place, Vedamanickam began to teach and preach the Christian faith to his people. He later met Rev. William Tobias Ringeltaube, a young missionary and begged him to come to his native place and baptize people. In 1816, Rev. Ringeltaube placed Vedamanickam in charge of the church, in which members from both Sambavar community and Nadar community worshipped together. Vedamanickam was accepted as a leader by all its members. (See Firth, pp. 156-157 and J. W. Pickett, p. 38-41)

Narrative 2

Periah from the village of Tallakondapaud was a Madiga by caste, but was a deeply religious person. He went to Godavari District to buy hides of the dead cattle killed by the epidemic. He stayed with his relative Vongole Abraham, enroute, who had already become a Christian. Abraham introduced Periah to Christianity. On his return to his village, Periah began to preach about Christ to his relatives and neighbours who opposed him vehemently. But, Periah and his wife and some others began participating in Christian worship. Rev. Clough, having come to know about the zeal of Periah and his wife concerning Christian worship, sent for them and taught them and baptized them in 1806. On Periah's insistence, Rev. Clough went to his village, reached and worshipped for five days and baptized twenty eight people. Through Periah's zealous work thousands of people got converted to Christianity by 1878. (J. W. Pickett, pp. 47-49)

Narrative 3

Rev. Clough organized relief work during the famine years of 1876-79 by taking a contract from the Government to dig a three and a half mile section of the Buckingham Canal. Large number of Madigas came for 'food for work'. During the nights they used to participate in Christian worship in which Rev. Clough used to preach. However, Rev. Clough refused to baptize any one when the famine was continuing. After the famine was over, people began to ask for baptisms, but Rev. Clough was not convinced of the genuineness of the christian commitment on the part of the people. They then gave a petition to Rev. Clough with the following words:

'We have learned about Jesus Christ. We now believe in Him as the only God and Saviour. We are poor; our huts are fallen down, and we have not much to eat but leaves; but we do not ask you for money. We will not ask you for a pie, even though we starve to death; but we believe in Jesus and he commanded us, we want to be baptized. We can die, if it is God's will; but we want to be baptized first. Be pleased to grant our request, and do not put us off any longer. May the Lord help us.' (Quoted in the notes by John C. Webster: *The Dalit Christians, A History,* p. 45-46)

Narrative 4

Ditt, a lame and illiterate, lived in a village called Shahabdike, in the District of Sialkot of Punjab State. He was from Chuhra community. He survived by buying and selling hides. He heard the Christian message from a Jat convert by name Nattu of the neighbouring village. Being interested to become a christian he persuaded Nattu to take him to missionaries in Sialkot in 1873. There, he requested for baptism as well as to be sent back to his village. Missionaries reluctantly agreed to both his requests. Back in his village he began to preach about Christianity to his family and relatives. Later, he took his wife, daughter, nephew and some other relatives to Sialkot to be baptized. It is said that this movement grew to such an extent that by 1891 there were 10,165 Christians. Regarding this movement one missionary writes in 1883 as follows:

'It is now over ten years since the movement began; it is not therefore, a mere temporary impulse. At first, one made a profession of faith in Christ, and it was principally through his efforts that the work spread through the neighbouring villages, then through the friends and relatives of those who first believed.' (Quoted by John C. Webster, p. 49)

The above narratives are only to indicate the basic nature of the mass movements. There are hundreds of stories like these in different parts of India during the 19th and 20th Century. What the above stories emphasize is that the initiative was taken by the oppressed communities themselves, some by individual leaders and at other times by a group of people together. Further, mass movements were not from one community but from different communities depending on the interest that they have shown in the Gospel. Missionaries did not seek them, but the community leaders or groups from the community sought the missionaries. It is this aspect that made J. W. Pickett to conclude as follows:

'The real founder in Travancore was not Ringeltaube, but Vedamanickam. In Kistna it was not Darling but Venkayya. In Sialkot it was not Gordon but Ditt.' (p. 56)

Narrative 5

This truth is not only applicable to missions of 18th and 19th Century but also to the 20th Century. One example can be quoted in this regard. Bishop Leslie Newbigin, in his autobiography '*Unfinished Agenda*' quotes from his own letter written in 1940, concerning an incident that took place in one of the villages in Kanchipuram District of the Madras Diocese, of which he became the Bishop later. The letter is quoted here verbatim for its effectiveness in story telling.

"Early in January two men came to our Mission Hospital here from a village of which we had not heard, named Tirupanamur. They said they had come on behalf of their village to ask us to send someone to tell them about Christianity. The Hospital Catechist promised that someone would come, and two or three days later three of us set off to look for the village. After many inquiries, and much wandering about in territory which was new to all of us, we arrived after dark at the village. In the middle of the village was a small, well-built temple. To our surprise, the temple was immediately opened, a lamp brought and ourselves invited to sit down inside. In a few minutes a large crowd was gathered round the porch of the temple, and the leading man, having made us sit down, spoke to us in words that reminded me of Cornelius welcoming Peter. In effect, he said: 'We have invited you to come, and we are glad that you have come. Now here we are, and we know nothing about Christianity, but we want you to tell us all about it from the beginning'. The Catechist, whom by general agreement we had made our spokesman, replied by asking why they had invited us, and in particular how it came that they invited us into the temple. They answered that they had asked us because some of them had been in the Mission Hospital, and what they had heard and seen made them want to find out more about this Christian way. As for the temple, they were not using it, and they were wondering whether the idol was any use at all, or whether they should not go over entirely to the Christian way. So, they asked us to tell them all about it.

It was wonderful to see the eagerness with which they listened. Here were people who were really in earnest, and their attention never wavered. The Catechist began from the idol in whose temple we were sitting, drawing from the people, by question and suggestion, their admission of the futility of worshipping the work of their hands. Then, he went on to appeal to the sense in all of them of a supreme creator God, and to the common situation of guilt before Him. Then came the change from argument to announcement as he told them of Jesus, and of the life which He gives. When the meeting at last came to an end, the majority had expressed themselves as satisfied that this was the truth, and they wanted to be instructed further. They had responded to my suggestion of sending a teacher with the promise of house and food and welcome for him, and the unfettered use of the temple for Christian teaching and worship." (pp. 63 and 64)

ii. Secondly, Mass Movements were a Rural Phenomenon

Missionary headquarters were in cities and towns. Their concentration was in attracting people of higher castes thinking that a higher caste convert would be able to convince the lower caste person easily about the truth of Christianity. Further, missionary approach was to individuals based on their philosophy of individualism. Hence, their presence in the rural areas were minimal, if not totally absent, before the mass movements took place. Yet, mass movements became a reality and spread throughout India in due course of time. History has demonstrated that these movements emerged from villages rather than from urban centres. Probably, it is this aspect of village centric movements that made the critics to think that they were motivated by economic considerations and not of genuine commitment for Christian faith. Hence, they categorized these converts as 'Rice Christians'. On the contrary, the above mentioned historical narratives disprove any such allegations as baseless and not true. To verify this fact, one has to only visit villages where Christians are residing. Their economic conditions have remained deplorable, but their faith in Christ is unshakable. However, the question still remains, that is, why village movements and not urban? To answer this question one needs to take the prevailing social conditions which have been described earlier into serious consideration. Centuries of oppression and marginalization have left the psyche of Dalits wounded. Atrocities against Dalits increased in villages due to strict regimentation of religious and social conditions imposed by high caste communities. As a result, Dalit feelings were repressed and suppressed. It is in this context, that Dalits have developed their own system of approach to life in their own religio-social contexts.

Three of the prominent approaches to life are mentioned here. The first one is *Pessimists View*. Majority of Dalits have come to the conclusion that their living conditions have been miserable for centuries and will remain so for centuries to come and so accept it as 'fate', some even considering it as 'karma' of the past. The second approach is creating a '*Counter Culture*'. They need gods to protect them but not the gods of the oppressors. They need gods who are blood-thirsty and gods who are ferocious and gods who are angry. These gods did not reside in magnificent temples in far-away places but resided in a hut or a small place like them just outside the village premises. They need to be worshipped not with flowers but with animal sacrifices. Their musical instruments are not melodious Veenas used in the temples but noisy drums. Their dance is not the methodical and rhythmic and gracious steps performed by trained dancers but ecstatic and exuberant outbursts of energy in a group. Even, death has a different meaning for them. It is not a solemn occasion to mourn but joyous occasion to celebrate with dance and alcohol, because the dead person has overcome all the trials, tribulations and humiliations meted out to that person in this world. The third approach to life is '*Exploring Alternate System*'. Those whose spirits have not been crushed completely kept their hopes alive and they began to explore alternate systems to express their spirituality. They looked for systems either within the Hindu tradition or outside Hindu tradition. For this purpose they explored all possible reform movements from within Hinduism, such as Buddhism, Sikhism, Lingayatism, Arya Samaj etc. and from outside Hindu traditions such as Islam and Christianity. So, mass movements of 19th and 20th century were not the only unique experiments that the Dalits undertook. Probably, the movement to Christianity might have been on a larger scale than in the other movements because Christianity offered better opportunity for worship and social acceptance. All that the Dalits desired was an opportunity to worship the Lord like any other believers and where their human dignity was upheld. Christianity met those conditions and so the movement took place in the villages, which are the nerve centres of human life in India. It should be noted here that all the three approaches adopted by Dalits are in the realm of religious experience; and it has always been a peaceful movement and never an aggressive or confrontational movement.

iii. Thirdly, Mass Movements were Movements of Families or Group of Families

We have earlier noted that nowhere in India have the people turned to Christ '*en masse*'. It should be noted from the narratives mentioned above that families and groups of families within a community accepted Christ. To understand this phenomenon we need to look into the social structure once again. One of the stable institutions found in the Indian social structure is family. Western missionaries with their emphasis on individualism have failed to recognize this important aspect of Indian life. In India, individual is not the basic unit of society, but family is considered the basic unit of society. This is applicable to any caste or religion. For instance, if one asks what the membership of any congregation or a Church in the West, the reply would be number of individuals on the roll. If the same question is asked in India, the reply would be numbers in terms of families. Family is defined not only as husband, wife and children, which is normally addressed as 'nuclear family' but also it includes parents, siblings, their spouses and children, which is called 'joint family.' Family also includes relatives which is called 'extended family'. Family provides nurture, protection and security to all the members. They share assets and liabilities, as well as joys and sorrows. Particularly among the Dalits, individuals have to depend upon the families for their survival. Therefore, family provides an important institutional mechanism in taking policy decisions about the future of that family. If the head of the family is a highly respected in the family circle, his decision will become decisions of the entire family or majority of the family members. Further, we have earlier noted that Dalit tradition is 'oral culture' and not 'written culture', therefore, the communication is oral, person to person, or person to other family members by way of story-telling or sharing experiences. Particularly, if the narrator is a person of integrity having the interest of the family at heart then his experience or his narrative will be accepted as the decision of the entire family. This is how families or groups of families have accepted Christ. It is this aspect of group decision, that was suspect in the minds of missionaries in the initial stages. This is also the reason, why intellectuals within the community and orthodox Hindus from outside the Christian community questioned the genuineness of the Christian commitment, on the part of the people involved in mass movements. The question, which has remained unanswered even today is, 'Is salvation available only to individuals – and that too, only after an intellectual and rational acceptance of Christian faith? Or is salvation available to even families or groups of families? Is there a scope for 'leap of faith' to become recipients of salvation? If it is not possible, then how would anyone explain the Pentecostal experience where Peter declares 'You will receive the gift of the Holy Spirit. For the promise is for you and your children and for all who are far off, every one whom the Lord our God calls to himself'. (Acts 2:38-39) Or again what does it mean when Paul calls upon the jailor to 'Believe in the Lord Jesus, and you will be saved, you and your household' (Acts 16:31) Theologians have refused to entertain such questions leave alone attempting to answer them. But, the people involved in the mass movements did believe in the saving power of the Gospel, however inadequate their understanding of the faith might have been.

d. Missionary Response to Mass Movements

As mentioned earlier, missionaries were critical of these mass movements, initially. They did not know how to respond to these movements. John C. Webster quotes from the Third Decennial Missionary Conference held in Bombay, at the end of 1892, which raised a number of questions in response to these movements. (p. 38). These questions are significant for our understanding of the perplexity prevailing in the minds of missionaries, in the initial period. They are: 'Are these movements the work of God? What opportunities and dangers are inherent in them? What forms should our responses to the Dalits take? Can and does Christianity in fact provide what Dalits are seeking? Should we try to ameliorate their social condition? If so, do we work on behalf of all the Dalits or confine our efforts to those who have become Christians? How will work among Dalits affect the rest of the work we are doing?' However, when once the missionaries were convinced of the genuineness of these movements, they went all out to strengthen these movements. Here again, their methodology was the Biblical methodology of preaching, teaching and healing. But, in implementing this method they devised entirely new strategies suitable to the context they were facing. They are:

Spiritual nurture

The primary concern of the missionaries was how to provide spiritual nurture to vast number of people who had become christians. It was impossible for a limited number of missionaries stationed in urban centres to provide Christian nurture to new converts living in far-away villages. Hence, 'natural' leaders from among these village Christians and talented women were selected by the missionaries and were trained on the job and sent back to their villages as 'evangelists' and 'Bible women'. They were to report to missionaries once a month about the progress of the work when they came to receive their 'honorarium'. They were also given instructions for further work for the following month. Missionaries visited the village congregations on special occasions like Harvest Festival or other Christian festivals. Thus, the spiritual nurture of the new converts was ensured by the constant interaction of the Evangelists and Bible women on day to day basis.

Education for Change

Missionaries were also concerned about the future of these congregations and they realized that the only way of building up a Christian community was through education, which not only removes ignorance but gives a better understanding of Christianity. But, education was not made available to the Dalit communities in those days. Hence, they began Elementary Schools in all these villages in the localities where Christian communities were residing, and in the vernacular language. The School was open to all irrespective of caste considerations both for male and female children. This policy was entirely different from the policy that the Missionaries adopted earlier in starting High Schools and Colleges in cities and for those who already had access to educational facilities. They appointed the Evangelists to double up as teachers to the school children and spiritual leaders to the Christian communities. The purpose was not only to make children literate, but also build up their character based on Biblical values. Further, in the School social integration was practiced between high caste and low caste children. Thus, education was to be a life changing process. In this venture missionaries became pioneers in ushering egalitarian society.

Empowerment of women

One of the programmes which brought about drastic change in the attitude of men and women was introduction of women's education. In a context where women were confined to the four walls of their homes and denied any participation in public affairs, the introduction of women's education became a turning point for change in the attitude of men and women in terms of their understanding of Sati system, child marriage, or devadasi system and such practices. Through education women were conscientised and empowered to fight against all these evil practices. Missionaries, rather the wives of missionaries and women missionaries whose work has not been adequately acknowledged became the pioneers in these ventures. Empowerment of women was one single activity of the missionaries which transformed the lives of thousands of women and laid the foundation for a modern India.

Breaking barriers

For the first time missionaries realized that individuals or families or groups of families accepting Christ did not transform the social systems and structures. They were convinced that individual salvation is also linked to a conducive social atmosphere. The systems and structures that dehumanize human beings and discriminates one from another on the basis of caste should be changed whether it is within the Church or outside the Church. Two examples from history can be quoted in this regard.

The first one is what has come to be known as 'upper cloth rebellion'. Though Vedamanickam was the pioneer in accepting Christ and few of his relatives and friends became christians in Travancore area under the leadership of Ringeltaube, from 1810 onwards a group of people from 'Shanar' community which is now called 'Nadar' began to accept Christ. Under the leadership of Charles Mead, the successor to Ringeltaube, a large number of people became christians. At that time, one of the prevailing social practices was that women from Nadar community should not wear any clothes above the waist. Missionaries desired that women come to worship covering their upper part of the body as well. So British Resident issued a proclamation permitting the use of Jacket called 'cooppayam' on the part of Christian Shanar women and prohibiting the use of the upper cloth on the part of Hindu Shanar families. Hindu Shanar women resented such a move. Further, Christian Shanar women began to wear not only the upper cloth but also dress like high caste women. High caste women opposed this change in dress code vehemently because their caste identity would be affected very badly. The conflict became so intense that the Maharaja of Travancore had to deploy a detachment of high caste regiment to crush the unrest. (See Dewan Madava Rao's letter to General Cullen, the British Resident dated 12th February 1859 as quoted in M. K. Kuriokose: *History of Christianity in India*: Source Materials. P. 184-187) The missionaries responding to this situation, took a bold and firm stand in expressing solidarity with the cause of exploited women both Christian and Hindu Shanar women. They wrote a very strong letter dated 26th March 1959 to Lord Stanley, Secretary of State for India (See M. K. Kuriokose pp. 187-189). This stand on the part of missionaries helped C. E. Trevelyan of Madras Presidency to instruct the British Resident in Travancore General Cullen to interfere in favour of demands of the Shanar women. (M. K. Kuriakose, pp. 189-191) Thus, missionaries stood firmly against social customs and practices that dehumanized a section of society.

The second example is from within the Church. One of the basic tenets of the Christian faith is that in Christ all are one and there is no discrimination between one to the other. For the Scripture expressly stipulates as follows: 'For as many of you were baptized into Christ have put on Christ, there is neither Jew nor Greek, there is neither slave nor free, there is neither male nor female, for you are all one in Christ Jesus. And if you are Christ's then you are Abraham's offspring, heirs according to promise'. (Gal. 3:27-29) Jesus himself broke the social customs that discriminated human beings on the basis of religious beliefs and practices. He accepted the anointing by a sinful woman and that too in the company of Pharisees who were very strict in following 'purity' and 'impurity' perceptions. (Luke 7:36 ff) He ate with tax collectors and sinners in their house. (Matt. 9:9ff) For Jesus any custom which discriminated and segregated one section of people from the other had to be broken down. No discrimination on the basis of colour, race, class, caste and gender is permissible in Christian faith.

However, it can also be observed that the Church has failed to live upto these Biblical injunctions and practiced racial discrimination, colour prejudice, gender bias, class distinction and caste segregation throughout its history. On the other hand, being conscious of God's grace, the Church also had the determination to overcome such practices, wherever and whenever such practices raised its ugly head. Even, in the New Testament when the needs of the poor widows of Helenist background were neglected by the Christians of Hebrew background, the disciples in consultation with fellow believers took steps to redress their grievances (Acts 6:1-7). Again when Christians from the Jewish background tried to impose the custom of circumcision on the Christians of Gentile background the first ever Council of the Church had to be convened in Jerusalem to resolve the issue (Acts 15 and Gal. 2). The serious conflict was resolved by the whole Church saying 'for it seemed good to the Holy Spirit and to us to lay on you no greater burden'. (Acts 15:28) Similarly, 'Black Theology' is essentially articulation of faith against the racial discrimination of Afro Americans by the White supremacists. 'Feminism' is basically assertion of human dignity of women against male domination. Likewise, Latin America's 'Liberation Theology' is fundamentally an articulation of faith against class distinction that prevails in their society. Dalit theology is an articulation of faith from the perspective of the struggles and aspirations of Dalit people in India.

One of the important issues that confronted the Protestant Missionaries from the beginning was caste system. Their attitude to caste system was particularly difficult due to the ambiguous position adopted by the exiting Churches of the time concerning this issue. Syrian Churches had accommodated caste system. Roman Catholic Church had 'tolerated' caste system within the Church. The Tranquebar Mission had permitted high caste and low caste groups to sit separately within their first Church building called 'Jerusalem Church' with the low caste Christians taking part in the Holy communion only when all the high caste people had received the same. Being influenced by the Lutheran Mission's attitude towards caste within the church some of the early Anglican Missionaries who had contact with Lutheran Mission tolerated caste system. But, later Missionaries and particularly Bishop Wilson stood firmly against caste system within the Church. He sent a pastoral circular in 1833 instructing the congregations to desist from caste practices within the Church, and emphatically stated that 'the distinction of caste must be abandoned, decidedly, immediately and finally.' (C. B. Firth, p.162) He followed it up with his visits to congregations in the South Tiruchirapalli, Tanjore and Madras preaching about the scriptural injunctions against caste practices. In particular, in Madras Vepery Church, he invited people to come to the Lord's Table to receive communion only if they believe in the egalitarian principles. The story is told that the Collector of Madras and his wife made a christian from Pariah background kneel in between them to receive the Holy Communion Cup. It is also said that out of five hundred communicants only about ten or twelve left the church without receiving communion (M. K. Kuriakose, p. 121)

The confusion in holding variety of positions with regard to caste within different denominations is precisely due to difficulty in determining whether caste is a 'religious institution' or a 'civil/social/cultural institution'. Duncan B. Forester (*Caste and Christianity*, p.18 f) quotes two social anthropologists in this regard. The first one is Professor F. G. Bailey, who held the view that caste is a 'peculiarly rigid and extreme form of social stratification. It legitimates itself to those within it, and it has not necessary connection with Hinduism or with ideas directly derived from Hindus. Hence, it is a civil/social/cultural institution.' On the other hand, Professor Louis Dumont is of the view that caste is 'integrally connected with Hinduism, and quite inconceivable apart from the Hindu context which provides the ideology without a grasp of which no adequate understanding of caste is possible'. Its hierarchy is based on religiously sanctioned concepts of purity and pollution. Hence, it is a religious institution distinctive only to Hinduism. The debate among the scholars continues even today. One notable feature of the debate is that scholars from high caste background defending that caste is civil institution and hence to be retained for the stability of society, whereas scholars from low caste background, including Dr. B. R. Ambedkar arguing for the 'annihilation of caste'.

The Protestant Mission opposed caste practices within the Church from the beginning as they considered caste as incompatible with the demands of the Gospel. Resolutions drawn at the South India Missionary Conference, held in Ootacamund in 1858 demonstrates the consensus arrived at with regard to the issue. As they are important for the churches even today the resolution is reprinted here:

'Resolutions on caste'

1. That this conference regard Hindu caste, both in theory and practice, as not a mere civil distinction, but emphatically a religious institution, and viewed in this, its true character, it is the monster evil in India. So paramount and all-prevailing in its power and influence, so tyrannical and cruel in its laws and regulations, so stern and exacting in its demands, so terrific in its denunciations of present and future, punishment for the slightest offence, and yet to changeful and accommodating in its manifestation that it is no marvel that millions have for ages fallen prostrate before it and that no arms of flesh can deliver them from its thralldom.
2. That it is the duty of all missionaries to spare no pains, on all proper occasions, to expose the absurdities and falsehood, and denounce the wickedness of caste, to show its great injuriousness to all classes of its voteries and its great obstructiveness to all efforts for the improvement of their temporal condition as well as its soul destroying influence.
3. That it is also the duty of all missionaries and churches to require its unreserved and unequivocal renunciation with all its outward manifestations, by all those who take up the profession of Christianity and join the ranks of the Redeemer. No man should be regarded as worthy the name of Christian who refuses to renounce caste and to remove all its outward marks or who objects to any kind of intercourse with any other Christians, simply on the ground of distinctions.
4. That the greater vigilance is indispensably necessary to prevent the return of this evil spirit after it has once been cast out, and to guard against the power of habit which it has to deeply inwrought into the very souls and hearts of men. Let a holy sagacity and unbending firmness be constantly employed in detecting and opposing all its workings, in all the intercourse of the Christian life.

5. That it is the duty of all Christians to unite in protesting against all recognition of caste in all public acts of Government, whether direct or indirect and in the whole of the military and civil services. Caste should be a thing entirely unknown in its connection.
 (M.K. Kuriakose p.176-177)
 From that time onwards all Protestant Missionaries sincerely followed the resolution of the Missionary Conference and stood firmly against the practice of caste within the Church.

e. Spiritual Formation and Economic Emancipation

Missionaries did not indulge in secular politics and commerce as organized activities. Firstly, because of their conviction that the Church and State are separate. Secondly, it was their conviction that the motive behind commerce is making profit, whereas the motive of the missionaries was to serve. The aim of the missionaries was to lead individuals to commit themselves to Christ, and not to make profit as a business concern. Spiritual formation based on alternate world view as revealed in the Bible was their primary concern. However, they soon realized that to be effective in their mission work they had to take the religious, cultural and social context seriously, particularly when dealing with the vulnerable sections of society, they had to combine service with spiritual formation. Worship Services, Bible Study Centres, preaching, cottage prayer meetings were some of the ways in which they introduced spiritual formation.

On the other hand, they started educational institutions and health care centres to provide wholistic approach to personality development. The purpose was to treat soul, mind and body as an integral whole. Spiritual growth for the inner being, development of mind through education and promotion of bodily health cannot be carried out in isolation, rather, it has to be achieved in combination with one another. This is what the missionaries aimed at, so they provided spiritual growth through the Church, development of the mind through educational institutions and maintenance of bodily health through health care centres. We should never make the mistake of treating these concerns as independent institutions having nothing to do with the other. Different emphasis may be there, but only when they are taken together they will have transforming effect on the individual concerned. Spiritual formation and service to humanity went hand in hand. It was always service with sacrifice without expecting any reward. Commerce or profit making motive was never the concern of the missionaries.

However, all these service institutions gradually brought freedom to the beneficiaries. Let us analyze this aspect especially from the point of view of the vulnerable section of people. Village schools started by the missionaries provided an opportunity to those who were not allowed entrance to schools to study. After primary school they were brought to urban centres and provided higher education through Boarding Homes and High Schools. Brighter children were encouraged to pursue university education, while for others job oriented courses were offered. Similarly, to provide health care various professional courses were introduced and needed personnel were trained. At the end of the course, the concerned persons found jobs either in the church, church related institutions, government offices or private concerns. Thus, the service institutions started by the missionaries became a stepping stone for economic activities. It brought economic emancipation for the individuals concerned.

This economic freedom changed the outlook and life-style of once vulnerable people. Those, who were destined to follow caste bound traditional menial jobs are now able to opt for decent, meaningful jobs. Those, who were bound by economic deprivation are now able to lead a dignified life. Those, who were socially ostracized are now able to forget their miserable past in the urban environment. In short, education started by the missionaries brought about economic emancipation for many in the long run.

Thus, as we have observed above, spiritual formation undertaken by the missionaries, based on biblical perspective has had an impact on whole of life. Spiritual formation resulted in personal salvation, human compassion, social transformation as well as economic emancipation. It covers individual life, community life and the life of the society around the faith community. All these changes take place in this world and not in the coming world. Spiritual formation is to transform this world, which is the Mission of God.

f. Legacy from Dalit Spirituality

We have noted in the earlier chapters, that the Indian Protestant Church have become recipients of inheritance from the Vedic religions and heritage from the Western Church through the missionaries. But, in this chapter we have also noted an upsurge of families from different Dalit communities into Christianity. In fact, it is these communities, who formed the majority in the early Church. They did not come empty handed, but they brought their own brand of spirituality into the church which the Church has failed to acknowledge. Three of their spiritual contributions need to be recognized here. Firstly, community spiritualty, the Vedic religion emphasized on self-realization and spirituality for service. The Western form of Christianity stressed in individual and spirituality, worshipping community as community spirituality. To this western Christianity, had also added spirituality for engagement as a third principle. But, Dalit communities brought in the concept of community spirituality as a life-style. Their style of worship is in community and not in individual capacity as the Vedic religions; their cultural activities were in community and not as individual talents; their survival depended on one another rather than individual abilities. Therefore, they came into the church as families or groups of families and not as individuals from the high caste groups. This community spirituality is a contribution from the Dalit religions to the Indian Church.

Secondly, spirituality of suffering – Dalit suffering begins at birth and ends only when a person dies. They are religiously isolated, socially ostracized, economically marginalized and culturally alienated. Life is full of suffering for them. Liberation is only through death; hence they celebrate at death. But, they have tolerated this suffering century after century, yet in the midst of all these sufferings they work for the benefit of others. They do not get any reward for their hard labour. Rather, being conscious that their hard work brings benefit for others they execute their work sincerely. This Karma Marga is their spirituality. Suffering for others welfare is their spirituality. It is this spirituality of suffering that has attracted them to Christianity and not any economic 'inducement' as insinuated by high caste critics. Dalits identified their suffering with the sufferings of Jesus Christ on the Cross, who suffered to bring about salvation for human beings. They found refuge in the God whom Christians believe, as a God who accepted them as His children as against their gods who turned them away. They found in the Christian Church, a people who treated them with human dignity, and that is why they decided to follow Christ. In turn, they highlighted the necessity for suffering for others, or following the Way of the Cross in the Mission of God.

Thirdly, importance of oral tradition – Dalits being illiterates, their channel of communication was only through personal conversation or through public announcements via a messenger. Recipients of the Gospel, themselves became messengers of the Gospel through oral communication and conversation. They received God's grace and in turn passed on that grace to others in the family and the community as channels of grace.

This is one of the very important principles in spirituality. Those who received God's grace must in turn, pass on that grace to others. This is another specific spiritual input from those who accepted Christianity from Dalit religions. In the course of history, the Indian Church developed a concept of 'personal evangelism' – communicating the Gospel from person to person. This concept certainly stems from the communication channel adopted by the Dalit religions.

Chapter 4

Religious, Cultural and Social Resurgence

Any movement, which disturbs the status quo of the existing order is bound to attract reactions - sometimes in a gentle manner and at other times in a violent manner. They can also be appreciative or depreciative; endorsing or critical. They can also pave way for corrective measures. When it affects a religion, it definitely arouses rational, emotional as well as communal feelings leading to violent outbursts at times. This is true not only in history, even in modern times it happens. For instance, in spite of Article 25 in the Indian Constitution assuring all citizens the right to 'freely profess, practice and propagate religion' and the State is called upon to make laws for 'social welfare and reform for throwing open of Hindu religious institutions of a public character to all classes and sections of Hindus,' there are many temples which do not allow entry to Dalits and women on the basis of tradition. When either a group of Dalits or progressive women try to enter such temples, it always creates tensions, violent outbursts to such an extent that police intervention becomes necessary.

In the case of formation of new communities in Christianity, it unintentionally disturbed the existing social order in Hindu society. The reasons being differences in theological, ideological and sociological understanding. Theological, because belief in one God as against belief in many gods. Secondly, ideological because of the concept of equality of human beings, both in the sight of God and in human relationships as against practice of superior and inferior treatment given to human beings in Hinduism. Thirdly, the difference is also sociological in nature. Hindu social order is based on caste system, whereas the Christian communities have been organized in such a way that it transcends all sociological barriers. For these reasons, whenever new Christian communities were formed, it invariably attracted some reactions, both at the ground level as well as at the intellectual level. Some of the reactions that were generated both within the Christian community as well as outside the Christian Church form the subject matter of this Chapter.

1. Reactions from within the Christian Community

a. Orientalists

We have noted in Chapter II that during the 17th and early part of the 18th century, two powerful movements swept across Europe, namely a philosophical movement called Enlightenment and the other was the Pietistic movement. The missionaries who came to India, being influenced by Pietistic movement, emphasized on the personal encounter with Christ. In their desire to prove the superiority of Christianity over and against Hinduism, they mainly took Hinduism as it was practiced in those days and pin-pointed the negative aspects of Hinduism. In some cases like Alexander Duff, the approach to Hinduism could even be described as 'aggressive Evangelism', though all missionaries cannot be clubbed under this category. On the other hand, Orientalists being influenced by Enlightenment philosophy felt the need to discover the 'essence' of Hinduism by studying Hinduism in its original context and not based on contemporary popular Hinduism which was becoming 'a decrepit religion' (a phrase used by Max Muller) of the later version. As a result, Sanskrit being the language of the Hindu Scriptures, Vedas being the original and earliest Hindu Scriptures including the Bhagavad Gita got published in English language. This, in a way, not only helped the European Scholars to get acquainted with Sanskrit and Hinduism, but also popularized Hinduism in its essence. Therefore, Mission in India by Missionaries and popularizing of Hinduism by Orientalists are to be treated as contemporaneous acts. Distinguished scholar among the Orientalists was Oxford Indologist, Max Muller, who published his work on 'Rigveda' between 1849 and 1875. He was of the opinion that Vedas which are the oldest written Scriptures present the essence of true Hinduism as against the subsequently written Puranas and Tantras. He writes: 'There is no authority whatever in the hymns of the Vedas for the complicated system of castes; no authority for the offensive privileges claimed by the Brahmanas,; no authority for the degraded position of the Sudras. There is no law to prohibit the different classes of people from living together, from eating and drinking together; no law to prohibit the marriage of people – belonging to different castes; no law to brand the offspring of such marriages with an indelible stigma.' (As quoted by Duncan B. Forester, p. 62) It is said that the Orientalists' influence in the formulation of the policy of 'neutrality' by the Government was very much there which in a way indirectly helped Hinduism against the policy advocated by Missionaries of 'strict toleration on an equal basis'. (See Duncan B. Forester, pp. 56-57)

b. Christian Communities

Accepting the Lordship of Christ and becoming members of the newly formed communities has transformed the lives of believers in many ways. Firstly, the very understanding of God and his nature. It changed their outlook on the world as being real as against unreal or *Maya*. It made them to consider other human beings as created by God and therefore to be treated with dignity. However, they also had to necessarily decide their relationship with Hinduism and the communities that they originally belonged to. This was not an easy exercise. Some of the beliefs and practices as found in Hinduism offensive to Christian beliefs and practices had to be rejected. While some others which are having common significance had to be adopted. This dilemma has prompted at least three different reactions from the early Christian communities.

- Rejection of beliefs and practices offensive to Christian faith; beliefs in many gods and worship of idols were totally rejected as Ten Commandments specifically states that there is only one God and worship of images and idols are prohibited. Subsequently, anything that has association with many gods and worship of idols of Vishnu, Shiva, Krishna, Rama and other gods as well as symbols and rituals associated with worship of idols are rejected. Similarly, practice of caste system was rejected as it is contrary to Biblical teachings.
- Adoption of some philosophical concepts: The three approaches in spiritual quest namely, Gnana Marga, Bhakti Marga and Karma Marga have been accepted. Christian communities unhesitatingly use Gnana Marga (rational, cognitive and intellectual approach), Bhakti Marga (emotional, contemplative

and meditative approach) and Karma Marga (action oriented, ethical and altruistic approach), though reluctant to acknowledge the source openly. Some of the philosophical concepts which are adopted will be discussed in the next point.

- Cautious adaptation of cultural practices: As we have seen earlier, culture encompassed every part of individual as well as corporate life. Some have religious significance while others have cultural values. So, the early Christian communities had to sift the religious from culture and adopt only cultural practices suitable to their faith. For instance, naming of the persons who had accepted Christ. Some adopted only Biblical names such as David, John, James etc. while others used Indian names sans religious connotations such as Krishna Prasad became Deva Prasad (God's gift) or Vishnu Priya became Deva Priya (One whom God loves). In some other cases, names which have common cultural significance are adopted such as Vasanthakumar (Son of spring) or Nirmala (Pure). When it comes to worship, from the beginning efforts were made to accommodate both Western culture as well as Indian culture. While the liturgy has been drawn up mostly using Western format, it also gives scope for 'silent meditation' in the worship service which is purely Indian spiritual format. Hymns accompanied by Western musical instruments represent a universal nature of Christian faith, whereas Lyrics accompanied by Indian musical instruments represents Indian particularity. Women seating separately or covering their heads, does not necessarily represent gender discrimination but cultural customs.

The most difficult part was to define the relationship between the newly formed Christian communities with their earlier Hindu communities. Initially, individuals who became Christians were either disowned by their families or they, themselves disconnected their relationship with their families leading to criticism, that Christianity alienates people from their cultural roots. Then, when hapless people who were helped by missionaries to settle down in a new locality, it was criticized as promoting 'Mission compound mentality'. It was the conversion of groups or families that changed the very nature of relationship between the two communities. As we have noted earlier, not all members of the families or groups became Christians. Some have remained in their old communities. Since they were relatives either close or distant they continued with their social relations unabated. Their cultural interactions in family functions and community activities continued. The new converts remained within the village and in their own homes surrounded by other neighbours as before with whom their interaction continued without any break. Some even established marital relationship between the two community persons without raising any eyebrows. Thus, Mass Movements or group and family conversions have laid a new foundation in building relationship between the two communities – from cultural alienation and cultural isolation to cultural inclusiveness.

c. Indian Christian Scholars

The reaction of the early Christian communities towards Hindu communities were mostly devices falling under practical realm and confined to oral culture. The reaction of Indian Christian scholars would necessarily have to be in the realm of written culture because scholars have responsibility of communicating theological truths, not only to the present generation but also to the future generation.

Theological articulation does not arise in a vacuum. It has to relate itself to the existing systems, religious beliefs, cultural practices and social conditions. In order to achieve this goal, Indian Christian thinkers had to overcome two major difficulties. One, theological formulations that they had received from the West were clothed in Western Philosophical thoughts of Plato, Aristotle, Kant, Hegel etc. To make their theological thoughts meaningful to Indian people they had to necessarily use philosophical systems available in India. Second difficulty was the attitude of some of the missionaries who considered the entire Hindu way of life as alien to Christian truth. This was not helpful in making the Gospel relevant to Indian context. The Indian Christian thinkers felt that while some beliefs and practices of Hinduism need correction, the Hindu view of life needed to be taken seriously for any theological articulation. Hence, they began to see Indian philosophy, religion and culture as a framework to articulate their theological concerns. Just to give a glimpse of different approaches adopted by Indian thinkers, not entering into their contents, arguments and discourses, a few such approaches, all drawn from the Protestant traditions, are presented here for the benefit of those congregation members who are not habituated in reading theological write ups.

Nehemiah Goreh

Nehemiah Goreh was earlier called Nilakanta Sastri. Goreh, from a Brahmin family from Maharashtra was an established Sanskrit scholar and an expert exponent of traditional Hinduism. After his conversion to Christianity he took the name of Nehemiah, became an ordained minister of the Anglican Church and widely known as Fr. Goreh. He entered into dialogue with Keshab Chandra Sen who was the founder of 'Church of the New Dispensation' concerning his interpretation. His best known published book is '*Shaddarshana Darpana; or Hindu Philosophy Examined*' (1860). The English translation is entitled '*A rational refutation of the Hindu philosophical systems*'. Many scholars considered this work as a standard work on Hinduism written from a Christian point of view. He employs Advaita philosophy to explain his theological convictions. He refutes the epistemological existence of *Paramarthika* which is Brahman, *Vyavaharika* which includes the world, human souls and the personal God of Iswara, and *Pratibhashika* or illusory soul, illusory existence is inconsistent with the Biblical doctrine of '*creatio ex nihilo*', i.e. creation out of nothing. The Christian understanding alone gives full sovereignty to God and hence real and true. Therefore, for Fr. Goreh, the concept of God as presented in Christianity is supreme as this God is the creator of the world, upholder and sustainer by divine will, above whom there exists nothing. However, he states that some virtues such as *Ananyabhakti* (undivided devotedness to God), *Vairagya* (renouncing the world), *Namrata* (humility), *Ksama* (forbearance) are fundamental truths found in Hindu Scriptures, which could be described as 'preparatio Evangelis' in Hinduism which are the entry points to accept Christian truth for a Hindu devotee. Salvation for him is emancipation of individual soul from the bondage to ignorance (Maya) which can be secured only through right knowledge (Gnana) and ultimate bliss is to have union with Christ experienced in the Eucharist which is the fulfillment of the ancient Hindu quest for deeper spiritual bliss.

A. J. Appasamy

Bishop Aiyadurai Jesudasan Appasamy was born in a Christian family whose parents were converted to Christianity from Saivism. After his studies in Tirunelveli, he spent seven years in America and England and obtained his doctoral degree for his thesis *The Mysticism of the Fourth Gospel and its Relation to Hindu Bhakti Literature.* On his return he served the Church as a teacher, pastor and then as the Bishop of the Coimbatore Diocese of the

Church of South India during the years 1950-1959. He has written several books but the most illustrative of them are *Christianity as Bhakti Marga* (1928) and *What is Moksha* (1931).

Appasamy used Visistadwaita philosophy as propounded by Sri Ramanujacharya as a frame work for his theological exposition. His exposition of St. John's Gospel based on Bhakti Marga of the Visistadwaita is considered original and illuminative even today. For Appasamy, the union between God and Christ is not a metaphysical one, but rather a moral unity with a 'completeness of harmony in thought and purpose'. Likewise, the relationship between Christ and his believers is one of unity in purpose and will. The relationship between Father and Son as well as Son and the believer cannot be divorced from one another. Rather, they are intrinsically linked with each other. Therefore, Christian life is to surrender oneself to Christ through Bhakti in thought, will and feeling, in fact the whole personality. Moksha or salvation is therefore to enjoy the communion, fellowship and eternal bliss in the presence of God in Christ where the identity of individual is retained and not merged totally with the ultimate being as in the case of Advaita philosophy. This experience of eternal bliss is both personal as well corporate in the company of fellow believers.

M.M. Thomas

Strictly speaking, Dr. M. M. Thomas cannot be clubbed under Protestant Churches, as he hails from Mar Thoma Church, which was part of the original Syrian Church. However, Mar Thoma Church with its emphasis on tradition combined with modernity and also a sense of commitment for evangelical mission as its calling is definitely a progressive Church in its outlook and practice. M. M. Thomas being a loyal member of the Church till his death demonstrated these qualities in his life, vocation and theological articulation. His exposure to a number of international bodies including the World Council of Churches and his study of Marxist ideology and Barthian theology made him go beyond the tradition to explore new avenues for his theological articulation. He then adopts 'Humanism' as his platform to reconstruct his theological formulations.

For M. M. Thomas, 'the mission of salvation and the task of humanization are integrally related to each other even if they cannot be considered identical'. *(Salvation and Humanisation*, p. 8) For him, perfect humanization has taken place in history, through the incarnation, passion and resurrection of Jesus Christ, who was not just a 'divine human being' but a historical person, sharing the struggles and aspirations of humanity.

God is already at work in the world. It is therefore, the duty of the Christian Church to recognize the presence of the Lord in the world and work towards achieving a common goal of true humanity, which creates conditions of 'greater human dignity enhanced human creativity and mature human living'. (*The Christian Response to the Asian Revolution* p. 29) Therefore, the Christian Church needs to work together with people of other faiths to realise the dignity of the human person and the fellowship of people as the fundamental values of our society transcending all barriers placed by religious communalism. Because of this emphasis on 'faith in action', Thomas has been described as pursuing 'Karma Marga' in his theological articulation by Robin Boyd in his book '*An Introduction to Indian Christian Theology*' p. 314) even though, Thomas himself does not acknowledge such a description about his theological approach. However, as mentioned in earlier pages, M. M. Thomas' call for 'Spirituality for Combat' at the Nairobi Assembly of the World Council of Churches in 1975 justifies such a description without much hesitation.

S. J. Samartha

S. J. Samartha hails from Mangalore in Karnataka State. He served as a theological teacher in Karnataka Theological College, United Theological College and Serampore Theological College. He has also served as Director of Programme for Dialogue of the World Council of Churches. He was a highly respected scholar in Karnataka and in fact all over the world.

For Samartha, religion is a reality and pluralistic in nature. One needs to recognize the significance of multi-religious context in the salvation history of human kind. The Church has a mission to the world, i.e. to co-operate with God, who is at work in the world in and through Jesus Christ in reconciling the world unto God himself. The day the Church claims exclusive right over God's mission over and against the claims of people of other faiths, the Church becomes arrogant and self-centred and thereby loses its fervor. Therefore, in a religiously plural world, Christians are called upon to co-operate with people of other faiths in order to participate in God's continuing activity in this world. Mission, therefore is 'God's continuing activity through the Spirit to mend the brokenness of creation, to overcome the fragmentation of humanity and to heal the rift between humanity, nature and God.' (*One Christ – Many Religions*, p. 170) Jesus Christ points beyond himself to God and God's Kingdom and therefore the Church as 'the community of people whose lives are transformed by

Jesus Christ and who being rooted in him and empowered by him are committed to move people in the direction of the Kingdom' (Ibid, p.174)

All the above mentioned theologians had one thing in common. That is they broke away from the traditional way of theologizing which was conditioned by the Western way of thinking. Instead, they adopted the Indian system to articulate their concerns theologically. Further, all of them were genuinely Christo-centric in their approach even though their interpretation of Christology differed from one another. However, there was a lacuna in their approach. The framework for theologizing centred around philosophical, humanistic and religious systems with their emphasis on doctrines and concepts which did not reflect the struggles, aspirations and hopes of vast majority of people who had accepted Jesus Christ as their Saviour. As can be observed, the above representative theologians were all from upper caste background and therefore their theological articulations were based on what is now known as 'the Brahminic tradition' or 'Vedic tradition'. The reflection on Brahminic or Vedic traditions, demands a rationalistic and systematic approach whereas the experience of ordinary people accepting Christ was based on Bhakti Marga or even Karma Marga. Hence, there was a deep gap between theological thinking of scholars and the practice adopted by congregation members.

Arvind P. Nirmal

Against this background a new movement in theological articulation began in the seventies. A group of theologians who were basically from the Dalit origin began to reflect from the point of view of Dalit converts to Christianity. Noted among them are A. P. Nirmal, M. E. Prabhakar, M. Azariah, James Massey and V. Devasahayam. These theologians deviated from the philosophical propositions of the past and began to discover their own roots and analyse the social conditions that existed at the time of the conversion of their own forefathers and mothers. The result was 'radical' in the sense that their ancestor's stories and the experience were entirely different from what had been described in theological articulation of the day.

In this process they were illumined by the progressive movements taking place in the literary world, both within and outside India. There was the flowering of 'Latin American Liberation Theology' during this decade. The Women's Liberation movements came to the Centre of day to day debate in all spheres of life. The struggles and aspirations of Black people in asserting their own spiritual distinctiveness and their cry for liberation from oppressive racial structures in which they were placed were some of the movements that caught the attention of the world, including the intellectuals hailing from Dalit communities in India. Simultaneously, a number of Dalit scholars in almost all important languages of India began to articulate the socio-economic and cultural conditions in which Dalit communities were placed which formed the basis for Dalit aspiration for liberation. Encouraged by all these movements but not confined to their methodical approach of theologizing the Dalit theologians in India formulated their own strategy of theologizing. A. P. Nirmal has been cited here as a representative of these theologians for this new way of doing theology.

In two of his articles entitled '*Towards a Christian Dalit Theology*' and '*Doing Theology from a Dalit Perspective*' which were published by the Gurukul Lutheran Theological College and Research Institute and edited by A. P. Nirmal himself, he outlines the basic feature for Dalit Theology. For him, Dalit Theology is distinct from the earlier theologies in three different ways. One, it is a theology *about* the Dalits, two it is a theology *of* the message addressed to the Dalits and three it is a theology *from* the Dalits themselves. According to Nirmal, three essential components are necessary for a Dalit Theology in the making. The first one being discovering Dalit roots which he describes as 'Historical Dalit consciousness' which is the primary dictum for Dalit Theology. It is recalling into memory the *pathos* or suffering of the people of the Dalit communities. Therefore, the starting point for Dalit theology 'is a story of the afflictions – the bondage, the harsh treatment, the toil and tears of the Dalits. A genuinely Dalit Theology will be characterized by pathos, by suffering' (p. 60) Secondly, the Dalit theology leads to a confession or a faith affirmation of a group of people who have experienced liberation in God through Jesus Christ from such pathos. Therefore, Dalit Theology is doxological in character. Liberation experience makes Dalit Christians to become faith sharers and faith receivers. Thirdly, Dalit Theology must also focus on the liberative motifs for entire humanity. The goal of Dalit theology 'is realization of our full humanness or conversely, our full divinity. The ideal of the '*imagio-dei*' the image of God in us. To use another biblical metaphor our goal is the 'glorious liberty of the children of God', (p. 62) because, God works in and through the weaker, the downtrodden, the crushed, the oppressed and the marginalized. This is because brokenness belongs to the very being of God. God's divinity and his humanity are both characterized by his dalitness. He is one with the broken. He suffers when his people suffer. He weeps when his people weep. He laughs when his people laugh. He dies in his peoples' death and he rises again in his peoples' resurrection.' (p. 70)

2. Reactions from Hindu Communities

a. Reform Movements in Hinduism

English education introduced by the early missionaries had twin purpose of creating an inquisitive mind with a scientific temper on all matters including religion as well as to point out Christianity as the only true religion. A few students were convinced of the arguments of the Missionaries and accepted Christianity as their new religion. But, many others began to look deeply within themselves and convinced of the innate vitality of their religion but at the same time required some reforms to overthrow some of the evil practices that have crept into the fabric of Hinduism. Only a few such reform movements are mentioned here to indicate the kind of social reform that took place through these movements.

Brahmo Samaj

Founded by Ram Mohan Roy in Bengal is a combination of Western and Eastern traditions. He took the Upanishads and Brahma Sutras as authoritative sources of Hinduism and prohibited some of the evil practices as non-scriptural. His reforms were:

1. Only spiritual contemplation and no idol worship and sacrifices
2. Abolition of sati.
3. Attack on polygamy
4. Denounced caste distinctions.

Prarthana Samaj

This is an off-shoot of Brahmo Samaj, being inspired by a lecture delivered by Keshab Chandra Sen in 1864. The most important person in this movement was Mahadev Govind Ranade who later became an eminent judge of the Bombay High Court. He took the religious traditions of saints and prophets and declared that Prarthana Samaj is like a Protestant movement in Hinduism. Some of the reforms that they attempted are:

1. Disapproval of caste
2. Introduction of widow marriage
3. Encouragement of women's education
4. Abolition of child marriage

Arya Samaj

Founded by Swami Dayananda Saraswati in 1875. Unlike Ram Mohan Roy and Mahadev Govind Ranade, Swamy Dayananda had not gone through English education. He was a Sanyasin and a great Sanskrit scholar and his spiritual resources were from oriental scriptures. He rejected all forms of worship and practices of Christianity and Islam as alien to Aryan faith. Some of the articles of faith in Arya Samaj were as follows:

1. Infallibility of Vedas.
2. The four stages of human life, namely, Brahamachary, Grihasta, Vanaprasta and Sanyasa are necessary steps for achieving salvation.
3. Believed in karma and rebirth.
4. Advocated three movements, namely, *Shuddi* – a process of reconversion of those who have been converted to Islam and Christianity, *Sangatana* – uniting all Hindus under one banner to defend itself from the onslaughts of other religions and *system of education* – establishment of Sanskrit schools and teaching Vedas.

Ramakrishna Mission

Founded by Swami Vivekananda is one of confluence of many streams. He combined the Indian spirituality with the Western secular ideas in this movement. He introduced all the three Margas effectively – Bhakti Marga of his Guru Sri Ramakrishna Paramahamsa, the Gnana Marga in his own exposition of Vedanta Scriptures and the Karma Marga of doing good for the benefit of all sections of society and particularly of the poor and down trodden. He organised Mission Centres both in India and abroad, and exchanged his disciples to share with one another. Mission Centres were open to all irrespective of their colour or caste. The Mission is a great example for combining effectively of the religious teaching, social service, medical relief and imparting of education.

b. Renascent Hinduism

Early Missionaries highlighted the evil practices prevailing in Hinduism. In response to that the reform movements worked towards removing evil practices and bring about reforms in their beliefs and practices. The Renaissance movements operated at a different level altogether. They had twin purposes, namely, to create awareness among the masses to be proud of their religion and culture and the second one was to present the strengths of Hinduism and not the weaknesses to the world, that is, to present Hinduism as a religion of peace and harmony and not a religion of hatred and discord. In order to achieve these twin purposes, multi-dimensional approach needed to be employed. For the intellectuals, a theoretical exposition of the Vedanta philosophy and for the masses practical methods of applying the philosophical principles in their day-to-day life. Renaissance movements, therefore are not a one-time effort, but a continuous process over a period of time. Many eminent thinkers from the Hindu community have contributed towards achieving these goals. For the purpose of our study we can only quote a few examples.

Even though, the orientalists had initiated the study of Vedic scriptures and culture as important tools in understanding Hindu way of life, it was actually Swami Vivekananda who brought to focus the strengths of Vedanta when he addressed the Parliament of Religions at Chicago, USA on 31st May 1893 by stating that Hinduism is a religion of tolerance and Vedanta is a philosophy of life which accommodates all and leaves out no one. Swami Vivekananda's rational exposition of Vedanta to the outside world and practical ways of uplifting the masses at the grass-root level brought Hinduism at once to a new consciousness.

Mahatma Gandhi should be credited as the greatest human being in India who could instill spiritual fervor in ordinary men and women and mobilize them for action. For, Mahatma had certain qualities which were visible to ordinary people that attracted them towards him. His faith in God; his ability to draw spiritual energy from the ancient scripture; communicative skills to translate scriptural values to even illiterates; his willingness to apply those values not only to others but to himself first and foremost and his alertness to socio-economic and political situations prevailing in the country gave him a distinctive personality, which made ordinary people to follow his leadership throughout India. Through *Swadeshi* movement, which emphasized on the use of services available within India, rather than relying on the services from outside India, he attempted to transform economics in the light of Hindu spirituality. Through the *Sathyagraha* movement, Mahatma was able to mobilize the entire country to use their spiritual energy in a non-violent way to fight against injustice. Thus, spiritual energy was converted into a political action. Therefore, it can confidently be concluded that in Mahatma Gandhi Renaissance reached its zenith.

Dr. S. Radhakrishnan, an intellectual giant has served the nation in many capacities – Professor of Philosophy in the Universities of Madras, Mysore, Calcutta and Banaras; Chair of Eastern Religions in Oxford, Vice

President and later as President of India. Through his erudite and scholarly lectures, articles and books he presented a comprehensive philosophy of life, which has caught the attention of the whole world. For Dr. Radhakrishnan religion is at the core of human lives. Only a spiritual revival can cure the ills of the world. Spiritual experience is the basis for the philosophy of religion, which allows different types of religious experiences. This in turn leads to mystic experience of the ultimate reality. Dr. Radhakrishnan expounds this spiritual experience through a systematic treatment of Advaita philosophy. His scholarly writings have made such an impact that 23 world renowned scholars have written essays covering Dr. Radhakrishnan's thoughts and contributions in a volume of 883 pages published in New York in the year 1952.

Simultaneously, literature, art, dance, drama and music were developed in all the regional languages in India. Research in ancient and modern languages were undertaken. The outstanding literary figure was Rabindranath Tagore, who was awarded the Nobel Prize for literature. Universities were established both in India and abroad to promote Indian philosophy and culture. Renaissance movements, therefore created an awareness among masses hither to unheard of concerning Indian way of life, its philosophy, its culture, and its ability to accommodate all kinds of views without surrendering its own cherished values. Among the educated, it created a sense of pride and ownership about the inherent strengths of Hinduism. As a result, Hinduism which was earlier confined to its own sects and sub sects has now become a universal faith recognized as one of the great religions of the world.

c. Militant Hinduism

Hindu Reform Movements focused their attention on bringing about reforms in faith and practices which were attacked by Christian Missionaries as evil practices; whereas Renaissance movements were involved in raising the consciousness of the ordinary Hindus to be proud of their religious, cultural, social heritage that they have received through Hinduism. Simultaneously, they also presented an intellectual and rational exposition of religion and philosophical concepts to the whole world through lectures, conferences and literature.

Conversion to Christianity also resulted in groups of orthodox Hindus opposing conversion. They could be categorized as 'Defenders of Hinduism'. Initially, it was used to be small groups of high caste people trying to prevent low-caste people from converting to Christianity through

Baptism. Since they were also influential people they would organize local villages to impose social boycott on the newly converted Christians. Afterwards, with the help of like-minded people from cities, they would put pressure on the new converts to return to their original faith. If someone or a group would like to return, they would organize 'Ghar Wapsi Programme' –'returning home', through some rituals. Today, educated and urbanized Christians, who are critical of the faith of the illiterate Christians of the villages must realize that if at all Christianity has remained as a force to reckon with in India, it is mainly due to the steadfastness of these illiterate Christians, in their new found faith in Christ. However, let us now return to the topic of 'Defenders of Hinduism'.

This sporadic opposition to conversion got a boost when 'Hindutva' philosophy came into prominence. The term Hindutva was first used by V. D. Savarkar, a Hindu Ideologue in the year 1923, who was imprisoned by colonial authorities on charges of inciting political revolution for 50 years in Andaman and later in India. The story goes that Savarkar used pointed pebbles and thorns to scribble on the walls of his cell in prison to record his thoughts undetected by prison authorities and memorized them. Later, when he was shifted to Indian jails, he used paper and pen given to other political prisoners and smuggled his writings through them when the latter were released. In the year 1923, when Sarvakar was still in jail, the book entitled '*Hindutva*' was brought out by Shri V. V. Kelkar, an advocate in Nagpur without mentioning the name of Savarkar, as he was still in prison.

In the above mentioned book Sarvarkar discussed important issues such as who is a Hindu? What constitutes the essence of Hindu community? And what binds them together, in spite of vast number of differences in beliefs and practices?

In order to arrive at a comprehensive definition and cogent rational explanation, Sarvarkar makes a distinction between 'Hinduism' and 'Hindutva'. For Sarvarkar, Hinduism deals with beliefs and practices of different sects both Vedic and non-Vedic traditions, whereas Hindutva deals with totality of culture, history, religion and nationhood of people. In his own words: 'Hindutva is not identical with what is vaguely indicated by the term Hinduism. By an 'ism' it is generally meant a theory or a code more or less based on spiritual or religious dogma or system. … Hindutva embraces all the departments of thought and activity of the whole being of our Hindu race.' (p. 4)'

Sarvarkar examines history and comes to the conclusion, that the word 'Hindu' occurs in history even prior to Vedic period and it essentially means the land 'from the Sindhu to Sindhu from Indus to the seas'. (p. 82) The first essential quality of Hindutva is a geographical one. Secondly, not just a geographical description, the people in the land are bonded together by a common blood by way of JATI, which is described as race. Thirdly, people living in this geographical area are also bound by common civilization and culture. Civilization consists of 'thoughts, action and achievements'. Civilization of Hindus begins with divine language namely Sanskrit. He says, 'Our gods spoke in Sanskrit, our sages thought in Sanskrit, our poets wrote in Sanskrit. All that is best in us – the best thoughts, the best ideas, the best lines – seeks instinctively to clothe itself in Sanskrit. To millions, it is still the language of their gods; to others it is the language of their ancestors; to all the language *par excellence*; a common inheritance, a common language that enriches all the family of our sister languages (vernacular languages). The language Sanskrit is a vital nerve thread which runs through all and leads to a harmonious whole. The common law which is called Hindu Jurisprudence binds all people into unity, thus creating a Rashtra, a Jati, with a common Sanskruti (culture) expressed through Sanskrit (mother tongue). Therefore, sages, saints, literature, festivals, ideals and outlook on life, originating in this land become essentials of Hindutva. So a Hindu is one who considers the land from Sindhu to Sindhu from Indus to seas as his/her fatherland or motherland.

Secondly, one who is a descendant of Hindu parents, claiming to have blood of the ancient Sindhu and the race that sprang from them in his/her veins (p.110) is a Hindu. Thirdly, he/she who treats the Sanskruti emerging from the land as Holy is a Hindu. Hindutva, therefore, is a philosophy of life; and not just confined to doctrines and codes. Using the above arguments, Sarvarkar goes on to demonstrate that Sikhs constitute a Hindu community as their faith originates from this land; whereas Muslims and Christians cannot be called as belonging to Hindu community as they do not pass the second test of Hindutva, namely, considering the land as Holy, since their Holy Lands are situated outside the geographical locations of Hindustan and their heroes, festivals and Sanskruti are different from Hindu civilization. This matter was also discussed in the Supreme Court on several occasions in the constitutional benches. Finally, it was discussed in Civil Appeal No. 2835 of 1989 whose judgement was pronounced on 11.12.1995. Its Constitution Bench has also come to the conclusion that Hinduism incorporates all forms of belief and worship without necessitating the selection or elimination of any. Whereas, Hindutva can be described as a way of life. Further, quoting Dr. Radhakrishnan, the judgement goes on to add, 'Aboriginal tribes, savage and half-civilized people, the cultured Dravidians and the Vedic Aryans were all Hindus as they were the sons of the same mother.' Also, quoting from the Constitution of India, Article 25 and Explanation II the judgement further states that "Hindus shall be considered as including a reference to persons professing Sikh, Jains or Buddhist religions'.

This Hindutva has been accepted as a cardinal principle around which Rashtriya Swayam Sevak (RSS), calling itself as cultural organization. Many other affiliates of RSS are having their own independent organization such as Hindu Mahasabha, Bajrang Dal, Vishwa Hindu Parishat, Sri Rama Sena and Hindu Sena just to name a few, are the organizations which are wedded to this Hindutva philosophy. Bharatiya Janata Party, has also adopted Hindutva as its ideology in 1989. While for RSS and its affiliates Hindutva is a cultural ideology; for BJP it is a political philosophy. Therefore, Hindutva revolves around two axes – the political and the cultural. But, Hindutva is constructed on the basis of Hindu religious consciousness. It is this Hindu religious consciousness which provides the foundation for Hindutva philosophy. This Hindutva is now being presented as 'Cultural Nationalism'. From the foregone discussion 'cultural nationalism', therefore, means 'to building a nation – a motherland and a Holy land using the medium of indigenous culture based on Hindu religious consciousness. While the RSS and its affiliates promote cultural unity of all sects, beliefs and practices sans 'outside' faiths, namely, Christianity and Islam; the BJP is trying to create 'Hindu Rashtra' based on Hindutva philosophy. In either of the above, Christianity and Islam do not seem to have any place. The promoters of Hindutva philosophy deny the ownership of cultural heritage to Christians and Muslims and virtually categorize them as second class citizens by questioning their patriotism.

At the ground level fringe elements among the Hindutva adherents usurp the assumed power to safeguard 'Hindu culture' by organizing moral policing – threatening women who wear certain style clothes of saying those clothes do not portray Indian culture; cow vigilantism – accusing people of killing cows considered holy in Hindu tradition; honour killing – punishing those who have married outside caste and preventing inter-religious marriages between Hindus and Muslims as well as Hindus and Christians accusing the minority partner as indulging in proselytism.

d. Dalit Movement for Human Dignity

That ' a view from below' is entirely different from 'the view from above' is what we have noted, when we discussed the reaction from Dalit theologians, represented by A. P. Nirmal, same is the case with Dalit thinkers. Their reaction to religion is based on their analysis of socio-economic and cultural realities. Undoubtedly, Dr. Bhimrao Ramji Ambedkar is one of the foremost thinkers, who stood firmly for upholding the values of human dignity for Dalits. For, he was a Dalit himself and had experienced personally as to what it meant to lead a life as a Dalit. For the purpose of this study, we will consider his views on Hinduism and Christianity.

Dr. B. R. Ambedkar

Ambedkar was born into an untouchable Mahar caste in Maharashtra. His ancestors, the Mahars were forced to hang pots around their necks and tie brooms to their hips so that they may not pollute the path they tread. He was given an admission in a government school in Satara, where he was made to sit away from his classmates on a gunny bag so that he would not pollute others. With a scholarship awarded by Sayajirao Gaekwad, a progressive Maharaja of Baroda, Ambedkar was able to complete his graduation, a rare distinction for a Dalit boy. Again, with the scholarship given by Gaekwad he was able to pursue his studies at Columbia University in New York. Thereafter, he got admission at London School of Economics and obtained a degree in Law. Even with all these educational qualifications on his return Ambedkar was made aware of the harsh realities of the caste system. His junior colleagues treated him with disdain. He found no accommodation for himself. Finally, in order to escape the harsh reality he masqueraded as a Parsi and rented a place to live. But, when the owner found out that Ambedkar was an untouchable, he literally threw Ambedkar out on to the street. Arundati Roy, who wrote an essay on Ambedkar and Gandhi, entitled 'The Doctor and the Saint', as a precursor to the write up by Ambedkar on '*Annihilation of Caste*', quotes from Ambedkar's biographical notes, which describes the deep humiliation that Ambedkar felt at that time. In his own words,

'I can even now vividly recall it and never recall it without tears in my eyes. It was then for the first time I learnt that a person who is untouchable to a Hindu is also untouchable to a Parsi'. (p. 98)

Dr. Ambedkar was an established scholar, a well-known lawyer, a prolific writer, an acknowledged leader and a committed social activist. He had studied Sanskrit and was thorough with Vedic Scripture. Therefore, his views on Hinduism spring not only from his personal experience but also from his knowledge of Hinduism. His views on Hinduism are drawn mainly from his write-up, 'Annihilation of Caste'.

For Dr. Ambedkar, caste is an obnoxious evil present in Hinduism. It cannot be reformed, it has to be annihilated to establish justice for all and particularly to the oppressed people. He writes, 'There cannot be a more degrading system of social organization than the caste system. It is the system that deadens, paralyses and cripples the people from helpful activity'. (*Annihilation of Caste,* para 17.7 on page 276). Even as a student in Columbia University, Ambedkar argued that 'Caste could not be equated with either race or class, but was a unique social category in itself – an enclosed, endogamous class. (Arundati Roy, p. 7)

Ambedkar was a strong votary for the values of liberty, equality and fraternity and above all justice for all. As Chairman of the Drafting Committee appointed by the Constituent Assembly on 29th August 1947, Dr. Ambedkar ensured that these three essential fundamental rights become part of the preamble of the Indian Constitution. He believed that social justice is a fundamental right. But, social justice cannot be achieved unless social imbalances are removed. This imbalance can be removed in India only if social order is radically transformed. The social order in India originates from Vedic Scriptures which is the root cause for the emergence of caste system. Ambedkar believed that caste system has its genesis in the *Purusa Sukta Hymn in the Rigveda*, which states that 'the mouth of Purusha became Brahmin, his arms Kshatriya, his thighs Vaishya and Shudra sprang from his feet.' Therefore, for Ambedkar social injustice originates from the religion itself. His social analysis of the prevailing social order led him to portray caste as 'the monster that crosses your path. You cannot have political reform, you cannot have economic reform, unless you kill this monster (Annihilation of Caste, p. 233). He wrote that caste system is monstrous for a number of reasons; it is not just a division of labour but also a division of labourers; division of labour and labourers are hierarchical – grading one above the other; division of labour is not spontaneous or based on choices but by birth; it is not only hierarchical but also hereditary – a person born into high caste enjoys all privileges and a person born into low caste suffers all kinds of disabilities; it is also based on the concept of Karma – a person born into high caste enjoys privileges because of the good work that he has done in the past life and a person born into low caste suffers because of the evil deeds of his past life. Dr. Ambedkar further argues that the caste system has killed public spirit. In his own words:

'The effect of caste on the ethics of the Hindus is simply deplorable. Caste has killed public spirit. Caste has destroyed the sense of public charity. Caste has made public opinion impossible. A Hindu's public identity is his caste. His responsibility is only to his caste. His loyalty is restricted only to his caste. Virtue has become caste-ridden, and morality has become caste bound. There is no sympathy for the deserving. There is no appreciation of the meritorious. There is no charity to the needy. Suffering as such calls for no response. There is charity but it begins with caste and ends with caste. There is sympathy but not for men of other castes.' (p.259)

Further, Dr. Ambedkar writes that caste system has 'completely disabled lower classes of Hindus for direct action – on account of this wretched caste system they could receive no education. They could not think out or know the way to their salvation. They were condemned to be lowly; and not knowing the way of escape, and not having the means of escape, they become reconciled to eternal servitude, which they accepted as their inescapable fate.' (p.275)

Ambedkar does not hold grudge against the practitioners of Vedic religion. He says, '... Hindus observe caste not because they are inhuman or wrong-headed. They observe caste because they are deeply religious.' (p.286) The problem is with the religion which promotes caste system and not with the people. Hence, reforms within Hinduism by allowing inter-dining or inter-marrying can only bring about cosmetic changes but not change of mindset. Therefore, caste can only be destroyed if the sacredness and divinity attached to it is destroyed. This means that the scriptural authority which sanctions such segregation is destroyed; that is, destruction of the authority of the Shastras and Vedas.

Dr. Ambedkar's view of Indian Christianity is elaborated in an articale, 'Caste and Conversion'. Dr. S. Lourdunathan, Professor of Philosophy at Arul Anandan College and a Roman Catholic by faith, briefly describes Dr. Ambedkar's attitude towards Indian Christianity in his book '*Theology as Social: Relevance of Ambedkar in Theologizing in India*'. I have paraphrased the same from Dr. Lourdunathan's book. The salient points are:

- Dr. Ambedkar defends the concept of 'conversion'. For him, conversion from Hinduism has both ethical and spiritual imperative. It essentially means 'a sense of felt need to change from one disagreeable form of life to an agreeable form of life'. Dr. Ambedkar further affirms that 'the conversion of Indians to

Christianity is not one of militant compulsion or deceit as it has been popularized by reformers in India.' (p.30)

- Dr. Ambedkar recognizes that a large number of people who have been converted to Christianity were from Dalit communities because 'Hinduism is inconsistent with the self-respect and honour of untouchables'. (p.37)
- Analyzing Christianity from a historical point of view, Dr. Ambedkar recognizes the existence of three main streams of Christianity, namely, Orthodox, Roman Catholic and Protestant traditions which promote denominational differences.

  Dr. Ambedkar appreciates the good work done by the Christian Missions, in the areas of work among children, among young people, among women, among poor people and among the sick and the needy.
- However, Dr. Ambedkar was highly critical of Christianity for the following reasons:

  - Treating the Gospel as purely spiritual having no effect on social life (p.54)
  - The complete absence of desire on the part of educated Christians to take up the cause of the community and fight for it. (p.55)
  - The absence of any urge on the part of Dalit Christians to break from the bondage of oppression.
  - The failure of the Church in not providing proper teaching to 'mobilize, agitate, educate and organize the masses for effective political action.
  - The failure of the Church in building and sustaining a community life which transcends the barriers of race, language and caste. As a result, there is no community feeling behind the phrase 'Indian Christians'. Indian Christians are not bound together by what is consciousness of kind which is the test of the existence of a community.' (p.58)
  - Dr. Ambedkar concludes his work with a prophetic call to Christianity. In his own words:

    'I am deeply interested in Indian Christians because a large majority of them are drawn from the untouchable classes. My comments are those of a friend. They are not the strictures of an adversary. I have drawn attention to their weaknesses

> because I want them to be strong and I want them to be strong because I see great dangers for them ahead. They have to reckon with the scarcely veiled hostility of Mr. Gandhi to Christianity taking its root in the Indian social structure. But, they also have to reckon with militant Hinduism masquerading as Indian Nationalism. ...Let all Indian Christians ponder.' (p. 58-59)

3. Constitutional Safeguards and Legislative Bills

Strictly speaking, it is an anomaly to consider this section as 'Reactions', for the constitutional safeguards are meant for the welfare of all and prejudiced against none, though some legislative measures may appear to be against Christian and Muslim communities in their desire to protect the 'interest' of Dalit communities. However, this section is included here, because it has a tremendous impact on the very understanding and implementation of the Mission of God by the Church.

The objectives of the 'Constitution of India', is to secure to all its citizens, JUSTICE, LIBERTY, EQUALITY and FRATERNITY. In the words of Dr. Ambedkar, in his concluding speech in the Constituent Assembly, 'Liberty cannot be divorced from equality, equality cannot be divorced from liberty. Nor can liberty and equality be divorced from fraternity'. (Quoted by Dr. Durga Dass Babu in his '*Introduction to the Constitution of India*, 2008, p.25) In order to achieve these objective, the Constitution provides 'Fundamental Rights' to all citizens as sacred rights and Directive Principles to States to ensure that these Fundamental Rights become cardinal principles in making laws and in governance of the country. The Constitution aims to provide political justice by way of 'adult franchise' which allows every adult to participate in the elections to parliament and state legislatures and local bodies to determine the type of government that the people want. It aims to provide economic justice to all its citizens by providing equal opportunity in education and appointments (Article 16). It aims to provide social justice to all its citizens by removing all social imbalances. It is this social justice, particularly to the disadvantaged section of society, that we are concerned herewith.

a. Constitutional Safeguards for the Disadvantaged Communities

Article 15 prohibits any 'discrimination on grounds of religion, race, caste, sex or place of birth'. It further removes all disabilities, liabilities, restrictions or conditions with regard to:

- Access to shops, public restaurants, hotels and places of public entertainment; or'
- The use of wells, tanks, bathing ghats, roads and places of public resort maintained wholly or partly out of State funds or dedicated to the use of the general public.'

The Constitution also provides equal opportunities for Backward classes and Dalit communities with regard to education and employment through Article 15(4), (5) and Articles 16 and 29(2). More specifically the Constitution abolishes 'untouchability' and makes the practice of untouchability as an offence punishable in accordance with law. (Article 17) Further, the State is required to promote 'educational and economic interest of scheduled caste, scheduled tribes and other weaker sections' and in particular protecting 'them from social injustice and all forms of exploitation' (Directive Principles, Article 46)

All the above rights, we may recollect, were denied to scheduled castes and scheduled tribes historically. Indian Constitution has corrected these historical mistakes and abuses.

b. Positive Affirmation

With a view to empower the scheduled castes and scheduled tribes to participate in Parliament and Legislative Assembly of the States, seats have been reserved in proportion to their population by way of Special Provision in Articles 330 and 332. Further, in matters of employment or appointments also, certain percentage is reserved based on their population as against the total population. Also under Articles 338 and 338 – A National Commission for Scheduled Castes and Scheduled Tribes is set up to safeguard the privileges, to investigate specific complaints, to advise the Government on the socio-economic developmental works and to recommend measures for effective implementation of privileges available under the Constitution for the Scheduled Castes and Scheduled Tribes.

c. Legislative Bills

The Constitution of India confers on all citizens 'Freedom of conscience and profession, practice and propagation of religion' in Article 25. It also guarantees the 'right to establish, maintain and manage religious and charitable institutions' in Article 26 to all religious communities. Article 25 ensures that individuals have the right to 'freely profess, practice and propagate' his or her own religion'. But, this right is not an absolute right. It is subject to restrictions imposed by the State in the interest of 'public order, morality and health'. Similarly, the right given to religious groups to establish, maintain and manage religious and charitable Institutions is also subject to restrictions imposed by the State in the interest of 'public order, morality and health'. Further, the State can also impose restrictions on 'economic, financial, political or other secular activity which may be associated with religious practice'. (Article 25, (2) (a)). Further, the Constitution also empowers the religious and linguistic minorities to establish and administer their own educational institutions. Again these fundamental rights given to minority communities are subject to reasonable regulations by the State.

Arising out of the above mentioned fundamental rights, three basic issues have been debated ever since the Constitution came into force. The first one is what is the redressal mechanism if a person or a group feels that the freedom to profess and practice their faith is violated by the introduction of newer forms of worship and practices in which that person or group is not familiar with or not happy with? Constitution provides in Article 32, by empowering such a person or group, to approach the Courts for the redressal of their grievances. More on this when we discuss the litigant nature of Church of South India later.

The second issue is 'Does the right to 'propagate' in Article 25, include the right to 'convert' also? Obviously, the Christian Church believes that the two are integrally related to each other based on the commission received by her from the Lord in St. Matthew 28:19-20 which states: 'Go therefore and make disciples of all nations, baptizing them in the name of the Father and the Son and of the Holy Spirit, and teaching them to obey everything that I have commanded you?' On the other hand, intellectuals and influential people of Hindu communities began to oppose 'conversions' as not genuine change of heart but achieved through 'inducement or allurement'. Even, before attaining Independence, there were several initiatives to ban conversions, such as the Rajgarh State Conversion Act of 1936, the Surguja State Hindu Apostasy Act of 1945 and the Udaipur State Conversion Act of 1946. After Independence as early as 1955, a Private Member's Bill called 'Indian Converts (Regulation and Registration) Bill' was introduced in the Parliament, which was opposed by the then Prime Minister. The problem became acute with the submission of Nyogi Commission report, set up by the State Government of Madhya Pradesh in the year 1954. Nyogi was a retired High Court Judge. He was scathing in his attack on Missionaries. It is ironic that a person who was against conversion ultimately got himself converted to Buddhism, in a mass conversion ceremony. As a result of Nyogi Commission report, the Madhya Pradesh passed 'Freedom of Religion Bill' in 1968 and Orissa in 1967. Then Arunachal Pradesh passed 'The Arunachal Pradesh Freedom of Indigenous Faith Bill' in 1978, Chattishgarh in 2000 and Himachal Pradesh in 2006. Even Tamil Nadu passed a Bill in 2002, but repealed it in 2003. In all the above Bills enormous restrictions on conversions have been imposed and also they provide punishment to those who indulge in conversion by 'force, inducement or fraudulent means'. The Orissa and Madhya Pradesh Bills were challenged by the Christian community as ultra – virus to fundamental rights. But, the Supreme Court in *Stainlaus Vs State of Madhya Pradesh, AIR 1977* rejects the contentions of Christian community *in toto***.** The Supreme Court Order essentially means that a right to propagate does not include right to convert and the State has the right to intervene in any such activity in the interest of 'public order, morality and health'.

Thirdly, do the minorities have absolute right to establish and administer educational institutions without any interference by the State? This matter also has been discussed thoroughly in all platforms, including judicial forums. Some of the Supreme Court decisions can be found in the following court proceedings: St. Stephen's College vs University of Delhi, 1992; TMA Pai Foundation vs State of Karnataka, 2002; P A Inamdar vs State of Maharashtra, AIR 2005; Secretary, Malankara Syrian Catholic College vs T. Jose, 2007. Quoted below are the gist of the general principles accepted by the Supreme Court:

- The Minority communities have a right to establish and administer educational institutions of their own choice, but they do not have a right to mal-administer them.
- The State can impose reasonable regulations in the larger interest of the State and the nation.
- While imposing such restrictions the State should be mindful not to destroy the minority character of the institution.

d. Presidential Order 1950

There is no definition of scheduled castes and scheduled tribes in the Constitution. In fact the words 'scheduled caste' and scheduled tribes' are used by British government in the place of 'depressed classes' to describe 'untouchables', which became official from 1936 onwards. The framers of the Constitution took these phrases to describe a group of communities who suffered discrimination, disadvantage and segregation due to the practice of untouchability at the hands of the mainstream communities. When the Constitution provided provision for 'positive discrimination' or 'positive affirmation' for these communities to overcome historical injustice, it became necessary to identify these communities in order to extend the 'privileges' mentioned above. The Constitution through Articles 341 and 342 empowers the President of India in consultation with the Governor of the concerned State to draw up a list and publish a notification specifying 'the castes, races or tribes ... which shall for the purpose of this Constitution be deemed to be scheduled castes or scheduled tribes in relation to that State'. Exercising this power, the President of India published an order called 'The Constitution (scheduled castes) Order, 1950 (CO 19)'. In this order a sub clause was introduced in paragraph three which states '... no person who professes a religion different from Hindu, shall be deemed to be a member of a scheduled caste'. This list published by the President cannot be varied by any subsequent notification. The Parliament by law can only add or delete from the list so published (Clause 2 of Article 341 and 342). So, the list is published by the President except by way of a law passed by the Parliament to add or delete from the published list. Exercising this power, the Parliament added 'or Sikh' to the word 'Hindu' in 1956 and in 1990 it further added 'or Buddhist', so essentially only Christianity and Islam have been deleted from the list. Of course, those who promote the inclusion of the words 'or Sikh or Buddhist', take their cover under Article 25 (2) (b) explanation 11: where it states 'In sub clause (b) of Clause (2) the reference to Hindus shall be construed as including a reference to persons professing the Sikh, Jain or Buddhist religion'.

The problem is not the list itself but the list has been used to extend the privileges envisaged under the Constitution in terms of protection, reservation, appointments and promotion to scheduled castes and scheduled tribes. Christian and Muslim communities feel that this is a discrimination perpetuated by the majority community against minority communities on grounds of religion by violating the rights of equality of opportunity in matters of public employment ensured in Articles 14 and 16. As a result, the minority communities have made several representations to the government and even organized several protests. But, the situation has not changed and it is not going to be changed in the near future.

We need to take another development in this context. The Constitution also empowers the President to appoint a Commission to investigate the conditions of backward classes under Article 340. On the basis of this, two Commissions were appointed, one in 1953 with Shri Kakasaheb Kalelkar as its Chairman and the other in 1979, under the Chairmanship of Shri B. P. Mandal. The first one suggested 'caste' as a criterion to determine backwardness of a community; which did not have the consensus of all the Commission members. The second one based its recommendation on the 'element of inequality and discrimination' found in the caste system. When the Janata Government headed by Prime Minister V. P. Singh made an announcement to implement the Mandal Commission Report, it created unrest throughout India saying that 'merit' has been sacrificed at the altar of 'privileges' to certain communities. The debate continues even today. This situation gives room to raise a number of questions relating to the Constitutional provisions to equality and protection. A few of them are listed below:

- Can a Constitution which promises equality before law and prohibits any discrimination on grounds of religion, race, caste, sex or place of birth, deny reservation benefits to Christian and Muslims on grounds of religion?
- Can a 'secular' nation (Preamble) meaning 'respect for all religions' or 'neutrality towards all religions' practice discrimination towards Christianity and Islam merely because these religions emerge from outside India?
- Is the non-inclusion of Christianity and Islam prompted by people committed to 'Hindutva' ideology?
- Do the different phrases used in the Constitution, such as scheduled *castes* and scheduled *tribes* and backward *classes*, one based on historic social, economic, cultural and religious iniquities and the other based on socio-economic criterion, lead one to conclude that the Constitution unintentionally has brought division among the oppressed communities?
- Christian Church in general and Christians in particular have to ponder very seriously whether 'spirituality and caste system' can co-exist either in thinking or in practice, for spirituality unites all in the presence of God, whereas caste system alienates or segregates one community from another.

The spread of the Gospel brought changes in the lives of those who accepted Christ as their Saviour. In the process, it also gave birth to a variety of reactions from different quarters resulting in religious, cultural and social resurgence in the nation. The intellectuals among Christians could not think of labelling Hinduism as superstitious in which case it would amount to disowning one's own past. On the other hand, there were certain practices which were not in tune with their faith and had to be abandoned. In order to emphasize the essence of Hinduism some of them took some concepts from Indian philosophy and Hindu Scriptures and reflected Christian faith based on those concepts. Some others began to discern how God is acting in and through Hinduism and how Christ is already at work in Hinduism.

Among Hindu adherents it created three major reactions. The first group began to bring about reforms in Hinduism by giving up some of the evil practices like Sati, child marriage, denouncing caste distinctions etc. The second group worked tirelessly to raise awareness among Hindu practitioners and to inculcate pride in them of their religious, cultural and social heritage. They brought about renaissance in Hinduism. The third group is the militant group wedded to protect Hinduism under the banner of 'cultural nationalism'. They not only promote Indian culture as sacred but also enforce it through force and violent means.

Dalits on the other hand, inspired by the charismatic leadership of Dr. Ambedkar have begun to 'organize, educate and agitate' to gain their human dignity and obtain their rights. It can be described as socio-political movement.

The State also has introduced a number of legislations by way of constitutional safe-guards and legislative bills both at the Centre and the States, to enhance social justice, to protect the vulnerable sections from all social inequalities and to ensure their participation in decision making bodies.

Chapter 5

Spirituality and Community

We have noted from the above description that Indian Church in general and Protestant Churches in particular, are the recipients of inputs both from Hinduism and Christianity of the West. Some inputs have produced positive results while others negative results.

Firstly, we have observed that Hinduism is a complex phenomenon. Though, majority of Hindu scholars depict Hinduism as 'a way of life', it cannot be denied that Hinduism also portrays 'a view of life'. Both are integral to each other and for a wholistic understanding of Hinduism both the 'view of life' and 'way of life' need to be taken into consideration. Philosophical Hinduism encourages all Hindus to attain self-realisation, which is the goal of spirituality by following the three Margas, namely, Gnana Marga (path of knowledge), Bhakti Marga (path of devotion) and Karma Marga (path of action). Philosophical Hinduism also depicts that spirituality for service by doing one's duty without expecting reward is also a way of expressing one's own spirituality. This spirituality is available to all, irrespective of their status and position in the hierarchical social system.

Practical Hinduism provides scope for variety of beliefs and practices. It does not insist on right doctrine. It consists of rituals and rites, signs and symbols depending on the caste that one hails from. Worship is always individualistic. They can worship personal god (Ista Devata) or family god or even community gods. Therefore, practical Hinduism multiplies the beliefs and practices among its adherents.

While philosophical Hinduism and practical Hinduism are essentially individualistic in their approach, social structure in Hinduism is basically communitarian. The social life in Hinduism is organized rigidly on the basis of caste and its standing on the hierarchical ladder in the social system. The origin of caste system can be traced to religion or to different communities intermingling with one another or to ethnological amalgamation due to migration of different ethnic groups to India, or to functional division devised by earlier society by assigning different professions to different communities or even a combination of several factors mentioned above. However, caste system is rigid; hierarchical and tends to become communal – communal understood as erecting a boundary around the group, without allowing entry to other groups and promoting interest of its own group over against other groups. The introduction of separate housing colonies for different caste groups in a village set-up is an example to this segregation. Even, in cities we see caste groups preferring to live in the same locality where their own caste group members live, thus making social interaction extremely difficult, if not impossible. Further, caste system operates on the concept of 'purity' and 'pollution'. Those who have performed good deeds in the previous birth are born as 'Dwijas' or twice born, and therefore, they are pure. Those who have performed bad deeds are born as 'untouchables' and therefore they are 'impure'. Their presence itself pollutes the atmosphere. They are born only to serve Dwijas. The caste system operates predominantly at three levels, namely, 'purity of race', 'purity of culture' and 'purity of habits'. The low caste people are considered as 'impure' in all the three aspects. Hence, they are segregated and discriminated by the high caste people who consider themselves as 'pure'.

We have observed in the section under 'cultural Hinduism' that India does not have homogeneous culture. It has both written culture and oral culture existing side by side. They further got diversified into multi-cultural system during the course of history based on language, region, caste, beliefs and practices, customs and traditions. Therefore in India, culture is not homogeneous but heterogeneous. However, these diverse cultures are held together on the basis of certain inherent qualities which promote unity in diversity. They are: quality of tolerance – allowing different opinions, beliefs and practices to co-exist; quality of accommodation – utilizing one another talents and skills without sacrificing their own talents and skills; quality of assimilation – whenever it is convenient to both the groups merging with each other to achieve a common goal; quality of absorption – dominant system taking control of the weaker system.

Secondly, we have noted that Christianity was brought to India by the Western Missionaries bringing their own brand of denominational Christianity. All the Missionary Societies irrespective of their denominational background considered spreading the Gospel as their primary purpose of coming to India. However, the Protestant Missionary movement is unique in that this movement differed from other Missions in their understanding and implementing mission concerns. The early Protestant missionaries were the products of 'Enlightenment Philosophy' and 'Pietistic Movements' which swept the European continent during the 17th and 18th century. While the Enlightenment Philosophy encouraged acceptance of faith based on scientific and rational enquiry of the Scriptures, Pietistic Movement demanded self-surrender of an individual by having personal encounter with Christ.

Missionaries from different Missionary Societies had the Agenda of promoting their own denominational Christianity. Yet, they devised strategies in order to carry on their mission without much competition between one another. They extended co-operation with one another. They organized Decennial Missionary Conferences to discuss common issues to resolve conflicts. They accepted 'comity' principle, so that each one's territory is protected from the onslaughts of the other. These ventures not only helped them in concentrating on missions, but they have also become cardinal principles in forming the Church of South India in later years.

The methodology that the missionaries adopted in missions was the biblical methodology of preaching, teaching and healing. But, they were sensitive to the context in which mission had to be done. Hence, depending on the context they were creative in their approach. To the educated, their approach was critical study of the scriptures and by way of arguments, debates and discourses, creating a critical faculty so that they could accept faith after being convinced rationally. To the sick, suffering, despised and vulnerable section of society, they adopted a methodology of showing human compassion. They expressed solidarity with the struggles and aspirations of Dalits, marginalized and oppressed communities. In order to provide quality leaders for Church and society, the missionaries established various institutions catering to different needs of Church and Society. Bible teaching was central to their methodology. Values emerging from the Bible were the foundation on which personality development, community building, social transformation and leadership development could take place. Therefore, missionary contribution to the Indian Church is enormous and incalculable. Does this mean missionaries did not have any weaknesses? This question will be answered in Chapter VI.

1. Spirituality

The word 'spirituality' cannot be defined but can only be described, just as the New Testament writers only describe the word 'Church' and never define it. For, spirituality like the Church has different shades of meaning attached to it. Emphasizing one aspect of the meaning over against the other would ultimately lead to distortion. Spirituality, as the word itself depicts is in the realm of spirit – beyond the scope of physical nature. It is to discover the true nature of human beings from within and beyond oneself; it is to relate oneself to the ultimate being who is the source of all life. Spirituality is to realize that human beings are not the centre of the universe, but there is some power or person beyond the human beings, who is the author of the universe, including human beings who are the crown of His creation. Therefore, spirituality has to do with one's own relationship with this ultimate reality whom we call as God. In other words, spirituality is to realize the true nature of oneself in relation to the Supreme Being, namely God. In short, spirituality is to put oneself right with God. So, spirituality is a response of human beings to the goodness of God in creating him/her in his own image. To discover this unadulterated godliness called God's image dwelling within oneself, is the true spirituality. Therefore, spirituality necessarily begins with individuals and their response to God. But, each individual understands God in their own way and from the perspective that they have been comfortable with. Indian philosophy has prescribed three major paths to attain bliss. To an intellectual, who can rationally think and act, it has recommended Gnana Marga to study, discuss, debate on the values enshrined in the scriptures and arrive at a rational decision through enlightenment. To the majority of people for whom emotions occupy an important place than intellectualism, it promotes Bhakti Marga – a person can surrender himself to ultimate reality through prayer, meditation, ecstasy, mystic identification etc. To the vast number of people who are not able to articulate or to spend their time in discovering the path of Bhakti, the Indian philosophy prescribes Karma Marga to find meaning in their work by performing their duties justly and honestly and to consider their 'work as worship'. These three paths are not mutually exclusive. A person can adopt any one or group of them to attain self-realization. Further, the goal of self-realization is for an individual either to be 'absorbed' into the ultimate reality or to be in 'fellowship' with the ultimate reality or even to live in the 'domain' of the ultimate reality. These goals are also not contradictory in nature but complimentary to one another. Hence, according to Indian philosophy true spirituality is to realize oneself in relation to the ultimate reality, and to involve in unmitigated service to humanity.

Christian spirituality does not negate the understanding of Indian spirituality. Rather, it affirms the Indian spirituality and builds on that foundation. Like in Indian spirituality, Christian spirituality also emphasizes the need for individual efforts to attain salvation, which is a combination of Moksha and Dharma of the Indian spirituality. But here, the horizon of understanding spirituality is widened. Christian spirituality, like the Indian philosophy, recognizes that human beings are not the centre of the universe. It is God the Creator, who is at the centre of the universe. It is the duty of human beings to relate themselves to God – that is true spirituality. But, unlike in Shankara's philosophy which considers world as 'Maya' – unreal, Christian spirituality affirms world as real in line with Ramanuja's Visistadwaita philosophy and Madhwa's Dwaita philosophy. The difference in understanding the true nature of oneself arises at the very understanding of God and His relationship to the world itself. It is this difference which is crucial to understand the very nature of spirituality according to Christianity.

Unlike in Indian philosophy, the view of life in Christianity is derived from the Bible. The Bible begins with the story of creation. It is God who took initiative to create the universe and all that is in it. The first two Chapters of Genesis pictorially presents the creative activities of God. Light and darkness, water and dry land, plants and animals and everything that has life on earth are the creation of God. At the end of each day of creation God appreciated his own marvelous work and called it good. As a crown of his creation God created human beings, male and female He created in his own 'image'. At the end of the creation God caricatured his creation as 'very good'. He further blessed them to inhabit the created world and use the resources of the universe and prosper. God, further took human beings as partners in his creative venture by allowing them to name every living creature. Bible is also categorical in stating that there was a harmonious relationship between God and human beings and human beings and nature. There was a perfect communication between God and human beings.

The third chapter of Genesis describes how this harmonious relationship between God and human beings and human beings and the universe are destroyed, by misusing the God given freedom. It is because of the sinful nature of human beings. Sin, is disobeying God's command. It is to grab the power and position that belongs only to God, it is to put the blame on others in order to cover up one's own mistakes and faults. Therefore, sin alienates human beings from God, from each other and from the universe. The facts found in Genesis Chapter 3, are only representative in character. For the whole Bible, is a depiction of how human beings, communities, regimes, leaders at different times in history have disobeyed God's command of maintaining harmonious and non-exploitative relationship between God, human beings and the universe. The last two chapters of the Bible namely Revelations Chapters 21 and 22 again portray a vision for a glorious and harmonious relationship between God and human beings, between human beings to human beings and between human beings and the universe. Here, God is depicted as dwelling in the midst of people and people acknowledging Him as their God, river of life, providing the daily necessities of all human beings, all nations are brought under the reign of God. Then God will create a new heaven and new earth, where 'He will wipe away every tear from their eyes, and death shall be no more, neither shall there be mourning nor crying nor pain any more, for the former things have passed away'. (Rev. 21:4)

Therefore, the biblical view of life is that God is at the centre of created world. He is the prime mover and ultimately, all life should end in His presence. This world which is created by God is good and real. Human beings are created by God as a crown of His creation. It is through a responsible stewardship of the earth's resources that human beings perpetuate God's goodness. Failure to do so would result in alienation from God, human beings and the universe. Spirituality according to Christianity is therefore, to put oneself right with God. To discern the will of God in one's own life; and then to become partner with God in restoring the broken relationship to its original status of harmony and goodwill, as well as to work towards abolishing all human barriers that hinders proper relationship with God and human beings, between human beings and human beings and between human beings and the universe is the true spirituality. Christian spirituality, can therefore be described as 'spirituality for combat', to use the phrase coined by Dr. M. M. Thomas, when he addressed the WCC Assembly in 1975 as Chairman of the Central

Committee. However, since the word 'combat' comes from the military background, we can rephrase it to describe as 'spirituality for engagement'.

We can, therefore, confidently conclude that Christian spirituality in India is a result of two streams of spirituality coming together and forming a wholistic understanding of spirituality. Indian spirituality begins with individual quest for self-realization in relation to ultimate reality. Christian spirituality equally begins with the individual as a response to God's goodness to that person and to the whole world. Without this basic step there cannot be any meaningful spirituality in a person's life. Hence, the Christian spirituality's insistence on individual commitment to Christ or personal encounter with Christ is a prerequisite for any spiritual journey. The journey can begin at a particular point in one's own life, but that is not the end of the journey, but only a beginning. In this journey one can even reach the zenith and enjoy the bliss of being in the presence of God or in fellowship with God. But, the danger accompanying such an extreme individual self-realization is that it may lead a person to renounce the world. Then that kind of spirituality might help that individual to attain the desired goal of self-realization, but it is of no consequence for the well-being of the world and fellow travellers. This aberration was corrected in the Indian spirituality, when it advocated spirituality of service to other human beings, by way of performing conscientious duty without expecting any reward for the same. Therefore, Moksha and Dharma are the two sides of the same coin in a person's spiritual journey. Christian spirituality has always stressed the need for service to humanity without expecting any reward for the same as one of the cardinal principles of Christian faith. Christian spirituality adds one more dimension to 'spirituality for self-realization' and 'spirituality for service'. That is 'spirituality for engagement'. The third dimension of spirituality motivates individuals and communities to use their spiritual resources to engage themselves in concrete and actionable programmes aiming at transforming individuals, communities, organisations and institutions to become God's instruments in ushering new and harmonious relationships in society. Spirituality for Engagement does not believe in sporadic actions, but in sustainable and long term activities based on spiritual values derived from the scriptures. It calls for total involvement of the people and communities in God's creative activities and not as just spectators or bystanders. It engrafts others as partners in God's redeeming acts and not as recipients of charity.

2. Community

One of the neglected aspects of study and research is the role of community in shaping the destiny of individuals in Indian context. The Western scholars with their emphasis on individualism, did not find it worthy to examine the positive and negative impact that the community has on individuals. The Indian scholars have only considered caste as a basic unit of socialization. The Christian scholars have concentrated more on the normative principles of socialization rather than analyzing the existing sociological realities. Therefore, the role of community in shaping the destiny of individuals has largely remained unexplored. On the other hand, community has exercised and continues to exercise enormous influence in enhancing the quality of life in individuals and at the same time, erects boundaries in such a way that the individual would find it difficult to escape from its stranglehold. Therefore, it is absolutely necessary to understand the role of community in relation to individuals in Indian context to arrive at the proper understanding of spirituality itself, but first some preliminary remarks.

Community begins with the question of identity. There are some 'given' identities and others are acquired identities. It is easy to change acquired identities but given identities cannot be changed that easily. There will always be resistance to change. Each of us has multiple identities. They interact with one another and sometimes overlap with each other. The strong characteristics of identities ultimately take control in given circumstances.

Let me illustrate this point. I am born to my parents, namely, Suputhrappa and Kanakamma in a village in Mysore District. I speak Kannada. My family is a joint family and all of them became Christians, about one hundred years ago. Therefore, all of them are practicing Christians. In this description, one can see a number of identities. First, I belong to a particular family – a given identity. Secondly, my mother tongue is Kannada – again a given identity. Thirdly, a Christian – religious identity, which can be changed, but I will never do it because of my conviction that Christian faith is the only faith that I am comfortable with. There are other identities like I am educated, I am a Pastor, I now live in Bangalore etc. All these are acquired identities which are available to anyone else and so easily changed. These identities are necessary for the growth and progress of any individual, because these identities provide support, comfort, consolation, affirmation and encouragement. But, these identities also erect boundaries around individuals either consciously or unconsciously. For instance, the fact that I speak Kannada means that I am not, say, a Tamilian or a Malayalee or a Telugu. Further, the fact that I hail from Mysore region means that I am not a Mangalore Kannadiga or Hubli-Dharwad Kannadiga whose culture is different from Mysore Kannadigas, even though, they speak the same languages. If one considers my religious identity, I am a Christian and therefore I am not a Hindu or a Muslim. But, I am a Protestant Christian which means I do not belong to Syrian Orthodox or a Roman Catholic tradition. Further, among the Protestants I am a member of CSI. Therefore, I belong to a CSI community. All the above identities are necessary for me to define 'who am I?'. But, the fact that I am a CSI Christian should not prevent me from accepting a Roman Catholic or a Syrian Orthodox or a Pentecostal as fellow Christians, and this depends to a great extent on my spiritual values. Again, the fact that I am a Christian should not deter me from recognizing a Hindu as a fellow spiritual traveller pursuing a different path than my own. Further, this also depends to a great extent on the spiritual values that I cherish. So, while given identities cannot be changed spirituality provides scope for an individual to transcend the limitations placed on individual by the boundaries that identity creates. But, the problem is while individuals may be able to transcend human barriers, it is the organized communities through their strict codes, rules and regulations that have a crippling effect on the behavior and conduct of individuals, more about this a little later.

Community's participation in the life of an individual in India begins at the birth of a child itself, nay, even before it and ends only at the death of that person. When a young mother is expecting a child and the pregnancy is at an advanced stage the family invites women from the neighbourhood who have already attained motherhood to come and bless the expectant mother and the future arrival. Arrival of a new baby calls for celebration in the neighbourhood.When the actual birth takes place, it is again a time for celebration for the community along with the family by sharing sweets with one another. The child is born into the family and not just to the parents. Therefore, ownership, protection, safety, nourishment of the child belongs to the whole family and not just to the parents. Take a labour class family for instance, when both the husband and wife go to work to earn their daily bread, the care and protection of the child is left to another child of eight or ten years, mostly female child, even though she herself needs such care. When a child grows up he or she actively participates in the peer group, formed informally among the children of the community through games and extra-curricular activities, which has a tremendous impact on the behavior and conduct of the child. Children participate enthusiastically in community activities such as games, sports, festivals and cultural programmes. Marriage is not just a family affair but a community affair. Death again is an occasion where the entire community participates in comforting and consoling the family. So, the life of an individual is intrinsically linked to the community life. In the process, the individual develops emotional and psychological bond with the community and the community in turn, claims the ownership of individuals within their community. Therefore, to think of individualism without reference to communitarianism, is erroneous in Indian context.

The word 'community' is used with different connotations in different contexts. It can be used to describe a group of people living in a specific locality as found in a statement, 'the village communities living on the banks of river Ganga are apprehensive of flood situation during monsoon season'. Here community refers to people living in a geographical location, irrespective of their faith, caste and class, or gender issues. It can also be used to describe a sociological reality or ethnic groupings such as 'tribal community' or 'Dalit community'. It is used to describe cultural leanings of a group – for example – community of musicians. It is also used to emphasize the religious character of a group – such as a Catholic Community or a Protestant community or Hindu community. It is also used to describe a small unit like a congregation as well as a large entity of the whole body. For example, the CSI Community which meets at Kothanur or the entire CSI population covering the four southern States as well as throughout the world by referring to them as CSI Community. It can also be used to describe a national character of a group – like when we say the Indians community living in United States of America. Thus, the word community has a rich variety of meanings attached to it, depending on the context in which it is used. However, it should be noted that community is a generic term which has been accepted by all across religious, social and cultural divides in society. A community, therefore, consists of members who exhibit a general equality, shared beliefs and practices, similar interests with common goals. A community exists for the benefit of all its members and governed by its own chosen/elected members based on conventional as well as written statutes.

Community is an organized entity. Any organization needs rules and regulations for its survival as well as growth. So, each community formulates their codes, legislations, rules and regulations for its members to follow. Any deviation in observing these rules and regulations will attract punishment. For example, a person may like to marry outside his or her caste, but, that would be considered as a deviant behavior and the person concerned and in some cases even the family members are punished ruthlessly by the community. Thus, even though the community has a positive role to play in the growth of an individual, it can also become a hindrance for the same individual to exercise his or her freedom. Further, the avowed goal of every community is to assist its members in every way, to achieve a better quality of life. In order to achieve these goals, community interacts with political parties, educational institutions, social scientists, economic advisers, cultural associations, commercial ventures and similar entities, who exert their own influence on the life of the community. The community uses all these opportunities to help its members to come up in life. We have instances of many communities in India who have used all these openings judiciously, carefully and systematically and as a result have now become influential communities, whereas at one time in history they were a 'no people'. Thus, community plays a vital role in the upliftment of individual members as well as the larger community itself.

However, there is also a flip side to community in India. Each community, in their efforts to enhance the quality of life to its members, creates layers and layers of boundaries around them either consciously or unconsciously, making transcending the barriers more and more difficult. Further, in that process they tend to forget or overlook the needs of other communities and particularly communities of lesser privileged people. Sometimes, communities want their progress even at the cost of other communities. This becomes more pronounced, when the demands of a particular community is clubbed with political motivation. Political parties treating different communities as vote-banks and powerful communities in turn demanding reservation, concessions and privileges for their respective communities, has made mockery of the whole reservation system, which was originally thought of as a step towards 'positive affirmation' of the dispossessed and the disadvantaged section of society. Any community, which seeks progress of its members and not being mindful of the other communities will ultimately end up as communal group – a group which whips up the passion of its members over against others, in order to protect the interest of its own members. This creates hatred between communities, and would end up in destroying the peace and harmony prevailing in society. Unfortunately, in India we are at a stage where 'community' and 'communal' have a very thin line dividing them. This is applicable to all communities irrespective of their religious, social and cultural affiliation.

It is my contention that only a proper understanding and application of spiritual values would help us rectify this dangerous trend in public life.

3. Salient Features of Early Christian Communities in India

The marks of a true Christian are: call, community and commission – all originating from Jesus Christ Himself. Firstly, Christian life begins with a call from God. Initiative for a true spiritual life of an individual begins with God's call. It does not rest with human efforts. The one who recognizes this 'still small voice' working within him/her and responds to it appropriately is called upon to begin this spiritual journey. The call may come in various ways such as in a dream, or listening to a testimony of someone who has experienced Christ or hearing the word of God or receiving comfort and counseling in a difficult situation. The ways are innumerable. The call can also come through different agencies – such as parents, teachers, community, peer groups etc. It is left to the individual concerned to discern such a call and respond appropriately. Appropriate response means to have a personal encounter with Christ; to surrender totally to Christ; to acknowledge his/her utter unworthiness before Christ; to cast oneself to the mercy and grace of Christ; to commit oneself to re-order life based on that personal experience and to 'lead a life worthy of calling'. From this perspective, baptism should be viewed as bestowal of God's grace upon the person (God's promise) in response to the pledge that a person makes or parents make on behalf of the person to God. This is the beginning of a spiritual journey and not the end of it. One has to continue to respond to God's call afresh, when he or she meets with new challenges in life.

Secondly, people who have had personal encounter with Christ and also engrafted into the body of Christ no longer remain as isolated individuals, but become members of a community consisting of those who have made similar commitment to Christ. Each individual, needs to grow together with other fellow believers, by learning, sharing and caring for one another. The individuals whom Jesus called by name to become his disciples, became a community of disciples around Jesus. They were not a perfect community, but a community growing together under the leadership of Jesus. Likewise, early Christians in the Acts of the Apostles also formed themselves into a community of believers. So, participation in the life of the community is an essential step for any Christian in his or her spiritual growth.

Thirdly, the call of God is not for self-aggrandizement, but for mission – a call to become partners with God in His act of restoration, reconciliation and re-creation. Jesus sent out his disciples in Mission. (Luke 9) He also sent out other disciples for the same purpose (Luke 10). Mission of God is the goal of every individual who has responded to God's call and every community, which bears Christ's name. With this perspective in mind, let us now, look at the salient features of early Christian communities in India. 'Early Christian Communities' here denotes 'early Protestant communities'.

a. Worshipping Communities

The early Christian believers were small in number. It consisted of individuals or groups who had accepted Christ as their Saviour. They were found in different villages. The first thing that they did was to come together either in their own village or in neighbouring villages, once a week, to worship. One of them who had been instructed or trained for that purpose by the missionaries would be the leader of worship. They gathered together either in a humble house of a believer or in a thatched hut erected for that purpose, by the believers themselves. Massive and grand Cathedrals and Church building were not there, yet they were happy to worship in a simple and obscure place. For them, place was not important but gathering had great significance. In the context of these people not being allowed to enter into temples, worship in a inconspicuous place meant a great spiritual awakening. Further, in the context of worship being individualistic in Hinduism worshipping together meant a community in God's presence. Therefore, they could joyously sing and pray, cry and clap, listen to stories from the Bible and share their experiences with others; even though, they could not articulate their faith in a coherent manner. By completely surrendering themselves to God they could experience the bliss of God through worship. Every time they met for worship, it was a mountain top experience for them – experiencing the majesty and glory of God himself (Mk. 9:2 ff). Whenever Holy Communion was celebrated, it was a banquet presided over by the Lord himself, for it signified sharing a meal hosted by the Lord but also sharing of the meal with other believers. This symbolic act had great social significance for them in the context of inter-dining not being allowed in Hinduism. Worship provided them spiritual strength and courage to face challenges in the world. Those who were 'no people' earlier had the realization that they became 'God's people' now; which was the best blessing that they could get in this world.

b. Christ Centered Communities

Those who accepted Christ experienced a new vigor in their life by listening to the stories about Jesus, his ministry, his suffering on the Cross. Jesus' solidarity with the sinners, tax-collectors and despised section of the society made them feel at home with Him. His empowerment of the neglected and marginalized women and children touched their hearts; His compassion for the sick and the dying brought tears to their eyes; they could identify their sweat with the sweat of Jesus at Gethsemane; the blood of Jesus on the Cross – resembled their own blood on their blistered palms; Jesus' suffering on the Cross, for the sake of humanity made them remember their own suffering at the hands of the oppressors; His death on the Cross brought home to them, their own day-to-day experience of near death at the injustices meted out to them. But, the resurrection of Jesus gave them a new hope that the oppression that they were experiencing, will come to an end and a new life is possible. Therefore, Jesus Christ became a 'prime mover' in their lives; He occupied a central place in their lives. For them, Jesus was not an idea but a reality; not a mythical figure but a historical human being. The debate about 'Jesus of History' and 'Christ of Faith' by the Western scholars had no relevance because Jesus of history is also Christ of Faith for them. There was no dichotomy between the two. Jesus Christ is the only one who could redeem and liberate them from their wretched position.

c. Bible Based Communities

Even though the majority of early Christians were illiterates, they were conscious that their lives changed for better after listening to the stories narrated from the Bible. The supreme inspiration for change in life style came from the biblical stories. Hence, Bible became a sacred book for them. Bible was important for them for the following reasons: firstly, it reveals the true nature of God. 'God is love', they learnt from the Bible as against their earlier practice of worshipping ferocious gods who were out to avenge all atrocities heaped on them. Biblical God, they realized is the God, who loves the world and in order to save the world and human beings, He did not spare even His own beloved Son but sent Him that all may have eternal life. (John. 3:16) and everyone may enjoy 'life in fullness' (John. 10:10). Secondly, Bible narrates the stories of Jesus – his life, ministry and mission on earth. They are historical narratives and not just doctrinal statements, hence are very valuable for illiterate Christians like them. Thirdly, Bible depicts the human nature in its totality. Like a mirror, the Bible pin-points the true nature of human beings. It shows the capacity of human beings to acquire divine nature and at the same time, it demonstrates the abysmal level, to which human beings can fall due to their sinful nature. Finally, Bible provides a spiritual framework on which an individual or a community can weave an acceptable life 'worthy of calling'. For the above reasons, the early Christian community built their new life on biblical principles. Bible was not one of the many books for them, but rather one and only sacred book available to them. Their life was shaped on the values that emerged from the Bible, because it contained 'all things necessary for salvation' in their understanding. They never worshipped the Bible but only considered it as 'Holy Bible'. The question of bibliolatry never occurred in their thoughts ever.

d. Communities Under Grace

These communities were conscious of their limitations. They could not boast of their past achievements as the high caste people did. They were aware of their historical past. Even as members of a new community they did not have any political influence or economic power, or even social standing, but they were conscious of their standing in the eyes of God, as they had heard many sermons preached on the biblical text which reads as follows:

"Consider your own call, brothers and sisters, not many of you were wise by human standards, not many were powerful, not many were of noble birth. But God chose what is foolish in the world to shame the wise; God chose what is weak in the world to shame the strong; God chose what is low and despised in the world, things that are not, to reduce to nothing things that are, so that no one might boast in the presence of God. He is the source of your life in Christ Jesus, who became for us wisdom from God and righteousness and sanctification and redemption." (1 Cor. 1:26-30)

It was this assurance from the scripture which gave strength and courage to early Christian communities to face criticism and hostilities heaped on them by self-proclaimed protectors of the status quo in social life. They had no one to protect them but God Himself. They depended on mercy and grace of God even for their survival as a community.

e. Mission Focused Communities

If one wants to be convinced that ordinary, illiterate and unsophisticated people are also equally good communicators like the intellectuals one must read the History of Missions in India. Therefore, if one were to read with discerning eyes, he/she would discover that the carriers of the Gospel were these ordinary Christians themselves. While intellectuals communicated through writings, art and culture, ordinary people communicated through 'conversation'. While intellectuals use concepts or theories to communicate their ideas, ordinary people use their life experiences as communication tools. This is actually what happened in the early Christian communities. Small house groups eventually became large congregations. Christian communities spread from one village to another. It was mainly due to the personal involvement of the village Christians in communicating the Gospel. From the head of the family to other members of the family and then to the relatives and then to the members of their own community or caste group the gospel was spread. In this mission work, village school teachers and Bible women, both of whom were local leaders, played an important role by sharing their life-changing experiences of their personal encounter with Christ. 'Go or send' is a missionary call given by the missionary organisations in modern times. But, for the early Christian communities 'going ' out of their context was impossible, while 'sending' someone was unaffordable. So, they decided to 'be' the missionaries themselves in their own context. The villagers around them knew their early life-style and the change that has taken place in their life after accepting Christ. Hence, when these early Christian communities communicated the Gospel, they believed and in turn some of them accepted Christ. In this way, the early Christian communities became mission focused communities.

It is my conviction that opposition to Christianity in India, is not primarily due to the fact that Christianity has not originated in India like Hinduism and therefore, it is a foreign religion. But, mainly because the way Christian communities were organized by not following traditional values of purity and impurity, high caste and low caste, sophisticated culture and demeaning culture but spiritual values emerging from their commitment to Christ resulting in transcending all human barriers and formation of new communities in the life of early Christian communities. Of course, they were not perfect communities. Human sinful nature has peculiar ways of infiltrating even the spiritually motivated communities, as we have observed in early Christian communities in Act 5. Likewise, even in early Christian communities in India the sin of hierarchical caste system has entered through a group of caste Christians and it is bothering the Church even now.

Chapter 6

CSI: A Pilgrim Church

The formation of the Church of South India, consisting of four denominational traditions, namely, Anglican, Methodist, Presbyterian and Congregational, and inaugurated on 27th September 1947 in St. George's Cathedral, Madras has attracted and continues to attract a wide variety of reactions from different sections of society in general and Church members in particular. To those who were accustomed to see God's intervention in history, it was 'a second miracle after Pentecost' for they had never witnessed or read 'Episcopalians and non-Episcopalians joining together to form a United Church in Church history'. To the theological puritans, it was 'sacrificing theological truths at the altar of convenience'. To the traditionalists, it was an 'attempt at syncretism'. To the denominational promoters, it was a 'compromise' and to the ultra-evangelicals it was neglecting evangelism with its emphasis on organization. To the social activists, it is suppressing the prophetic voice by the Institutional Church. To the skeptics, it is a litigant Church. But, for the vast majority of the faithful it is 'an agreement to walk together in obedience to the will of God, as Marcus Ward describes. Based on this understanding, Marcus Ward, who was a Professor of Theology at the United Theological College and a representative of the Methodist Church in Union Negotiations Committee describes the Church of South India (CSI) as a 'Pilgrim Church', a phrase which he uses as a title of his book, while evaluating work of the Church in the first few years of its formation. This phrase 'Pilgrim Church', truly describes the nature and function of the CSI, even today. Let us therefore, look at some of the characteristics of a pilgrimage as prevalent in the earlier times.

The word 'pilgrim' is always associated with a journey to the sacred places or shrines. It is a religious act and not a social obligation. It is undertaken voluntarily and never by coercion or through inducement. The desire to go on a pilgrimage springs from the heart. The reasons for undertaking pilgrimage may vary from person to person. To one, it may be a fulfillment of the vow made earlier; to another it may be an act of thanksgiving for the blessings received; to yet another it may be to experience and to enjoy being in the presence of the Lord. But, ultimate goal of having 'Darshan' of the Lord and being in the presence of the Lord is the same for every pilgrim.

The word 'Church' indicates corporateness. It is a collective group. Therefore, 'Pilgrim Church' indicates pilgrimage undertaken together as a group of believers. It is a community journey in which individuals participate voluntarily. It is not just the desire of individuals to experience the presence of the Lord. Individuals join others with similar desire and organize a pilgrimage tour, the groups may be from a village or group of villages drawn from different caste groups or even economic status. All of them decide to undertake such a pilgrimage. As the journey would be long and arduous; and the terrain rough having to cut across forests or mountains and requiring to camp in the wilderness on their journey, the pilgrims necessarily have to decide to take only essential things leaving non-essentials back in their homes. Accordingly, the CSI members gave up non-essentials like, caste affiliation, ritual practices and denominationalism. Instead, they armed themselves with deeper individual and community spirituality with a desire to serve humanity without expecting any reward. They have to leave the comforts of their homes to stay in tents and forgo luxuries to lead a frugal life. But, these hardships do not deter the pilgrims from their determination to have darshan of the Lord.

During the course of their journey individuals and groups begin to converse with each other, share their life's concerns with each other and even share their meals with one another. Sometimes, unexpected calamities may strike them, such as, robbers attacking them, or heavy rains causing floods or even someone falling sick. In all these events, they help each other forgetting their differences of caste, language or economic status. In the process, a community transcending all the barriers begins to emerge. By the time they reach the shrine, the community life wherein caring and sharing already is in practice, becomes a reality. Finally, when they are in the presence of the Lord, three realities interact with each other, namely, the Lord, the individual and the community of believers. Both the individual and the community enjoy the bliss in the presence of the Lord. This is the highest point of their pilgrimage.

There is another aspect related to the pilgrimage. The pilgrims may stay in the vicinity of the shrine for some time, but afterwards they return to their original homes as transformed people. They share 'prasadams' with people in their native place; they narrate their encounter with the Lord to the people around; they describe how difficult the journey was, but worth the trouble because they have become recipients of God's blessings. Therefore, the quest for spiritual journey begins with individuals, forms a community on the way, and leads them to the presence of the Lord which motivates them to share their spiritual experience with those who did not have such experience. This is the ultimate aim of a pilgrim church. The Church of South India is committed to such an understanding of the Church.

The pilgrim journey which started on 27th September 1947 continues, even today. Every worship service and other spiritual activities conduced act as fuel stations replenishing the spiritual energy spent on the way. Individuals, with deep commitment to Christ have joined and continue to join the journey. Communities of innumerable number of congregations have been 'walking together in obedience to the will of God'. In the process the CSI has become recipient of great many blessings from God. In turn, it has also shared these blessings with the people of other faiths and particularly with the poor and the marginalized. But, the journey has not been smooth. There have been ups and downs in its journey; seen bickerings and frustrations; faced problems of the magnitude of 'Typhoons' and 'Tsunamis', yet the CSI has not given up its pilgrim journey rather it continues its journey with all firm determination. For, it is conscious of the ever present guiding hand of the Lord telling the community of the faithful, 'Take heart, it is I: do not be afraid'. (Mark. 6:50). With this assurance from the Lord the journey of the faithful continues unhindered.

1. Shared Vision

Preparation for the journey itself was elaborate and time consuming. It was a dream of a few visionary leaders to establish a Church bereft of denominationalism, but deeply rooted in Indian soil. With unwavering commitment for the mission of God, these individual visionaries began to share their concerns with others of the same mindset, which culminated at the 'The Tranquebar Conference on Church Union' in 1919. The fact that the Conference had 33 Christian leaders from Anglican and SIUC denominational background, of whom only 2 were non-nationals, clearly indicate the seriousness with which they approached the issue at hand. At the end of the Conference, they issued a call for the union of churches, which has come to be known as 'Tranquebar Manifesto'. In response to this call participating churches sent their representatives to a Joint Committee to discuss and debate the issue. The Joint Committee began its work in 1920. The Wesleyan Methodists joined the Committee from 1925 onwards. The scheme of Union was first published in 1929. It was revised seven times before it was finally accepted in 1947. The method that they adopted was to discuss, debate, argue and enter into dialogue with each other. The findings of the Joint Committee were sent to their respective Synods and Councils of the negotiating partners, so that the representative bodies might discuss and comment on the same. This way the vision of a few individuals got transferred to representative bodies, and thereby the individual visions became a shared vision of all the participating bodies. This was a long drawn out procedure, but a process through which consensus, was arrived at. It took 28 long years of negotiations to arrive at a consensus but a consensus which awakened the consciousness of the universal church for a different possibility.

2. The Object of Negotiations

As mentioned earlier, the object of negotiation was to 'establish a united church bereft of denominationalism, but deeply rooted in Indian soil with an unwavering commitment for the Mission of God.' The object, therefore, is three dimensional – United Church; National Church and Mission focused Church. As a working formula, to achieve the above objects the leaders adopted three principles, namely, 'self-supporting, self-governing and self-propagating church'. Church historian C. B. Firth, attributes these principles as originating from Rufus Anderson, Secretary of the American Board, who visited India in 1854-55. (*An Introduction to Indian Church History,* p. 261) However, these principles became the cardinal principles for the union negotiators upon which they visualized a new Church.

a. United Church

The fact that the four denominations have joined together to form a new Church is a reality now for the last 70 years. Further, a number of books and articles have been written on the process and the issues involved in negotiations. Therefore, it is not necessary here to once again repeat the same, except to recapitulate the principles involved in working towards a United Church, 'The Basis of Union', which is a historical document retained in the Constitution of the Church of South India. The purpose of the union according to this document is:

"The Uniting Churches affirm that the purpose of the Union into which they hope to enter is the carrying out of God's will as this is expressed in the Lord's prayer – 'That they all be one … that the world may believe that thou didst send me'. It believes that by this Union the Church of South India will become a more effective instrument for God's work, and that the result of Union will be greater peace, closer fellowship and fuller life within the Church and also eagerness and power for the proclamation of the Gospel of Christ. It hopes, that the Church may be a true leaven of unity in the life of India, and that through it there may be greater release of divine power for the fulfillment of God's purpose for His world." (*The Constitution of the Church of South India,* Ch. II, clause 2, p.4)

From the above statement, we can draw at least three basic principles involved in the Union negotiations. Firstly, union of churches is a divine will, expressed by our Lord through his prayer in St. John 17:21. Secondly, union will bring about greater peace and closer fellowship and fuller life within the Church. Thirdly, union will create new eagerness for the proclamation of the Gospel. To put it differently, the union will motivate the Church to be involved in the Mission of God in India, with a renewed commitment and therefore the negotiators believed that unity and mission are integrally and intrinsically linked to each other.

b. Mission Focused Church

Mission is the essence of the Church, the negotiators were emphatic in their conviction. Without mission the Church turns out to be a mere human organization having no trace of divine call. It was not only their conviction but a life experience. It was only through mission work that they or their ancestors were brought to the personal knowledge of Christ. This mission of God in reconciling the world unto Himself must continue and that is possible only if those who have had personal encounter with Christ become partners with God by becoming missionaries themselves in word and deed. The Church by equipping these 'Saints' for mission becomes an effective instrument for God's work, and thereby, She becomes 'a true leaven of unity in the life of India.'

c. National Church

The Basis of Union document also contains the following statement:

"They (the uniting Churches) further agree that the United Church must be an autonomous Church and free from any control, legal or otherwise, of any Church or Society external to itself". (Clause 13)

This statement has been retained in the Constitution of the Church of South India, Chapter II, Clause 18 on page 20. Not many Church historians and scholars have reflected on this clause in their writings, except for a casual reference here and there, probably because the early writers were mostly Westerners and they did not think that the Indian Church could actually be 'autonomous' and the later Indian thinkers took the 'autonomy' of the Church for granted. However, this statement underlines a very important step in the Union Negotiations. What was the context which prompted the negotiators to deliberate on this issue? What steps did they take in order to achieve the desired 'autonomous' nature of the Church? These questions need to be asked and answered, for a clear understanding of the nature of the United Church.

i. Political context

By the end of the eighteenth century the British rule in India was firmly in the hands of the East India Company – a commercial company – incorporated under a Charter of the British Parliament. The policy of the East India Company was anti-missions. The missionaries and Indian Christians had to face a lot of hardships at the hands of the East India Company authorities. It was only in 1813, when the Charter came for renewal the British Parliament took a lenient view towards missionary societies by making a provision 'sufficient facilities should be afforded by law, to persons desirous of going to and remaining in India for the purpose of accomplishing those benevolent designs, i.e. the introduction among the inhabitants of India of 'useful knowledge and religious and moral improvement' (C.B. Firth, p.158) With this relaxation new Protestant Missions opened their stations in India. By a further relaxation in 1833, the Continental and American Missions also opened their stations in India. Therefore, mission work in India is a product of different Missionary Societies coming from all over the world, and not confined to colonial rule only. The Missionary Societies, except the Anglican Church which catered to the spiritual oversight of the Chaplains and the English Churches – Civil and Military – which came under the Ecclesiastical establishment of the government, were never under political authority of the East India Company.

It was only in 1858, after the Sepoy Mutiny in 1857 the government came directly under the Queen's reign. The Sepoy Mutiny was directed against British rule and not a movement against Christian Missionary work. But, many missionaries and Christians became unfortunate victims of the furore, because of the mistaken notion that Missions are associated with the British. Many scholars consider Sepoy Mutiny as the beginning of the Freedom movement whipping up national fervor among Indians, leading to Independence in 1947.

ii. Missionary context

We have noted in Chapter III the enormous contribution made by Missionaries through their respective societies towards establishing Churches in India. Their main purpose was to create a new spirituality based on their experience in Christianity – a spirituality based on the scriptural values as against tradition. It included personal as well as corporate dimensions; it touched the minds, hearts and the life styles of those who responded to their preaching. They insisted on individual commitment to Christ, but also emphasized on the need to grow together as a community; their message covered all dimensions of human life namely, quest for spiritual salvation, compassion for the poor, solidarity with the oppressed and breaking down the barriers that existed in society. In this process, they neglected their health, donated their wealth to the mission work and at times, even sacrificed their lives for the sake of the Gospel.

Human as they were, the missionaries had one weakness in them cutting across their missionary organizations. Mission was initiated, organized, controlled and directed by the missionaries. Mission was *for* Indians and never *with* Indians. Indians were only recepients and not participants. They arranged for Evangelistic campaigns, but told the Indians as to how salvation needs to be understood. They established Churches, but retained the power to appoint Evangelists and Pastors; started Schools and Colleges and Hospitals, but the administrative control remained with them; purchased properties for the work of missions but registered them in the name of their respective Societies, Missionaries being the sole 'Power of Attorney' to administer properties; raised finances for the mission work, but never discussed the financial management with the locals. It is this paternalistic attitude of the missionaries that irked the Indian leaders. Independent thinkers, who were deeply committed to the ministry and mission of the church in India began to articulate their frustrations on different platforms. In order to highlight the prevailing context, a few statements are given here below:

V. S. Azariah, young missionary from 'Indian Missionary Society', to Dornakal was invited to be an Observer in the 'World Missionary Conference' in 1910 at Edinburgh where missionary representatives from all over the world met for the first time in history. In this Conference of more than one thousand representatives, he made the following bold statement, which shook the conscience of the Missionary Societies: "You missionaries are too generous. You insist on doing everything for us. You even make our mistakes for us". (Marcus Ward, p.157) He further went on to say – 'Through all the ages to come the Indian Church will rise up in gratitude to attest the heroism and self-denying labours of the missionary body. You have given your goods to feed the poor. You have given your bodies to be burned. We ask also for *love.* Give us *friends.*' (*Apostle of India*, p.6) V. S. Azariah who later became the first Indian Bishop in the Anglican Diocese of Dornakal was one of the leading persons to convene the meeting at Tranquebar in 1919.

Marcus Ward quotes from the Editorial of the 'South India Church', an official magazine of the newly formed Church of South India which described the foreignness of the Church of South India:

"It is foreign in its leadership, both central and local …and that is not the whole story! The Church of South India, is in fact a combination of several foreign churches and is, therefore, just as foreign as any of them was in isolation … It is not only foreign in its personnel; it is foreign in ethos; it is foreign in its administrative machinery; it is foreign in its theology; and above all, it is foreign in its material resources."

What about the desire of the average Indian Christians? What was his/her attitude towards Hinduism. P. Chenchiah, a leading figure in the 'Madras re-thinking group' along with A. J. Appasamy and V. Chakkarai, has this to say:

"There was a type of convert in the past who hated Hinduism and surrendered himself whole-heartedly to what is supposed to be Christianity. The convert today regards Hinduism as his spiritual mother who has nurtured him in a sense of spiritual values in the past. He discovered the supreme values of Christ, not in spite of Hinduism, but because Hinduism has taught him to discern spiritual greatness. For him, loyalty to Christ does not involve the surrender of a reverential attitude towards the Hindu heritage". (*Re-thinking Christianity in India*, p.48)

The above statements illustrate the context in which the union negotiators began their work. The assertive nature of resurgent Hinduism; the spirit of nationalism, coupled with ever growing anti-British feelings among the locals; creation of mass-based political and cultural organisations throughout India, and above all the desire of the entire that India be freed from the clutches of the British rule were some of the political realities which the negotiators could not be blind to.

Further, the Indian leaders were convinced that a lot of things had to be changed within the Church. The paternalistic attitude of the missionaries which did not encourage the local leadership; the method of aggressive evangelism adopted by the early missionaries and their attitude of condemning everything Indian as superstition; the organizational, administrative and financial control exercised by the missionaries which projected the image of the church as alien and not rooted in the soil; and the denominationalism imported from the West were some of the prominent reasons for the Indian leaders to think of a new Church with new credentials. If we place the three principles the union negotiators adopted namely, 'self-supporting, self-governing and self-propagating Church', in the context mentioned above, then we realize how powerful and purposeful those principles were in initiating a desired change. It was not easy for a Church, which was totally dependent on the missionaries for theology, personnel, administration and finances to become 'autonomous'. That meant, taking up the responsibility for ownership of the Church, undertaking stewardship of the resources as well as creating partnership for mission. It was an uphill task, but they ventured into it because their faith in Christ was deep and their love of the land was great.

The principle of self-supporting presupposes that infrastructural and financial resources comes from within. But, to raise the necessary funds for a vast number of ministries started by missionaries from the poverty stricken and economically deprived majority Dalit congregations, was not going to be easy. The principle of self-governing assumes that local leaders have to take charge of different ministries. They needed to be trained and necessary skills imparted. The principle of self-propagating requires theological and ideological commitment of the participants. They needed to be given proper orientation, teaching and nurture. The process of implementing such principles were necessarily time consuming and could not be achieved overnight, but had to be gradual. Union negotiators were aware of these difficulties, but willingly gave themselves to the task. As a result of the concerted efforts of those leaders and subsequent leaders today, it will not be an exaggeration to assert that the CSI has achieved the desired goals to a great extent.

A national church needs to reflect certain national characteristics. One important aspect of this characteristic is the concept of 'unity in diversity', as we noted earlier. India is a land of diverse culture portrayed through number of languages, literature, art and dance forms, customs and beliefs and mannerisms and practices. Our study of CSI history is normally confined to denominational unity, which culminated in the organizational unity. But, there were other factors which were brought together as a result of union negotiations. We do not know whether the union negotiators were conscious of those concerns, as no literature is available to indicate those concerns, but the end result was evident. Along with the denominational unity, four Dravidian languages namely, Kannada, Tamil, Telugu and Malayalam along with their sister languages; each having its own cultural specificities came together to form a United Church. Languages give identity to people, hence, it cannot be abolished, but has to be cultivated. People can express their faith meaningfully only through the language known to them. Further, each language acquires regional characteristics as well. The usage of language, pronunciation, mannerism and cultural moorings differ from region to region. All these factors influence our outlook in life. The United Church, therefore, brought together four different languages with their cultural values to the life of the Church. For a meaningful spiritual growth, these languages and cultural specificities need to be cultivated, encouraged and promoted. Unity in this sense is possible only through recognizing and promoting diversity in one faith and not looking for uniformity. It is with this intention that the Uniting Churches pledged themselves to "conserving all that is spiritual value in its Indian heritage, will express under Indian conditions and in Indian forms of spirit, the thought and the life of the Church universal". (Basis of Union, Clause 1, para 5)

Cultural diversity needs to be celebrated, but should not be allowed to segregate. All the beliefs and practices that dehumanize, alienate and segregate one from the other, need to be denounced and discarded. We have noted that different caste communities in different parts in South India responded to the Gospel. The missionaries, by taking a bold stand against the caste practices and prejudices within the Church, demonstrated that caste system is unscriptural. They insisted on the new converts to denounce caste system. The United Church by bringing together all these converts from high caste and low caste under one Church, proclaimed to the world that the United Church has transcended the barriers imposed by caste system to be united in one faith. This represented a radical shift from the traditional understanding of society. The United Church, is a community under the Cross of Jesus Christ, embracing all faithful as one family. The attempt by some people to retain caste identity within the Church under the guise of cultural moorings, goes against the very spirit of unity within the Church. It is significant to note here that the prayer of Jesus for unity is not only for his disciples, but also for 'those who will believe in me through their word'. (John. 17:20) Jesus was referring not only to the historical community, but to an eschatological community of believers as well. The faith of the historical community would impact on the eschatological community also, and so unity that transcends the barriers imposed by segregation and alienation in itself constitutes the mission of the Church.

The union negotiators had one more important task at hand and that is to define the relationship between the proposed National Church and the parent churches from the West. Does nationalism mean isolationism from the rest of the world? What is the relation between national church and the universal church? Does nationalism require detachment from the wider church? Does rooting the church in the soil mean disowning the past heritage? These were some of the issues that prompted the union negotiators to affirm 'the principles that it should maintain fellowship, with all those branches of the Church of Christ, with which the uniting churches now severally enjoy such fellowship, and that it should continually seek to widen and strengthen this fellowship … '(para 6). This concern has been retained in the Constitution of the Church of South India to maintain special relations not only with those Churches of the West, but also with wider ecumenical bodies. (Chap. II, Clause 18, p.20) Therefore, the Union Negotiators while emphasizing the national characteristics of the proposed church also envisaged a local church with a universal outlook. In this sense, the desire of the union negotiators to have an autonomous church 'free from the missionary control' should not be equated with the call for 'Quit India' from the members of the Freedom Movement in India. In the case of Churches, the relation continues without any control; but in the case of freedom movement, the relation was severed once and for all.

In short, the union negotiators prepared the ground for the Church to undertake pilgrimage. Over emphasis on organisational and denominational unity had camouflaged the achievements of the union negotiators in terms of spirituality, cultural diversity and integrating segregated communities. Taken together they provided deeper and inner spiritual strength to the faithful to undertake the pilgrimage ahead of them. This was possible because of their unwavering faith in Christ, love for the nation and a vision for a new church, as a community of caring and sharing. In fact, they have provided us with a vision for a new church distinct from the prevailing one – a new ecclesia. What then is the vision of our forefathers and mothers with regard to the forthcoming United Church? Briefly speaking, the vision can be summarized as follows:

The United Church is built on the bedrock of Jesus Christ, illumined by the Scriptures, and empowered by the Holy Spirit for the purpose of channelizing the grace of God to the communities of people around her. It consists of people who have had personal encounter with Christ, nurtured in faith by the community of faithful through worship and other activities. It embraces people of all castes, creed, colour and languages. It is united in Christ, celebrates diversity, transcends all barriers and girds itself to serve others. It is rooted in the soil and yet belongs to the Universal Church. It does not exist for itself but only to be in service to others. This is the vision – a utopia. The Church has not reached that stage. It is on the way. Hence, it is a Pilgrim Church.

This is also the vision of St. Paul for individuals as well as the Christian community. For Paul, the life of a believer is centred around Christ. A believer is baptized *into* Christ. (Rom. 6:3, Ga. 3:27) He/she participates in the sacraments instituted *by* Christ. (1 Cor. 11:24f). He/she shares in the sufferings *of* Christ (2 Cor. 1:5) He/she is buried *with* Christ by baptism. (Rom. 6:4) so that he/she may rise again from the dead to share His glory. (Rom. 6:5) Therefore, the believer is required to be in constant communion with Christ. Paul uses 'in Christ' (in Greek *en Christo*) as a comprehensive word. It is to live in fellowship with Christ or in the presence of Christ, just as Ramanujacharya's 'the goal of human soul is to live in the presence of the ultimate reality'. For Paul, 'In Christ' also meant to live by the side of Christ or in the domain of Christ, as in the case of Madhavcharya's ultimate goal of human soul is to live in the domain of ultimate reality. For Paul, 'in Christ' also meant to be grasped by Christ or to attain complete identity with the ultimate reality as explained by Shankaracharya, when he said that goal of human soul is to attain complete identity with the ultimate reality. In other words, for Paul the life of every believer should always be surrounded, encompassed and controlled by Christ.

But Paul goes beyond individual goal. For him, individuals are important, however, individuals not in isolation, but always in conjunction with other believers, individuals growing together in community. Paul explains this aspect of community vividly in Chapter 4 of his letter to the Ephesians – Paul recognizes the pilgrim nature of community life of Christian community. He begins the Chapter with the words 'walk worthy of the vocation wherewith ye are called'. (AV) – walking together towards the goal. What then is this goal? It is explained in verse 13, i.e.

- That all of us must come to the unity of the faith
- Must receive the knowledge of the Son of God
- Must reach the measure of full stature of Christ.

For Paul, Christian journey begins at baptism, confessing one Lord, empowered by one Spirit, where God is acknowledged as the Father of all. (Vs. 5) However, to reach this goal Christian community needs to be always mindful of and making conscious efforts to maintain the unity of the Spirit in the bond of peace. In order to achieve this, the believers need to imbibe, four essential characteristics in their attitude towards other believers, namely, lowliness – a life full of humility; meekness – spirit of submissiveness and not asserting one's own importance; long suffering – slowness in avenging anger or retaliating when hurt by others and forbearance – quality of continuing friendship in spite of the weakness of another. On the other hand, Paul urges all believers to recognize that 'every one of us is given grace – according to the measure of Christ's gift'. (Vs. 6) In other words, we need to recognize that every believer is endowed with certain gifts. Each one needs to recognize what the gift that he/she has received from Christ. The word 'grace' here means that the gift that we have received is not because of our merit, but purely out of His grace. It is an unmerited gift, so there is no scope for anyone to boast. Further, no one has all the gifts. The gifts are given not for self-aggrandizement, but to be used for the common good. Paul uses four passages to describe special gifts endowed on people. They are found in (1 Cor. 12:7-11; 1 Cor. 12:28-30; Rom. 12:6-8 and Eph. 4:11). These passages depict that there are no hierarchy in gifts. Each gift is as important as the other. For instance, the gift of a Sunday School teacher is in no way less than the gift given to a Presbyter or a Bishop, all have to exercise their gifts for the common good of the community. All need to use their gifts 'to equip the Saints for the work of the ministry as well as for building up the body of Christ'. (Vs. 12) Therefore, identifying one's own gifts and using them to equip the saints and to building up of the body of Christ is an essential requirement for all believers in the Church. Individual gifts are to be used always for empowering one another in the Church, and also to build up the body of Christ. Paul cautions in 1 Corinthians Chapters 12 and 14 that there are two types of dangers in understanding the gifts. The one is some people claiming to have the gifts that they have not been endowed with (1 Cor. 12:29ff) and the other is some claiming that their gifts are superior to other gifts. (Ch. 14) In such cases, the growth of the Church is hindered and the unity destroyed. On the other hand, when all the believers put to proper use their gifts then 'the whole body joined and knit together by every ligament with which it is equipped, as each part is working properly, promotes the body's growth in building itself up in love. (Ep. 4:16)

But, there is another dimension to this 'walking together in community'. New Testament Scholars are of the opinion that the verb 'grow up' in verse 15 can be translated either as a transitive verb, in which case the sentence would read as in many of the English translations of the Bible, 'We must grow up in every way into him who is the head, into Christ'. (RSV) If the verb is accepted as intransitive verb then the sentence would be translated as, 'We must allow others to grow up in every way into Him, who is the head, into Christ'. The first translation gives importance for the believers to grow together in Christ. The second one gives the possibility of, not only the believers growing together into Christ, but allows space for others also to grow into Christ. In short, unity leads to mission. This aspect of unity and mission is brought out very clearly by Paul in Colossians Chapter 1, Verse 18 ff where he says:

'He is the head of the body, the Church; He is the beginning, the first born from the dead, so that He might come to have first place in everything. For, in Him all the fullness of God was pleased to dwell, and through Him God was pleased to reconcile to Himself all things, whether on earth or in heaven, by making peace through the blood of His Cross.'

Therefore the spiritual journey of the Christian Church would end:

- When individuals recognize and treat others with respect and dignity
- When they use their gifts for equipping one another in the Church
- When the Church is built up in unity
- When the Church through its life and witness allows others to grow into Christ

- And finally when God in Christ reconciles the world unto Himself.

This is the goal set for the Christian Church by St. Paul as described in Verse 13 of Chapter 4 of his letter to the Ephesians. So, the pilgrim journey of CSI to achieve this goal continues.

Chapter 7

CSI: A Democratic Church

Every organization, be it spiritual or secular, civil or military, private or public adopts a structure found suitable to lits adherents for effective functioning. It draws rules and regulations, code of conduct for the members, privileges and responsibilities. Only, when the members function within this framework of structure then the organization can flourish. The Church of South India decided to incorporate democratic principles in its governance and organizational structure. In the context of the Freedom Movement, the Church opting for democracy for its organization does not raise eye-brows, rather it re-emphasizes the very nature of the Church – a Church which ensures peoples participation in its governance. But, the Constitution of the Church of South India, in its 'Governing principles of the Church', which has a binding effect of not only on the present day Church, but also on the Church to be evolved in the future, talks of unity at two different realms. It affirms that the unity that the Church seeks is 'fundamentally a reality of the spiritual realm (Chap. II, Clause 2, Para 2) as well as organizational unity of 'the Christ's Body into one organisation' (Para 4). In order to understand the import of these realities on the life and witness of the Church, we need to first analyse the principles under which they are formulated and incorporated.

1. Spiritual Unity

The unity that the Church seeks lies fundamentally in the spiritual realm. It springs from the bosom of the God-head. It is modeled on the relationship that exists between the Father and the Son and the Holy Spirit. It is given and not acquired. It does not depend on the merits of the faithful, but a grace bestowed on them by God through Jesus Christ. It is therefore, not a right to be demanded but a privilege bestowed on them. This spiritual unity is in the form of a prayer by our Lord for all his disciples – A prayer in the nature of a 'command' to be followed. Believers need to discern the spirit behind this command and respond to it appropriately. When the Lord's command is followed sincerely by the disciples it gives them the privilege to become participants in God's continuing Mission in this world; and they become 'a true leaven of unity' accelerating 'the greater release of divine power for the fulfillment of God's purpose for His world'.

In order to translate this spiritual unity in the day-to-day life of the Church, the CSI, based on biblical teaching as well as the heritage received from the West, has recognized three distinct units. They are linked to each other and cannot exist in isolation of the other. These are congregations/pastorates at the ground level, Diocese at the local level and the Synod at the national level.

A congregation or a pastorate is a 'basic unit of the Church of South India' – proclaims the Constitution. (Ch. VII, Clause 1, page 68) The requirement for forming a congregation at the local level is as follows:

- Fifty or more baptized people should come together for regular worship and fellowship.
- It should be recognized as such by the Diocesan Council.
- They should share common concerns with one another, i.e. they should share their spiritual gifts with one another for growing together.
- The members should take decisions on mission in its neighbourhood. (Clause 3 and 9)

All the above are in the spiritual realm. They need to be empowered for this spiritual task. Hence, they are always under the guidance of a theologically trained person called Presbyter, which literally means an elder, not in terms of age but in terms of wisdom in discerning and enhancing spiritual qualities of the members. This is not an office acquired through a process of election, but a divine gift received in obedience. In this way the congregation becomes a basic ecclesial community, having vertical relation with God through worship, horizontal relation with other fellow believers through sharing of spiritual gifts and reaching out to the neighbourhood through mission. In this process, a Presbyter plays a very important role as a spiritual mentor. The duties entrusted to the Presbyter in Chapter V Clause 18 onwards also emphasize the spiritual role of a Presbyter through pastoral visitation, preaching and teaching, leading in worship, administering Holy Communion, equipping the congregations for mission and ministry of the Church and encouraging the congregation members to participate in various ministries of the Church. Therefore, the primary focus of the congregation is Mission of God. They are the mission agents.

The second unit is the Diocese. The Diocese is a cluster of congregations or pastorates and institutions brought together as one unit in a particular geographical area, for providing a general management and good governance. But, it is also a theological reality. A cursory glance at the functions as described in chapter VIII unravels the purpose of such a reality. Firstly, it has the duty of *fostering* the development of the evangelistic, pastoral, educational and other work of the Church in the Diocese. Secondly, it has the duty of *co-ordinating* the work of mission undertaken by various agencies within the Diocese for this purpose. Thirdly, it has the duty of *assessing, empowering* and *initiating* new ministries within the Diocese by calling for reports, undertaking the survey and promoting formation of new movements such as 'Laity Association, Youth Movement, Women's Fellowship, Socio-Economic Institutions, Centres for Study and Dialogue and Movements for Justice, Peace and Ecological Concerns.' Fourthly, the Diocese has the duty to *recruit, train, ordain* and provide necessary human resources for the congregations and institutions. These are not just administrative matters but Mission concerns. But, suitable administrative systems are necessary for effective implementation of these mission concerns. In this task, the Dioceses have freedom to evolve their own strategies and methodologies. Therefore, we can safely conclude that the Diocese is primarily a mission organizing body, empowering the congregations and the Institutions in their mission work and initiating new frontiers of mission through a collective thinking process. It is with this intention, that the Diocese is put under the care of a Bishop, a name which originally meant a spiritual overseer. Is it a wonder then that the functions and responsibilities envisaged for the Bishop in Chapter V are exclusively spiritual in nature, such as pastoral oversight, leadership in evangelization, teaching, leading worship services, ordaining and overseeing the function of Presbyters and Deacons?

The third unit is the Synod. The Constitution boldly affirms, 'The Synod is the highest representative body of the Church of South India, its supreme governing and legislative body and the visible symbol of its unity' (Ch. IX, Clause 1). It is the highest policy making body. Its legislative decisions are binding on the whole church. It is the supreme governing body beyond which there is no other. It is the visible symbol of the unity of the whole church. The Constitution recognizes that these responsibilities entrusted to the Synod falls within the realm of spiritual reality. Here is what the Constitution says:

'In all its work the Synod should take time to wait upon God and listen to His voice, both in order that it may receive His guidance for its administrative work, and also that He may speak through it to the whole church and make His will known to it for the strengthening of its spiritual life and for the perfecting of its witness and service. In the evangelistic calling of the Church of South India, and should include in the business of its ordinary sessions a review of the mission and ministries of the Church both within its area and outside, in order that it may ascertain what progress has been made, and also receive the guidance of the Holy Spirit for the further development of the work'. (Ch. IX, Clause 18 Page 84) It is again with this intention of effective implementation of God's Mission that the Synod is placed under the guidance of the Moderator, elected from among the Bishops. The Synod, therefore, acts as the Legislative and co-ordinating unit of the whole church. In short, the CSI recognizes three important realities within the Church having different responsibilities, but linked together as one United Church. They are congregations as Mission agents, the Dioceses as Mission organizers and the Synod as Mission Co-ordinators. The Church needs to be mindful of these spiritual realities and responsibilities.

We need to recognize one more spiritual reality here. The CSI believes in the royal priesthood of all believers (1 Pet. 2:5). It proclaims that 'all its members have direct access of God and share in the commission and authority of the whole Church'. (Ch. V Para 1) Therefore, 'all alike are called to continue upon earth the priestly work of Christ by showing forth in life and word the glory of the redeeming power of God in Him.' (Ch. II Clause 7) Consequently, the ordained ministers, namely, Deacons, Presbyters and Bishops have no higher spiritual status than the laity of the Church. Those, who are called to the office of the ordained ministry are chosen for specific tasks. It is 'for the equipment of the whole church for the fulfillment of its ministry and thus to build up the body of Christ, Christ has given the gift of the ordained ministry,'. (Ch. V Clause A) Deacons for Diaconal services, Presbyters for the service of 'equipping the saints for the ministry and mission' and Bishops for overseeing ministry. There is equality in the sight of God, but different functions to fulfill. The CSI recognizes spiritual unity and equality of all believers. In exercising these different functions, the CSI believes that the model for the ministry is expressed in the servanthood of Jesus Christ. (Ch. V Para 2) We, only need to recollect Jesus teaching in the following words:

'You know that among the Gentiles, those whom they recognize as their rulers lord it over them and their great ones are tyrants over them. But, it is not so among you; but, whoever wishes to become great among you must be your servant and whoever wishes to be first among you must be slave of all. For, the Son of Man came not to be served, but to serve, and to give his life a ransom for many.' (Mk. 10:42 45) All the ministries in the Church are based on this spiritual truth.

2. Organizational Unity

Spiritual unity was achieved through dialogue, discussion, debate, arguments and listening to one another. This was a long drawn out process covering several years. But this spiritual unity has to manifest itself in organizational unity. The Church had to find an organizational structure which includes all the salient features of the Uniting Churches, yet, depicting oneness in purpose. There were three forms of government at work - Anglicans following episcopal form of government – that is the entire administrative system coming under the Bishop's authority. This system portrays a central authority, wherein spiritual and temporal authorities are combined in one person, namely, the Bishop. To this system the concept of 'District Superintendent' as found in the Methodist is added, a person having delegated authority of the head of the church, who acts as a facilitator of all activities in the prescribed area and represents the concerns of that area at the central level. The Churches from Reformed traditions considered that the words 'Bishop and Presbyter' are used as synonymous terms in the New Testament. Hence, they evolved a synodical system for its governance. According to this system, each congregation would be governed by a team of elders ordained for that purpose under the Chairmanship of a minister. The ministers and representative elders would then form a Presbytery in a prescribed area. The members of several Presbyteries would then form a

Synod, which acts as a final arbiter. In this system, the spiritual authority rests with the ordained and the temporal authority with the collective decision of the Synod. The third system was followed by Congregationalists. According to this system, each congregation is autonomous and the whole congregation in an annual session takes decisions in terms of its Ministry, Mission and governance. Even the appointment of the Minister is subject to the approval of the General Body of the congregation. In this system, the temporal authority rests with the congregation and the spiritual authority is minimized in the process. Each participating church in the union negotiations, insisted on retaining the essential elements found in their respective traditions. As a result, the CSI accepted the following as necessary elements in the life of the Church of South India:

'The Church of South India recognizes that Episcopal, Presbyterian and Congregational elements must all have their place in its order of life, and that the episcopate, the presbyterate and the Congregation of the faithful should all in their several spheres have responsibility and exercise authority in the life and work of the Church, in its governance and administration, in its evangelistic and pastoral work, in its discipline, and in its worship.' (Ch. II Clause 8 page 11) The task was to find a suitable administrative system, which affirms the above stated position.

The Church could not be blind to the system that is prevalent in the Hindu Religious Institutions. They were mostly organized under Gurukul system, under the leadership of a spiritual guru. Each Institution is autonomous, shaped as per the vision, ideology and teachings of the Guru. The succession is through nurturing and anointing of a person by the spiritual guru, and never by an election process. All the ministries connected with these institutions are headed by people, appointed by the guru from among those who enjoy the confidence of the guru. In this system, spiritual authority rides over the temporal authority.

The political situation in India, as we noted earlier, also demanded that the Church needed to adopt a system, which appreciates the uprising nationalist spirit all over India. The nation was in the process of adopting democracy as a form of governance for Independent India. In this system, the spiritual and secular authorities are distinct from one another. Democracy comes from the secular world. But it has features which are in consonance with the spiritual values. It emphasizes the participation of people in deciding their own government just as in spiritual realm, wherein all believers are called to participate in the mission of God. It recognizes social equality irrespective of caste, colour, creed, class or social standing just as in spiritual realm, wherein all are equal in the sight of God. It is 'a government *of* the people, *by* the people and *for* the people' – a phrase, coined by Abraham Lincoln in his inaugural address, when he was elected as the President of the United States of America and continues to be popular, even today. This indicates that the ultimate authority rests with the people. CSI is emphatic in declaring that 'the privilege of participation in the government of the Church is confined to adult communicant members of the Church ... Adult communicant members shall mean, persons who have attained the age of 21 years, have been duly confirmed, and partake in the Holy Communion'. (Ch. IV clause 4 page 32)

For these reasons, the CSI adopted democracy as a form of government in order to bring about organizational unity from the congregational level to the Diocese and to the Synod of the Church. Undoubtedly, this is the best form of government. The people can choose their own representatives to determine the policies and programmes of the Church. They are no longer the spectators, but active participants in the decision making process. They are responsible for the destiny of their own organization. Further, the United Church has tried to combine two authorities, namely, spiritual and temporal into one structure demonstrating that there need not be a dichotomy between the two authorities. This attempt on the part of the United Church to incorporate two authorities into one, needs to be appreciated. However, just as the salient features of the United Church were retained to form one church in the spiritual realm, democracy also needs certain necessary elements which are normally described as 'pillars of democracy' for its effective functioning. Individuals cannot participate in the government directly. Hence, the elected representative body functions on behalf of people. These elected bodies represent *legislative wings* at the congregational, diocesan and synod level. They take policy decisions. In order to implement these policy decisions, there needs to be in existence another forum, which is described as *executive wing*. The officers at the pastoral level, the officers of the diocese, the conveners and heads of institutions at the diocesan level, constitute this body. Their duty is to implement the policies taken by the legislative wing. As such, the Executive is responsible to the legislature. Thirdly, if a person or group of people feels that wrong policy decisions are taken, or injustice has been meted out by implementing such wrong policies, then they need to have a forum to appeal for re-dressal of grievances. In a democratic set up it is *judiciary*, which is independent of the legislative wing or the executive wing. Fourthly, there is a fourth estate called '*media*' which functions as a hawk's eye observing, investigating, articulating and educating the public of the policies and progrmmes of the democratic organization. In this way, checks and balances are established at every stage in the organization.

3. Analysis of the Organizational Structure

The organizational structure is described in the Constitution of the Church of South India. But, several factors have influenced the making of this Constitution. The spiritual unity of all denominations was uppermost in the minds of the framers of the Constitution. Next, historical realities of the uniting churches in India and their specific contributions needed to be taken into consideration. Thirdly, political developments taking place at that time in secular India played a very important role in shaping up a Constitution. This third factor which has not received sufficient importance in the history of the Church is very significant. Consider this: India attained freedom on 15th August 1947 and the Church declared itself as an United Church on 27th September 1947. The Constituent Assembly approved the Constitution on 26th November 1949, on which date the Constitution received the signature of the President and was declared as passed. Also, certain provisions of the Constitution were given immediate effect. But, the whole Constitution came into force on the 26th January 1950, which is now being celebrated as Republic Day. The United Church, since its inauguration functioned under 'Scheme of Church Union in South India' which contained Basis of Union and the Constitution. The new United Church appointed a Committee to bring a draft constitution. This draft constitution was approved by the Synod and the Dioceses upto December 31st, 1951. Thereafter the Church of South India published the Constitution in 1952. Therefore, the Constitution of the Church of South India has to be understood from these perspectives, namely, spirituality – as the basis of the community, unity in diversity in its substance and democracy as a form of government. The framers of the Constitution need to be appreciated for holding these concerns together in balance. Emphasis on one over the other would result in conflict. Keeping this perspective in mind, let us now analyze the organizational structure in the CSI to assess its strengths and weaknesses.

a. Spiritual and Secular

The Church is not an isolated island. It is part of the larger society. Yet, the Church is *in* the world and not *of* the world. It is a spiritual organization in the midst of a secular society. In as much as the United Church has combined spiritual realm with the secular organizational structures, both realms are bound to interact with each other. The Church by ensuring that the presiding authority of the pastorate committee is a theologically trained presbyter, the president of the Diocesan Council and the Chairperson of the important key committees in the Diocese is the Bishop, who is not only a theologically trained person but also chosen and consecrated for that purpose, and the President of the Synod and the Chairperson of the Executive and Working Committee is the Moderator who is chosen from among the Bishops, has demonstrated that the spiritual concerns are the basic foundations on which the organizational superstructure is built. It therefore, points to the fact that spiritual values must be the basis on which all policy decisions are to be taken, beginning from the congregation to the Diocese and to the Synod. However, the fundamental spiritual concerns differ from that of the democratic society. In the spiritual realm, the basic thrust is to ensure individual commitment to Christ, maintain fellowship of believers and motivate congregations to be involved in the mission of God. The goal of a democratic organisation is to ensure 'justice, liberty, equality and fraternity'. The values of these two realms interact with each other. The intention of the United Church in bringing these two concerns into one unit is to ensure that the spiritual values are in operation in achieving the goals of democratic society – a lofty yet noble ideal, possible only if all concerned are committed to such an ideal and organizational structures pave the way for achieving such a goal.

As mentioned earlier, a democratic form of government requires certain institutions for its effective functioning. Legislative and executive wings have been given due importance in the constitution. But, all the decisions and implementations are for the well-being of the ordinary person - in the case of the Church the communicant members. All the communicants have the privilege of participation in the government of the Church. In other words, legislature and executive take decisions on behalf of these communicant members. What happens if these communicant members are not satisfied with the decisions? How to deal with a situation when a communicant member or a group of them feel that the decisions taken are not in the common interest of the whole church? What is the forum to discuss their grievances against the leadership of the church, either alleged or genuine? What is the communication channel between the leadership and communicant members? The Church has tried to provide two fora to meet such needs. The first one is official magazine or occasional Bishop's letters to the members of the Church. But, these can only serve to disseminate information and in some cases as educational material. The do not provide scope for discussion, debates or arguments. So, the aggrieved persons have resorted to use secular print, electronic and social media to air their grievances.

The second forum is a policy for redressal of grievances. The Constitution in Chapter XI has provided two different methods for this purpose – one to deal with disciplinary issues, be it individual members of the congregation or ordained clergy or even the Bishop. The other is to deal with the settlement of disputes. But, this process also suffers from lack of apparent neutrality. It is the Bishop who initiates the process of appointing a Commission or an Arbitration Board. But, in most of the cases the grievances are against the decisions of the Committees in which Bishop has participated as the Chairperson. In such cases, the initiative of the Bishop to settle the disputes would be viewed with suspicion in spite of the integrity and sincerity of the Bishop. In view of this, some members resort to approach the secular courts for redressal of their grievances. If the complainant is personally prejudiced against the Bishop, he/she might even resort to criminal complaint to harass the leadership to fall in line. On the other hand, the Church has no human as well as material resources to set up an independent forum to deal with such grievances. Therefore, the Church is caught up in this dilemma of providing an independent forum for redressal of grievances within the church. This may not be a problem for a Church which has not accepted democratic form of government as the members would be subjected to punitive measures by the spiritual authorities if they do not toe the line. The litigations in CSI have to be viewed from the above perspective. The cases against the Church heirarchy can be broadly categorized as follows:

- Affecting the faith of a person or a group of people, as in the case of some Basel Mission people going to the Court stating that the faith of the CSI in accepting the Episcopacy is different from the faith of the Basel Mission, which believes in equality of all believers. This case went up to the Supreme Court which decided that both the faiths are essentially same.
- There are cases filed for the redressal of grievances by individuals or by employees of the Church or its institutions.
- Cases arising out of election disputes beginning from the pastorate level up to the CSI Synod.

- Cases filed against the Church and its Officers concerning the alleged faulty decisions, administrative lapses, financial misappropriation and property mismanagement. In almost all the cases, the Church is only a defendant and very rarely a plaintiff.

It is to be noted, however, the people who resort to redressal of their grievances outside the Church constitute a negligible percentage. A vast majority of the people are disciplined enough to deal with their grievances within the framework of the Church and its structures. The Church is not a perfect society. In as much as it consists of human beings as its members, its structure also are not perfect. But, since the Church is also a divine institution, it is always under the grace of God. Therefore, it is capable of rectifying its mistakes and to introduce reforms to become a better human organisation. The New Testament testifies to this aspect of the Church. The disciples of Jesus, in spite of their deep commitment to Jesus Christ, were not perfect human beings. They aspired for power and position (Matt. 20:20ff) One of them, even went to the extent of betraying the Lord for pecuniary benefits. (Matt. 26:14ff) Leader of the team could not stand up for truth at the time of crisis. (Matt. 26:69ff) Yet, with all these weaknesses, Jesus Christ used them as his instruments to be his messengers throughout the world after His crucifixion and resurrection.

The early Church was not perfect either. In spite of their salvation experience and their commitment to Christ, they could not be described as a perfect community. The believers decided among themselves to pool all their resources to be used as a common resource for the common good of all. Yet one couple decided to portray pretention as truth, outwardly they wanted to showcase themselves as generous couple, but inwardly they kept some portion for themselves from the proceedings of the sale of their property. (Acts Ch. 5:1ff). There was a complaint of ill treatment of poor widows from one segment of the Church. (Acts Ch. 6:1ff) The division between Jewish Christians and Gentile Christians (High caste and low caste) had to be settled in a Council. (Acts Ch. 15, Gal. Ch. 2) The Corinthian Church was one of the prominent congregations of that time. Yet, Paul had to deal with a number of issues such as division in the church, law suits in the secular courts, sexual immorality, marital relationships, appropriate relationship with the people of other faiths, proper way of celebrating Holy Communion, order in public worship etc. Yet, in the midst of all these human weakness, Christ used His disciples, early believers and the early Church as mighty agents of God in transforming the world.

It was possible, because they surrendered themselves to the will of God, willing to rectify their mistakes under the grace of God and move forward with Christ committing themselves to the mission of God. The views of St. Augustine, one of the prominent Christian leaders of the fourth century, is illuminating in this regard. He maintained that 'the Church is holy, not because all its members are holy, but because its purposes are holy, and that the unworthiness of the minister does not affect the validity of a sacrament. This is because the real minister of all sacraments is Christ Himself, and the actual minister, Bishop or Priest, is only someone authorized by the Church to represent Him'. (Quoted in *From Jerusalem to New Delhi*, p. 61)

Secondly, no organization can function effectively, if the powers and functions of various categories of people within that organization are not defined properly. This is particularly relevant to the Church, where the spiritual realm and democratic structures are fused together. At the Pastorate level, the functions of a Presbyter are defined in the Constitution very clearly. But, what are the Presbyter's powers and functions when it comes to the democratic organization? Who is the implementing authority of the legislative decisions at the Pastorate level – the Chairman, Secretary or the Treasurer? Further, if a certain requirement like – auditing the accounts and submitting the same to the Diocese in the appropriate form is not completed in time – which in turn affects the entire Diocese to fulfill its responsibility – then who is to be held responsible – the Presbyter or the Treasurer? Can a Presbyter wash off his hands off saying that it is the responsibility of the elected Treasurer? The powers and functions of different authorities at the Pastorate level are not defined in the Constitution causing confusion in terms of accountability.

The problem becomes more complex at the Diocesan level. The Diocese has a responsibility of co-ordinating the work of all the congregations/ pastorates and the Institutions within the Diocese, big or small. It also has the responsibility of organizing various programmes and activities through different committees set up constitutionally. The administrative, financial and property management takes place at the Diocesan level. Further, it has the responsibility of organizing all the activities in terms of the legislations passed by the supreme body namely the CSI Synod. Hence, it becomes absolutely necessary for the Diocese to function properly. The CSI Constitution empowers 'Every Diocesan Council has the power to make rules and pass resolutions and take executive action for the general management and good government of the Church in the Diocese'. (Ch. VIII, Clause 5, p. 72) In terms of the above, each Diocese has framed its own Constitution, but here again powers and functions of various authorities are not defined properly and accountability fixed. Who is the administrative head? What is the relationship between the Bishop and the elected Officers? Who is accountable for what? Such questions have not been addressed in the Constitution. In particular, the Bishop's position seems to be vulnerable. In political terms, is the Bishop to be compared with the Chief Minister or the Governor of the State? The first one is Executive Head and the second is constitutional head. If the first one, then what are the Bishop's power? If the second, then who is the Executive Head of the Diocese? Or in the language of the secular organisations, is the Bishop, the Chairman and Managing Director or Chief Executive Officer of the Church? Does the Bishop have power to shape the organization according to his/her vision for the organization? The spiritual role of the Bishop has been defined very clearly in the Constitution, but it fails to describe his/her role in the administrative set-up.

This is further complicated by the decision of the Uniting Churches in their definition of Episcopacy. 'The Church of South India accepts and will maintain the historic episcopate in a Constitutional form', the Constitution proclaims. It further goes on to add, 'But, this acceptance does not commit it to any particular interpretation of episcopacy or to any particular view or belief concerning orders of the ministry, and it will not require the acceptance of any such particular interpretation or view as necessary qualification for its ministry'. (Ch. II, Clause 11, p. 13) This seems to be a compromise arrived at by the Episcopalians and non-Episcopalians to achieve unity of the Church. In practice, this clause meant the office of the Bishop is not like an Anglican Bishop in whom spiritual and administrative authority vests in one office. Since, the other Uniting Churches did not have the office of the Bishop, this clause meant the Bishop is only a Constitutional head without having executive powers. The Bishops in CSI have been asked to function under this peculiar situation where he/she is the head of the Church without having any executive powers depending solely on the collective decisions of the committees of which he/she is only a Chairperson. In the spiritual realm the Bishop is the head of the Church, but in terms of organizational structure, his/her powers and authority have not been defined clearly. For instance, there could be a clash of ideas and perspectives between the Bishop and the Diocesan Secretary. In such situations, the Constitution does not help us to decide who can say 'the buck stops here.' Or again the CSI Constitution specifically states, 'The Bishop of the Diocese shall have general oversight of the financial administration of the Diocese, but shall not exercise any direct control over the finances.' (Ch. V, Clause 10, p. 39) Using this clause can an elected Treasurer refuse to disclose financial details to the Bishop and act independent of the Bishop asserting that he/she is only responsible to the Committee? But strangely, the Synod requires that all financial statements from the Diocese to be co-signed by the Bishop with the Treasurer, casting the financial accountability on to the Bishop also. As a result in the history of the CSI, we have had saintly bishops who concentrated on spiritual well-being of the people, but branded as administratively weak bishops. We have also had administratively strong bishops who assumed administrative powers, but were criticized as not being spiritual. We have also had bishops who compromised with the 'powers that be' in the Diocese and enjoyed peaceful time at the cost of the development of the Diocese. On the other hand, we have also had bishops who took on the powerful and stood by the poor and the neglected in the Diocese and paid the price, sometimes even to the extent of facing untold miseries. If the Church had decided the powers and functions of various authorities within the democratic structure, such situation could have been avoided. Sadly, even after seventy years of its existence, the Church is yet to give serious thought to rectify this lacuna in its democratic functioning.

b. Accountability

Accountability determines the very nature of the organization. The vision is translated into a structure and the structure demands accountability. The Church being a spiritual organization derives its values from the Scriptures. These values such as honesty, sincerity, integrity and transparency have to be infused into the structure which in turn should reflect in its functioning. But, the faith of the Church is that every baptized and communicant member has both the privileges as well as obligations, as a member of the Church. It is the faith of the Church that every communicant member, having been a recipient of God's grace, saved by the salvific acts of Jesus Christ and empowered by the Holy Spirit has certain obligations to fulfill. Every member is called to lead a devotional life in private, participate regularly in public worship, maintain a good family life, participate meaningfully in secular life, involve in all Church activities and share in the Church's corporate acts of witness and service. (See Ministry of the laity, p. 48 & 49) It is spirituality that is underlying in all these obligations. But, spirituality cannot be measured by external apparatus. It originates from within. Yet, each of us know that there is 'a still small voice' within us cautioning us when we go wrong. In other words, every Christian needs to render accounts for the responsibility entrusted to him/her first and foremost to God, who is able to assess honesty, sincerity, integrity and transparency of a person. Similarly, the spiritual duties of a Presbyter is found on pages 43 and 44. A Presbyter need not function for the fear of higher authorities in the Church but they should certainly have fear of God in them in discharging their duties. There is no annual performance appraisal in the Church as in some secular organisations, but certainly, they have to render accounts to God every day, in their life. Similarly, the Bishop's duties are described on pages 35 to 39. In discharging his/her duties and particularly with regard to personnel management the Bishop needs to be fair and just to all irrespective of whether someone appreciates or denounces the Bishop. Bishop's office is essentially a spiritual office and the incumbent has to render accounts for his/her actions to God who is able to understand the intention of the Bishop behind every action.

The Church is also a democratic organization. As we saw earlier, the ultimate authority in a democratic society rests with the common people. The leaders in a democratic organization function for and on behalf of the Church members. The leaders, therefore, need to be fair and just to all members of the congregations, irrespective of their economic status or educational qualifications or their standing in the hierarchical order. Any instance of nepotism, favoritism and corruption by the leaders destroys the confidence of people. Therefore, all decisions should be transparent. This is possible only if the leaders are guided by spiritual values failing which they would only reflect their sinful human nature and not divine qualities of 'love, joy, peace, patience, kindness, generosity, faithfulness, gentleness and self-control' as mentioned by Paul in Galatians 5:22-23. In discharging the administrative functions, financial responsibilities and property management, the leaders will have to be transparent and be willing to be scrutinized by the members of the congregations. Thus, the leaders have to be conscious that they are not only answerable to God, but to the community of believers as well.

There is a third set of accountability which is more complicated. The Church as an organization runs a number of educational, medical, developmental and training institutions, along with these, programmes and activities covering socio-economic and environmental concerns should be added. Both the Centre and the States have set up statutory bodies to stipulate and regulate such activities. The Church cannot claim exemption under the pretext that they are managed by religious bodies. For instance, there are rules concerning admission, fee structure, qualifications for faculty, curriculum, discipline matters etc in an educational institution and the Church needs to comply with these. Sometimes, these rules and regulations may not be compatible with the avowed principles of the Church. In such situations, the leaders are forced to either compromise or suffer consequences. A classical example in this regard would be that in order to obtain certain grants from the Government the rules stipulates that the property on which the institution stands should be transferred in the name of the institution itself and not in a larger Trust like CSITA. This is not allowed in the Trust rules. If the required Government rule is followed then the leaders would be guilty of not following the Church's rules. If it is not complied with then the leaders would be accused of working against the interests of the Institution. Similarly, the Church is answerable to number of statutory bodies of the Government in conducting their activities through Institutions. The Dioceses through its Officers are primarily responsible to implement these statutory rules and held accountable for the same.

c. Management of the Properties

Management of property is another serious issue where accountability is always under a cloud. We may recollect that before the Union, the properties were vested with the respective Missionary Trusts. After the Union these properties were transferred to Church of South India Trust Association (CSITA) – registered under Section 26 of the Indian Companies Act 1913 (now Section 25 of the Indian Companies Act 1956) on 26th September 1947, as a Religious and Charitable Company, which has no business character and with no profit motive. Some of the Anglican Church properties which were under the 'Indian Ecclesiastical Establishment' were transferred to Indian Church Trust (ICT) with its headquarters in Calcutta by way of a parliament decision in 1948. These properties were also transferred to CSITA subsequently. (The Anglican Dioceses like Madras and Tirunelvelly, where they had established 'Madras Diocesan Trust and Tirunelvelly Diocesan Trust' respectively continued without hindrance) All the properties acquired subsequent to the Union are registered in the name of CSITA. The CSITA, therefore, has the following characteristics:

- A legal Trust
- A holding Trust
- A Trust registered under Companies Act
- A Religious and Charitable Trust

As a registered Trust, CSITA enjoys protection under law. At the same time, it casts responsibilities on the Trustees to act as per law. In as much as CSITA is a holding Trust, the Trustees are in a 'fiduciary' relationship with the beneficiaries. That is, the Trustees are bound to act in the best interest of the beneficiaries and never use the position to enhance his/her position or to get pecuniary benefits for self. There is a fundamental difference between a 'Private Trust' and a 'Religious and Charitable Trust'. A Private Trust has a demarcated beneficiary, but a Religious and Charitable Trust is established to carry out the specified objects of the Trust. These specific objects are mentioned in Clause 3 (a) to (q) in the Memorandum of Association of the Church of South India Trust Association. Simply put, the purpose of establishing a Trust in CSI is to carry out the 'Ministry and Mission' of the Church. Therefore, it has no business character or a profit motive. The purpose of establishing CSITA has been clearly expressed in Clause 4 of the Memorandum as follows:

'The income and property of the Association whencesoever derived shall be applied solely towards the promotion of the objects and purposes of the Association as set forth in this Memorandum and no portion thereof shall be paid or transferred directly or indirectly by way of dividend, bonus or otherwise howsoever by way of profit to the members of the Association …'

The CSITA is a holding Trust for all the properties of the CSI. This is made clear in the Article of Association of the CSITA, Clause 3. This covers all the Uniting Churches as well as the entire CSI, after inauguration. By way of an Amendment, the CSI Constitution also recognizes the relationship between CSITA and CSI as found in Clause 14 of Chapter IX on page 82. But, we noted earlier that the centre of activities of the CSI is Dioceses, the Diocese being the administrative and co-ordinating body. Recognizing this aspect, the Committee of Management of the CSITA, normally issues Power of Attorney to four of the Officers of the Diocese, including the Bishop, the Secretary and the Treasurer of the Diocese and one other Officer. Two of the signatures of the Power of Attorney are a must for each transaction. However, the Bishop's signature is mandatory and he/she can authorize another Power of Attorney in his/her place. The Power of Attorney Holders cannot act independently. They can only act on the basis of a resolution from the Management Committee of the CSITA, which in turn is taken only on the basis of the resolution of the authorized Committee of the Diocese. All sale/lease/mortgage of any property within the jurisdiction of the Diocese shall be through competitive tenders, after giving due publicity in the local papers. Thus, checks and balances are introduced in every transaction. It is the duty of the Power of Attorneys to supervise, administer, preserve and maintain the properties as per prescribed rules under the guidance of the appropriate committees in the Diocese. Yet, the problems are aplenty. They may be historical problems, encroachment problems or problems caused by vested interests. To impress upon those members of the Church who are not familiar with the administration of the properties in the Diocese, an example from our Diocese is narrated here.

This is the story of a portion of prime property in the Diocese, located in the centre of the city. The property originally belonged to the Wesleyan Methodist Trust Association which later was transferred to CSITA. In the year 1946, two unscrupulous people created a fake document claiming ownership of the property. The Wesleyan Missionaries challenged the fake document in a court of law. The case went on for years, and finally went up to the Supreme Court, which decided the case in favour of the Church in the later part of the seventies. In the meantime, a group of slum dwellers occupied the vacant land and established themselves there with the active connivance of the politicians who treated them as vote banks. All efforts by the Church to vacate the slum dwellers and take possession of the land proved futile. In the meantime, some Christian NGO's supported by foreign funds, entered the fray in support of the slum dwellers asking the Church to register the land in the name of the slum dwellers, whereas the Christian community was insisting on vacating the land mainly for maintaining hygienic environment. The Church was caught in a dilemma between the demands of the faith community and the mission to the poor. After a long protracted discussion, the Church decided to sell the land in 'as is where is condition'. This decision was opposed by the slum dwellers supported by NGO's through a case in a court of law. This matter also went up to the Supreme Court. The Church being conscious of its mission to the poor, agreed to pay for the construction of houses to the Slum Clearance Board for these people on the land given by the Government of Karnataka elsewhere. Thus, the problem arose in the 1940's could be solved only in the latter part of the 1980's. Many such examples can be quoted from all the Dioceses of the CSI.

The property is managed and administered at the Diocesan level. But, it is put to use at the congregational and institutional level. The CSITA properties are used for conducting worship services and other activities of the congregations and institutions like schools, colleges, hostels, boarding homes, hospitals, dispensaries, etc. These properties are used both for the community activities and for the public causes. Only condition for the usage of these properties is that the activities must promote the objects of the Association. The local sub-units are not entrusted with power of attorney, but they are entitled to use the property to achieve the objects of the Association. Thus, we see three levels of accountability. The Central Authority at the level of the Committee of Management of CSITA, with the responsibility to ensure that all legal requirements are adhered to promptly. The Administrative Authority at the Diocesan level which has a responsibility of protecting, preserving and administering following the rules and regulations stipulated by the Management Committee of the CSITA and the functional sub units, who have a responsibility of putting to use the property, in line with the objects of the Association. All three levels of responsibilities, need to be fulfilled properly in order to achieve the set goal. Failure to comply with the demands of the Act even by individuals or sub units or units or by the central authority would result in Breach of Trust and the same would attract penalties by the law enforcing agencies, and thereby cause enormous and untold miseries for the whole Church. This is not just a secular responsibility but a spiritual responsibility in as much as the objects of the Association are spiritual. Therefore, spiritual and secular responsibilities cannot be separated from each other, rather our spiritual values must guide our secular responsibilities for the good of the whole Church.

d. Management of the Finances

Financial management and accountability is another function of the Church, which determines the character of the Church. Proper financial management calls for integrity, honesty and transparency in dealing with the finances of the Church. It is not just a secular responsibility, but a spiritual vocation which forces the Church to be transparent in financial matters.

Resource Mobilisation

The Church raises its resources for its programmes and activities of Ministry and Mission by employing various methods. To recapitulate: one of the avowed goals of the Uniting Churches was to become a self-supporting Church relying on local resources. For a Church which was entirely dependent on the contribution raised by the Missionary Societies, it was an uphill task for the newly formed United Church to raise vast finances to cover the expenses of all the activities of the Church. So, they had to resort to drawing up of priorities. Accordingly, the pastoral ministry and mission activities occupied the top-most priority in their scheme of things. The leadership at that time encouraged the congregation members to contribute liberally for these two activities through biblical teaching and house visitations. In this process, the congregations coming from the congregational background gave a lead, for they were involved in supporting the pastoral ministry of their respective congregations from the inception to a great extent. As a result of the sustained Biblical teaching and pastoral visitations, the congregation began to slowly become aware of their responsibility of supporting the pastoral ministry. In order to support the pastoral ministry throughout the Diocese, be it poor or rich, urban or rural, a system of 'pooling resources' from all congregations and administering at the Diocesan level was introduced. Along with this, Church planting also became a priority for the congregation members since they need a suitable place to gather together for worship and other activities. Further, again, through sustained Biblical teaching the congregation members were convinced of their duty to contribute their mite for mission activities. As a result, we can boldly affirm that the vision of our fore-fathers and mothers in becoming a self-supporting Church has been realized to a large extent today. We can also affirm without hesitation that CSI congregations are giving congregations. The giving of the people can be broadly categorized under three headings, namely support for the pastoral ministry, Church planting and mission activities. These contributions are not forced but they are voluntary. Each individual or each family decides according to the measure of blessings they have received from God. While the urban congregation members give out of their salary or earnings the villagers contribute from their agricultural produce and livestock. Giving has become part of their spiritual discipline. They consider this as part of their response to the mercy and grace received from God. Hence, they contribute to God's work. Therefore, it is essentially God's money that the church is entrusted with.

Secondly, as we have noted earlier, the Missionaries started a number of institutions to achieve their goal of reaching the unreached. They were the witnessing wings of the Church, but wholly supported by the Missionary Societies. The United Church did not have the ways and means of raising the necessary financial support for these institutions, nor did the Missionary Societies support these Institutions for they themselves lacked financial backing from their Home Boards. Consequently, those institutions which were capable of raising resources became self-financing institutions. Some institutions were brought under the Government 'grant-in-aid' system. Many institutions were either closed down or handed over to the Government. Some institutions were financially supported by the Diocese. The finance, for the self-financing institutions came from the beneficiaries of the institutional service, while institutions under grant-in-aid system received part of the finances from the Government.

In order to augment the financial resources of various ministries and mission activities, the Church gradually also began to construct Income Generating Projects on the CSITA properties and derive income from them. So, the third source of income is from the property. Fourthly, some of the activities like child care through Boarding Homes and Hostels and community development programmes continued to receive foreign support through donor agencies having similar objectives. Therefore, resource mobilization in the Church has a multi-pronged approach each rendering accounts to different agencies fulfilling different requirements and obligations of those agencies.

Accountability

As in the case of property management even in the field of financial management the Church needs to be accountable to various authorities and statutory bodies. First and foremost, we earlier observed that the Church's money is God's money. Also, all those who are handling money either directly and indirectly are accountable to God. There needs to be 'fear of God' in every person handling money, only then they will be able to protect and use God's money, wisely. Only fear of God can remove deceit, mismanagement of funds, corruption and favouritism from the minds of people, who are entrusted with God's money. Unlike, in property matters, in the area of financial handling, vast number of people are involved beginning from the congregations, institutions, programmes and activities, Diocese and Synod. Most of them are rendering voluntary service either as elected persons or as nominated persons. Majority of them are not professionally trained in handling finances. In such a situation, only people with spiritual values imbibed in them can handle God's finances properly. A simple exercise like all collections from a Sunday Worship Service should be remitted to the Bank account on a Monday morning and for all expenses money should be drawn from the Bank and spent with proper vouchers and receipt, is not only a requirement in financial handling, but it is a spiritual discipline, because it is honesty and integrity of a person handling church's money that matters ultimately rather than his/her professional competence.

Secondly, the Church's money is contributed by God's people. They contribute liberally for God's work from their earning voluntarily. The congregation members are not only contributors they are also participants in God's ministry and mission. They need to know how their sacrificial contributions are utilized. With the de-centralized system of administration and accounting, members of the congregation may be aware of their own sub-units, but never the financial situation of the entire organization leading to all kinds of speculations based on hearsay. On the other hand, with the centralized system of administration and accounting, only the authorized elected members become aware of the financial situation leaving the vast majority of congregation members ignorant of the financial needs of the organization,. In such a situation, there will be no enthusiasm left for the congregation members to meet the financial needs of the entire organization. Therefore, the Church needs to devise ways and means of informing and educating people of God of the financial situation of the entire organization.

Thirdly, the institutions are governed by-laws, rules and regulations enacted by the Church, State and Central Government authorities. All institutions, be they self-financing, government aided or church sponsored have to function within the parameters of these laws, rules and regulations. At the end of the year, they need to render accounts to appropriate authorities. For instance, the Government has barred capitation fee in self-financing institutions and regulated fee structure any deviation in implementing these stipulations by any one institution would attract penalty, not only for the concerned institution, but would also put the entire organization in jeopardy apart from deviation in ethical principles.

Fourthly, Government of India has stipulated the conditions for receiving, maintaining and utilizing funds from abroad. These conditions are covered under Foreign Contribution (Regulation) Act 1976, and as amended in 1984. According to these Acts, the Church can receive foreign funds only through a specified branch of a Bank after registering itself with the Government of India. The amount so received is to be utilized only for the purpose for which it is received. The accounts need to be submitted to the Home Ministry in a prescribed form within the stipulated time. The CSI Synod has made arrangements for the Government to recognize each Diocese as a recognized unit to receive foreign funds. Any sub-unit within the Diocese receiving foreign funds would violate this Act, in which case the entire organization would face the consequences. The description mentioned above establishes the need for transparent and appropriate financial systems in the Church which is not only a requirement in law, but also a necessity befitting the nature of a spiritual organization. The financial system currently being used in the CSI is described here below.

The concept of unity in diversity which is a legacy of the union negotiation efforts continued in the United Church in faith and practice, in administration and even in financial management. The Dioceses, where Anglican presence was dominant continued with the centralized administrative and financial management system. The Dioceses, where congregational churches were dominant continued with the practice of administrative and financial management system as a decentralized system. Others followed a combination of both the systems. For instance, the salary of the Presbyters in the Anglican background Dioceses were disbursed through Diocesan Office. The salary of the Presbyters in the Congregational background Dioceses were disbursed in their respective congregations, through the Congregational/Pastorate Treasurers. The salary of the Presbyters in some Diocese which had the presence of the other denominational background, was disbursed through the District/ Area Chairpersons. Again, the salary of the Presbyters in the Anglican background Churches was reimbursed by the individual congregations/ pastorates to the Diocese. The salary of the Presbyters of the Congregational background Churches was the responsibility of the local congregations, and in case a local congregation was not in a position to meet the entire salary commitment, then the Diocese would meet the shortfall. In the case of other Dioceses a graded system of assessment based on the financial ability of the congregation/pastorate was levied by the Diocese to the congregation/pastorate. As a result, different accounting systems were practiced and continue to be so even today, in different Dioceses. Unity in diversity is put into practice even in financial management throughout CSI.

At this time, we must remember that when individuals and families make financial contributions to the Church, it immediately acquires two different characteristics. One, since the money is given to the Church for God's work it becomes God's money. Second, the money given to the Church also assumes the characteristic of Trust money, in as much as all the movable and immovable properties of the Church are vested in the CSITA. The CSITA being a religious and charitable company is bound to follow stipulation of law, rules and regulations under this Act. As a religious and charitable Trust the CSITA enjoys income tax exemption for all its income under Section 10 (23c)(v) of the Income Tax Act. The mandatory requirement to obtain this tax exemption is

- That all the accounts of the units, i.e. Diocese and the sub units, i.e. the Pastorates, Institutions and the Programmes and activities must be incorporated into the Annual Statement of Accounts of the Diocese and in turn in the Annual Statement of Accounts of the CSITA.
- That all these accounts should be submitted in the prescribed form duly audited.
- That a certificate, signed by the Diocesan Bishop and the Diocesan Treasurer, authenticating the incorporation of all accounts of the Diocese, Pastorates, Institutions, Programmes and activities big or small must be submitted to the Synod Treasurer for further incorporation into the CSITA accounts.
- That all these procedures must be completed within the stipulated period of the Income Tax Act. According to the statistics published by the CSI at the time of the Synod sessions of 2010, based on the details submitted by 20 Diocese out of 22 dioceses, there are 2187 pastorates, 11137 congregations, 39 degree colleges, 160 junior colleges, 207 secondary schools, 1859 elementary schools, 15 teacher training institutions, 14 B.Ed. colleges, 26 polytechnic institutions, 7 engineering colleges, 36 institutes for the physically and mentally challenged people, 69 hostels, 69 hospitals, 2 medical colleges, 23 nursing schools and 15 paramedical institution in the CSI. One can imagine the magnitude of the problems involved in collecting all the accounts at the diocesan level from all the sub-units and that too in a prescribed format within the stipulated form, but failure to incorporate the accounts of one unit time frame or one Diocese would ultimately result in cancellation of Income Tax Exemption not just to that Diocese, but to the entire CSITA as the CSITA is registered as one Company.

We can identify two major problems in fulfilling the demands of law in this arena. The first one is systemic failure. As we have noted earlier, the Churches continued the traditional and denominational practices in financial management, resulting in centralized, decentralized and mixed accounting system. Whereas, the legal demands of the company is to follow uniform system throughout the company so that accounting system is transparent and readily available for comparison and cross-checking. The second failure is lack of professional competence. The Church's accounts are handled by the elected Treasurers, rendering honorary services. Majority of the Churches cannot afford to have a qualified person to maintain their accounts. In many cases, the elected Treasurers are also illiterates, not being aware of the nuances of book keeping or digital account keeping. Majority of the Treasurers may not be aware of the demands of law as well. Their only qualification is their commitment to Church and honesty in dealing with God's money. The Church is yet to give serious thought to bring about a system which is in consonance with the principles of unity in diversity adopted by the Church and uniformity in accounting system of all units and sub-units of a company as required by law.

Chapter 8

CSI: A Mission Focused Church

1. Ministry and Mission

'Equipping the saints for the work of the Ministry' is a sacred duty entrusted to the Church by the Lord, Himself. It is a divine mandate. Individual believers and the Church as the body of Christ only need to respond to this call appropriately. Initiative for this task does not lie in human beings. It comes from the Lord, Himself. Every word in this Biblical mandate is rich with meaning, and therefore very important to understand the very nature and essence of the Church. The Dictionary meaning of the word 'equip' is 'to furnish one with necessary supplies', 'to provide with abilities and understanding', 'to put in order', 'to empower'. But, the way St. Paul uses this word is deeper than the above meanings. For Paul, ministry of equipping is 'given' to the Church and not 'acquired' by the Church. It is given 'for the perfecting of the saints for the work of the ministry' (Tyndale Commentary) or to use another phrase, it is 'to fit his people for the work of service' (Interpreter's Bible) or 'the bringing of the saints to a condition of fitness for the discharge of their functions in the body'. (Robinson in Tyndale Commentary) Therefore, for Paul, equipping implied that it is the duty of the Church to empower every Christian for the spiritual task of functioning effectively in the ministry.

For St. Paul the words 'saints' carries a theological significance. In all his letters, St. Paul always begins with two affirmations, one he being called 'to be an apostle' and the other is calling his addressees as 'saints'. Historically, the word 'saint' is always associated with 'holiness', more so, in the Indian context. The saint is one who has conquered the desires of the world and attained unity with the eternal. It also refers to moral and spiritual status of some people, over and above others. But, for Paul, the word 'saint' simply means 'God's people' those whom God has chosen as His people, rather than the human superior moral qualities of a group of people. For Paul, saints indicate people who have accepted the Lordship of Christ. He always addresses his letters to a group of people in a particular location such as 'Saints in Rome, Saints in Ephesus, Saints in Corinth, Saints in Philippi' etc. It means all those people who have accepted the Lordship of Christ in a particular location, and those who belonged to God through worship or those who believe in the sovereign reign of God in their lives. It never meant, people who are 'sinless' or those who have conquered 'sins'. For, after addressing the Corinthian Christians as 'saints', Paul goes on to point out variety of sins of Corinthian Christians in each chapter of his first book. They are 'saints' because they belong to Jesus Christ, but their human sinfulness continues because they continue to be human in spite of God's call to them as a 'set apart people' for the service of God in this world. The saints for Paul are the 'saved sinners', as described by Martin Luther. They are saved by the grace of God and called to His service. They have experienced the salvation offered by Christ but their human sinful nature continues to haunt them. Therefore, various translations use different words to describe 'saints'. The Revised Standard Version continues to use the word 'saints'. The New English Bible uses the word 'his dedicated people' and Today's English Version uses the word 'God's holy people'.

These saints need to be equipped for the work of the 'ministry'. The word for the 'ministry' in Greek is *diakonia,* which refers to menial service. While the term 'diakonia' is sometimes used technically to refer to a particular office in the New Testament such as found in Phil. 1:1; 1 Tim. 3:8-12 and Acts 6:2, it is more frequently used to refer to those who lived and worked in service to others. It is particularly used to indicate menial service. The concept is derived from the ministry of Jesus Himself in his life. Jesus said 'For the Son of Man came not to be served but to serve' (Mk. 10:45). St. Paul highlights Jesus' ministry by quoting an ancient hymn in Philippians 2:6-11, wherein he states that Jesus took 'the form of a slave'. St. John further demonstrates this concept in his gospel in practical form when Jesus washes the disciples' feet in Chapter 13. Therefore, 'equipping the saints for the work of ministry' in the New Testament means empowering the believers to undertake menial service, i.e. lowest level of service possible, which is not recognized by human society, but valued very highly in the sight of God, a service looked down by the society but regarded by God. The Ephesians passage clearly indicates that the equipping has to take place in the context of the Church. That is in the collective and corporate life of the Church or in the common life of the fellowship of believers. In this process, every one contributes to the growth of the other. There are no spectators, all are active participants. There are no hierarchies either, but each has different contributions to make. Each one by contributing his/her gifts in the common life of the Church, helps the whole body to be built up. In other words, equipping of the saints for the work of ministry is not done in isolation, but in the context of the common life of the Church. This equipping ministry to each other is a service to the other without expecting any reward. It is a selfless service, but enriching service and mutually beneficial service. The word 'ministry', is therefore used mainly in the context of the church and its service to one another within the Church. What is done to equip the saints and the selfless service offered by the saints to one another is normally referred to as 'ministry'.

The Church of South India, reflects the true spirit of New Testament ministry when it affirms, 'The ministry of the Church expresses the servant-hood of Jesus Christ' (Constitution, Chapter V, page 34). In the context of the common life of the congregation, the Sexton who cleans the Church, Sunday School teachers who shape the spiritual life of children, youth who participate enthusiastically, women who are literally the backbone of the Church through their prayers and service, men who provide organizational support to all activities, choir who inspires the members through their songs and music, elders who provide infrastructural facilities and the Pastor who unravels the mysteries hidden in the Scriptures – all play an important role in equipping the saints for the work of ministry. It is an interdependent ministry and not a mono-directed ministry; it is a mutually enriching ministry and not a belligerent ministry; it is a service oriented ministry and not an over-lording ministry. Mutual service offered in a humble manner without expecting any reward or credit for it, remains one of the chief marks of Christian Ministry.

The goal of equipping the saints is 'Mission' and not self-aggrandizement. St. Paul makes it abundantly clear that his ambition in ministry is 'to proclaim the good news not where Christ has already been named'. (Rom. 15:20) The encouraging, empowering and enabling ministry within the Church is to prepare the congregations to be involved in the Mission of God in this world. That is to reach out to people outside the Church, reaching the un-reached, proclaiming the good news to those who have not heard that good news is the ultimate goal of Church's ministry. Therefore, ministry in the Church is not an end in itself but a necessary step to move to missions.

In the history of the church, three important words have been used to describe the nature and functions of mission. Each word lays emphasis on a particular dimension of mission, but they cannot be isolated from one another. The first word used is '*Evangelism*' – derived from the Greek word '*Evangellion*' which means 'glad tidings', 'joyful news', 'the Gospel'. The verb '*Evangelisomai*' means 'to announce good news'. (Lk. 1:19; Acts 13:32; 14; 15) or to 'announce the good tidings of the Gospel' (Lk. 4:18; Matt. 11:5). In essence 'evangelism' is to proclaim the good news coming from God and not that of human achievement. It is to proclaim to the world what God is doing in this world. The second word used is '*Mission*' – derived from the Latin word '*missio*'. In order to avoid misrepresentation that Mission is a human endeavor the word ' mission' is always used in conjunction with another word '*Dei*' – '*Missio Dei*' is therefore, Mission of God. Mission of God is not what Christians as individuals or as a Church offer to the world, but rather how Christians as individuals and as a corporate body are involved in discerning and communicating God's redeeming activities in this world. The third word used in this context is '*witness*' - this word also has been taken from a Greek work '*martureo*' which means 'to testify', 'to depose' or 'to bear testimony', or 'to declare solemnly'. The word 'witness' is always associated with the legal trial. In the Mosaic Law to convict a person of any crime a single person's testimony was not sufficient. There had to be two or three witnesses to testify against the wrong doings of any person only then he can be convicted. (See Deut. 19:15) This was practiced even in New Testament times. See the efforts of the Chief Priests, the Elders and the scribes in their attempt to foist false witnesses against Jesus in his trial. At last two witnesses testify against Jesus with the words, 'This fellow said, I am able to destroy the temple of God and to build it in three days.' (Matt. 26:60). II Cor. 13:1 and Hebrews 10:28 also confirm this practice. Therefore, the word 'witness' comes from the legal background. It speaks of one who has a personal experience of the event that has taken place.

The word 'evangelism' lays stress on proclamation, that is, announcement through appropriate words God's redeeming activities in the world. The word 'Mission of God' emphasizes on the Christian presence in making known God's redemptive activities in this world. The word 'witness' portrays God's redemptive activity through a lived experience of an Individual or an organized institution. One is not divorced from the other, neither can they be complete without the other. All the three are intrinsically linked with each other. There is no dichotomy among these three concepts nor are they to be compartmentalized. They should always be considered as integral whole and never as divisible units.

Unfortunately, during the course of history, these words have been used to convey sectarian understanding of the concepts to suit their theological position and thereby distorting the truth. The word evangelism has been used predominantly in the context of proclaiming the Gospel to those who have not heard the Gospel. This in turn is associated with the so called 'Evangelical theology'. The word 'mission' is exclusively used in the context of social service rendered by the Church to the society at large. This in turn is associated with the so called 'liberal theology'. The word 'witness' is particularly used in the context of institutional activities of the Church, and thereby depicting the institutional character of the Church's mission. Sensing a danger in such a parochial understanding of the nature of mission, several attempts have been made to rectify the situation. The Lausanne Committee, on World Evangelism has tried to remove the dichotomy that exists between evangelism and social action with the following words:

'There are at least three equally valid relationships between Evangelism and Social Action. First, social activity is a consequence or even one of the principle goals of evangelism. Second, social action can be a bridge to evangelism, that means, the missionaries can move from temporal needs of the people to their deeper need of their relationship to God. Third, social action not only follows evangelism as its consequence and aim, and precedes it as a bridge, but also accompanies it as its partner. They are carried out in tandem as the two blades of a pair of scissors or the two wings of a bird. Neither is the other, but the one cannot be done without the other'. (Quoted by Udaykumar in *Mission Today, Challenges & Concerns,* p.26)

The World Council of Churches which is accused of as promoting liberal theology has published a booklet as early as in 1982, whose title is

'*Mission and Evangelism*'. In this booklet, the World Council of Churches, brings out the inextricable relationship that exists between Evangelism, Mission and Witness. It says: 'There is a growing awareness among the Churches today of the inextricable relationship between Christian unity and missionary calling between ecumenism and evangelization. Evangelization is the test of our ecumenical vocation'. It adds further, 'But, the common witness should be the natural consequence of their unity with Christ in his mission'. The World Alliance of Reformed Churches also produced a booklet entitled '*Called to Witness to the Gospel Today*' in 1982, in which the ministry of suffering has been emphasized for the Church to be an effective witness to the Gospel of Jesus Christ. Therefore, proclamation, Christian presence and Christian witness constitute the essence of God's Mission in this world. Evangelism, Mission and Witness are therefore, the nerve centre of the Church's life and ministry.

This ambiguity in using the words, Evangelism and Mission is reflected even in the Constitution of the CSI. The framers of the Constitution use frequently the word 'evangelism'. The Church is called to be an 'Evangelistic Church' (P.6) so that the 'work of evangelization may be more effectively fulfilled (P.7). Therefore, the CSI purposes ever to be mindful of its missionary calling ... for the evangelization of South India. (P.7) Therefore, the Church wishes to order its own life 'for the proclamation of the Gospel to those outside the Church'. (p.12) But, in the Preamble as well as in Chapter III the word used extensively is Mission. We may recall that the Preamble and a new Chapter called 'The Mission of the Church' is a later addition as a result of a review of the Constitution initiated in connection with the Golden Jubilee celebrations of the Church. Is this a correction to the failure of the Church in its original constitution to define 'mission'? Or is it an improvement of the earlier version? We will never know. Also note that the language used in the earlier version is 'pastoral' and the language used in the additional Chapter is 'theological'. But, the worst part is the addition of a new chapter on 'The Mission of the Church' has no bearing on the 'functioning of the Church' in its subsequent chapters. Hence, the additional chapter has remained a theoretical affirmation having no effect on practice. However, being a committed CSI Churchman, I have chosen to use the word 'Mission' in this book commensurate with the thinking of the Church, with a proviso that the word 'Mission' is inclusive of evangelism and witness.

There are three important aspects of Mission which are beyond human comprehension. The first one is that mission springs from the bosom of

God. It is God who is the 'prime mover' of mission, originating from His love for the world. (John. 3:16). It is God, who wants to reconcile the world unto Himself in Christ not counting the trespasses against human beings (2 Cor. 5:19) Secondly, Christ is the 'Perfecter' of this process of reconciliation. He achieved this through his incarnation, life, witness, death and resurrection. He gave his life on the Cross in order to bring people closer to God. It was a costly mission for Jesus. Even though Jesus knew no sin, but for our sake God made him to be sin. (2 Cor. 5:21; Rom. 3:25-26) God, through His gracious act removed the guilt of sin from human beings and made it possible to restore to them the original fellowship with Himself, in Christ. Thirdly, Holy Spirit is the 'Promoter' of this process of reconciliation, He reveals the hidden truth, He teaches God's people. He empowers them to become God's partners in Mission. Therefore, Mission originates from God. It is not the mission of human beings neither is it a mission of the Church.

This ministry of reconciliation must continue even after the earthly ministry of Jesus. St. Paul is categorical in saying that this reconciliation ministry is entrusted to the Church – not because of their 'holiness', but because of their experience of 'reconciliation' with God in Christ. In this sense, the Church occupies the privileged position of 'Ambassadors for Christ' – a group representing and carrying on the Ministry of Jesus on this earth.

There are certain qualities that are required of believers to become eligible to be the messengers of reconciliation. Firstly, they must have felt the call from within themselves. The call from the Lord comes in various ways and in different forms as well as in different contexts. The call is not uniform. Every individual needs to recognize this call and make an appropriate response. While for Peter the call was in the context of his day to day work, but for Paul it was in the context of hatred towards God's people. Yet, both of them responded to the call. Encounter with the Lord is the first requisite of becoming a messenger of reconciliation.

The second requirement is to become a part of the worshipping community. This is necessary because it brings God, individual and the other believers together. It gives scope for everyone to share his/her experience of encounter with the Lord, as well as learn from the others' experience. It lifts them from human level to divine love and unites them with the Lord. That is why the Church is called a 'called out' community – called out means set apart and not segregated from the others. They are set apart because of their experience of divine love and oneness with one another.

The third requirement is commissioning. Jesus not only called his disciples but also commissioned them to go out into the world as his representatives. There are two Greek words to explain this quality. One is '*apostollein*' from which the word apostle is derived. The other word is '*pempein*'. Both words convey the meaning of being 'sent'. God sent his son to this world. Jesus sent his disciples. (Luke 9) Jesus also sent the seventy. (Luke 10) Jesus says 'As the Father has sent me, even so I send you'. (John 20:21) A sense of being commissioned by the Lord is an essential requirement to be a messenger of reconciliation. This sense of being commissioned is different from being a disciple. It is true that one has to be a disciple of Christ to be eligible to be sent, but all the disciples need to have a sense of being commissioned to be his representatives in this world. As a matter of fact, apostolicity of the Church is to be understood in this act of commissioning rather than on the act of succession. Every Christian and every Church must possess this quality of being commissioned by the Lord to carry on the Mission of God in this world.

The next qualification required is to understand that all those who have received 'commissioning' from the Lord become 'co-workers in God's service'. (1 Cor. 3:9) Each person may have been commissioned for a different task, but they all become co-workers with one another in the service of the Lord. It is not who they are that defines them, but what they are that matters. Only those who are conscious of these requirements can become messengers of reconciliation.

But, can the Church in India truly become God's representative in this world? The Church is full of problems; bickerings within the Church; partisan politics; craze for power and authority; sometimes even caste prejudices; language bias; cultural superiority – all the evils prevailing in society are also visible within the Church. In such a situation how can the Church become an instrument of God? Pessimists would not think of any role for the Church. Secular ideologues would not give any credit to faith based communities and critics within the Church would question the credibility of the Church. But, an honest look at the history of the Church would reveal the fact that God has used his Church as his instrument in every difficult situation. Individually speaking, the one who denied the Lord became 'the rock' on which God's church was built. The one who persecuted Christians became the promoter of Christianity. The one who displayed his doubts about the resurrection of Jesus Christ became the founder of the Church in India.

The awareness of the failures of the Church by a group of faithful people led to Reformation of the Church. It is the ability of the Church to be self-critical and willingness to correct itself which is the first step of becoming God's partners once again. Then God empowers them through his Holy Spirit to actually become God's partners in Mission. When the Church becomes aware of its failures and expresses its willingness to change its direction, then God uses them to be His representatives in this world. When the disciples were afraid and locked themselves up in a closed room after the death of Jesus, God empowered them by sending His Spirit upon them which made them courageous to go into the world as God's representatives. When the believers learnt to be together in the presence of God, then God poured out His Spirit upon them so that they were able to understand one another in their own language/situation. God uses vulnerable Church as His instrument. Only the Church needs to realize its vulnerability and learn to seek divine power without depending on its own power and authority, then the Church will definitely be used as God's effective witness in this world. At this stage, we need to make a distinction between 'mission' and 'vision'. Mission is given, cannot be altered - it is eternal, it can only be perceived and received. Vision is human attempt to understand mission. It is contextual. The manner in which we perceive mission constitutes vision.

2. Three Different Models of Mission in the New Testament

The Bible reveals God's creative, redemptive and restorative activities in this world. These acts of God are communicated through prophets and kings and communities such as the Israelites and the Church. It used different media such as history and theology; poetry and songs. In the New Testament, God's saving activities are communicated mainly through life and ministry of Jesus Christ. This revelation needs to be continued in and through the life, ministry and mission of the church. One of the important means through which God's redemptive activities in the world is communicated is by using common day to day examples and metaphors. The New Testament is full of such usage. Here, we will use only three such metaphors to explain three different dimensions of mission entrusted to the Church.

a. Temple of God (1 Cor. 3:16, 17)

Religion has played an important role in the national life of Israelites in the Biblical period. When they led a nomadic life in the wilderness, it was the tabernacle which symbolized the presence of God going before them in their journey. When they came to lead a settled life, then they felt a need for a temple to represent God's presence in their midst. Even though, King David was desirous of building a temple (2 Sam.7:2) it was Solomon, King David's son who completed the construction of the first temple around Tenth Century B.C. (1 Kings 6:37:38) With the Babylonian conquest the temple was destroyed. The exiles who returned around 537 B.C. built a second temple on the original site which stood almost for five hundred years. The third temple was built by Herod which commenced in 19 B.C. and was completed only around 64 A.D. which was destroyed by the Roman Empire around 70 A.D.

'Temple' provided a powerful symbol for the religious life of the Israelites. In its structure it had three distinct parts, namely, priest court which had an inner sanctuary which represented the holy of holies. To this place, no human being can enter except the Chief Priest only once a year on the day of atonement. The second part is called inner court where women could assemble separately and men could enter into another court above the women's court. The third part was called the outer court, where Gentiles could enter which also served as a market place. The entire religious life of Jews is centred around the temple.

St. Paul used this ordinary metaphor of the day to day life to convey deeper spiritual meaning. Temple conveys that it is the 'house of God', a dwelling place where God resides or a holy place which represents God's presence. Temple also represents that a community of God's people is residing around the temple and they come into the temple precincts to have *darshan* of the Lord and to 'interact' with the Lord. It is a place where the divine and human meet, and so a holy place. But God's people dwell in a secular world, outside the precincts of a holy place. They also 'interact' with the secular world. In fact the offerings that they bring into the temple – holy place – is from the secular world. So, the secular and the sacred meet together in God's presence. In this process of secular and sacred meeting together the priest plays a vital role. He takes the offerings of the people and offers it to God and in turn he returns the same offerings to the people – with the blessings of God. In this process, symbolically the secular is sanctified by the blessings of God. The devotee then takes this as God's '*prasadam*' or blessed food and shares his/her blessings with neighbours.

By using this metaphor temple, St.Paul conveys that it is essential that sacred and secular interact with each other but only spiritual values must transform secular life. St. Paul further goes on to apply this metaphor into the life of the Church. The Church, a community of Christian believers is holy because God has chosen to indwell in them. This sacred presence of God must be available to all believers without any hindrance or profanity attached to it. The believers must be able to receive God's presence and blessings from the holy precincts and go back to the secular world with God's blessings to share the same with their neighbours. The task of the Church, therefore, is to interact with one another in the presence of God and carry those blessings to share with the secular world.

St. Paul also adds a warning that the moment the Church ceases to see its role as temple of God then it loses God's blessings and instead may become a 'curse' for others. Our Lord's act of cleansing the temple (Mk. 11:15-19; Matt. 21:12-17; Lk. 19:45-48 and Jn. 2:13-22) must be understood from this perspective. Was Jesus against economic activities that are necessary for survival? No – because Jesus recruited his disciples from among those who were involved in economic activities such as fishing and tax collection. What Jesus was up against was economic activity turning into an exploitative system. The trade practices should be just and fair. From time immemorial temple worship was always associated with offerings by devotees to God in response to His blessings. So also was the ritual practice in the Jewish temple. A devotee would offer oxen or sheep in the temple. If a person was poor then the offering would be reduced to turtle doves or pigeons. These animals would be sold in the Gentile court. In as much as it was an economic activity helping the devotees in fulfilling their spiritual obligation there was no problem. But the problem became acute when religious requirement was used as an excuse to introduce exploitative system of unfair and unjust trade practices with an ulterior profit motive. As a result, commercialization of economic activity and exploitation of the religious sentiments of the ordinary innocent people with the active co-operation of religious leaders and the traders became the order of the day. It was this unjust system that Jesus was up against. Hence, he protested against such unhealthy practices in the spiritual arena. The moment ,the Church allows secular concerns to camouflage the sacred values, then the Church turns the 'House of God' into a 'den of robbers'.

b. Light of the World (Matt. 5:14-16)

Jesus addresses his disciples as 'the light of the world'. We will not go into the details of other metaphors such as 'lamp stand' or the 'city built on a hill' used in this passage. Nor will we take into account variant readings such as 'bushel basket' (Matt. 5:14) or 'under bed' (Mk. 4:21) or 'jar' or … 'bed' (Lk.11:33). We will concentrate only on 'the light of the world'. Firstly, the light, when once it is lit and placed on a higher plane it gives light to all 'in the house'. But, the disciples are to be 'the light in their good works' in such a way that it draws attention not to themselves but to their Father in heaven.

How can we understand the role of disciple as 'light' pointing not to themselves but to their Father in heaven? We will be able to understand this only if we link this Jesus' saying with his other assertion in St. John's Gospel Chapter 8, verse 12 wherein he says, 'I am the light of the world. Whoever follows me will never walk in darkness but will have light of life'. Commentators Raymond Brown and John Marsh place this saying in the context of feast of Tabernacles. During the feast of Tabernacle four golden candlesticks which could be reached only by ladders were lit in the court of the women. It is said that this light was visible throughout Jerusalem. Jesus was teaching on the last day of the festival. (7:37) Using the metaphor of light, he declares that he was the light, not only of Jerusalem, but of the whole world. As a confirmation of his role as a light of the world, he opens the eyes of a blind man in Chapter 9, continuing the work of Him, who sent Jesus. Therefore, when Jesus calls upon His disciples to be the light of the world, he was actually telling them to reflect the light that originates from him. Just as the moon reflects the light coming from the sun to the world, the disciples are to reflect the light coming from Jesus to the world. Or just as the reflectors on the highway reflects the light originating from the vehicles so that the road becomes clearer the disciples have to reflect the light originating from Jesus onto the world.

There is another aspect to this light. Matthew talks about lamp giving light 'to all in the house'. Here is an image of a house and the light shining in the house. The light does not pass through opaque body, but the house needs to have windows and doors properly placed so that light can pass through every part of the house. The structure of the house should be transparent enough to allow the light to shine in the house. This means not only the life of the disciples but also the structure that they adopt for their house should be transparent enough for the light to shine. The life of the believers as well as the structure that they adopt for their organization should be transparent enough so that the light that originates from Jesus is visible in the world. Again the message from this metaphor is that the totality of life and ministry of the Church and its structures should make way for the fulfillment of the mission of God in this world.

c. Salt of the Earth (Matt. 5:13)

Again Jesus addresses his disciples as 'salt of the earth'. Commentators are of the opinion that the word 'earth' is used synonymously with the word 'world' in the Bible as found in Gen. 11:1; Matt. 10:34 and Luke 12:49. They are used to refer to the total universe and not just a part of the universe. The Church should be 'the salt of the universe'.

Salt has three distinctive qualities embedded within it. Firstly, salt is used in cooking. It is used to enhance the taste of the cooked food. The quality of salt is that it can dissolve itself in the food without losing its character of giving 'taste'. Secondly, salt is used in preserving the perishable items from decaying. Here, the salt signifies its value as a means of giving new impetus for the decaying substance to survive. Thirdly, salt is used as a fertilizer as a manure to the soil. Here the salt inter-mingles with the soil or permeates into the soil and helps the same to nourish the plants to give better yields. In all the three functions salt plays a vital role without which food does not taste good, perishable items decay and the soil does not yield good produce. But, in all the three roles salt is not visible but its influence is obvious. Jesus wants his Church to be the salt of this universe through its life and mission.

There is another aspect of salt that we need to be reminded of, salt is always used in proportion. Less salt means 'tasteless' or 'ineffective', more salt means 'excessiveness' leading to ill health. The Church needs to be aware of both these possibilities. Being a miniscule minority in India, the Church has always suffered from 'minority complex' leading to withdrawal from active participation in the life of the world. In such a situation the Church becomes 'tasteless' and 'ineffective'. We need to remember it is a 'pinch of salt' that flavours the food and not a 'mound of salt' that is required. On the other hand, the Church can also become 'arrogant' because of its emphasis on spiritual experience. In our enthusiasm to be relevant, the Church sometimes imposes too much salt. Recently, in a well researched article in the New Sunday Express Magazine on March 26, 2017, Ann Jain Rohatagi, points out that while WHO recommends 5 grams of salt consumption per day, 25 – 30% of Indians consume over 10.9 grams of salt every day – a 119% more than the recommended limit, leading to high blood pressure, brain strokes, cardiovascular ailments, kidney failure, stomach cancer, obesity and diabetes. Imposing excessive doctrines which we believe as sacred will not yield desired results, on the other hand, it will be viewed with suspicion. In such a situation the users throw it as 'worthless'. The salt metaphor teaches us that neither the minority guilt complex nor the majoritarian arrogant complex is useful in the mission of God. Salt has to be used judiciously and proportionately if the Church wants to partner with God in His Mission.

3. Perspective for Mission from the above Biblical Modules

All the three biblical modules discussed above have a tremendous bearing on the mission activities of the Church. They portray different dimensions of the mission but maintain a common thread running through them. They complement each other and not opposed to each other.

Temple of God establishes the ground for mission and reminds the Church that God dwells in the midst of people. The holy, transcendent, unapproachable God, free from the limitations of time and space has chosen to empty Himself and dwell among sinful human beings. His presence is available to those who seek Him in the midst of their life situations. For us, Christians, this transcendent God 'became flesh and lived among us' (John. 1:14) as 'Emmanuel – God with us'. (Matt. 1:23). Therefore, the transcendent God became an Immanent God through the incarnation of Jesus Christ. Those who seek will find Him in their own contexts.

This God dwells not only in the midst of sinful human beings but also in this universe, which is His creation and has been corrupted by the rebellious nature of human beings. The Mission of God therefore, is to reconcile human beings as well as the universe unto Himself. Thus 'this world' and 'the universe' is real, unlike in Advaita philosophy, which considers matter as unreal and only 'Brahman' or the ultimate reality as real. Temple of God module demonstrates that both God and the universe are real. In order to reconcile with God human beings need to come out of the 'secular world' and enter into the 'spiritual realm' to have the personal experience of the reality of God. This is the starting point for any meaningful reconciliation process. The offerings brought to the spiritual realm both in terms of persons as individuals and the material offerings they make to God are sanctified by the blissful presence of God. After being sanctified the seekers cannot stay endlessly in the presence of God, but take that presence, the blessings into the secular world and share the same with others who did not have such experience. Therefore, the reconciliation process begins when human beings realize the need for God's presence in their lives in their day to day context. Renouncing the world is not reconciliation, but transforming the world is the only option available.

Individual encounter with God is only a first step but not the end goal. Reconciliation is a process initiated by God and each individual has to appropriate this process individually in his/her life. But, reconciliation calls for 'collective' participation in God's mission. Those who have had this personal encounter with God are called to belong to a new community – a community where they 'share their experiences with one another' and 'care' for one another. To this community God has given privilege of becoming 'co-workers with God'. (1 Cor. 3:9) Mission is a task entrusted to the Church of God to bring about transformation in the lives of people and the universe.

Temple module recognizes the role of a priest in the temple. A priest is necessary as a representative of the people who takes their day to day concerns to God, and in turn passes on the blessings of God to people. This did not mean that the believers cannot have access to God's presence except through the mediation of a priest. Rather, it means that a priest is able to channelize God's blessings in the day to day context of the devotees. The author of the letter to the Hebrews lifts the role of a priest to a new level. Here, we must make a mention, in passing, that the New Testament scholars are not unanimous in deciding the name of the author or the date and time of composition. Very few scholars ascribe the authorship to Paul. Several theories have been proposed, such as the author may be Luke, Clement of Rome, Apollos and Barnabas. Further, some scholars put the date of composition before 70 A.D., and the others place it somewhere between 80 and 90 A.D. However, all scholars concede the fact that the letter to the Hebrews belongs to the 'Pauline corpus' and therefore, can be described as a continuation of Pauline thought.

What we are concerned here is the role of the high priest in the Hebrews. This role is ascribed to Christ which is 'according to the order of Melchizedek, rather than one according to the order of Aaron'. (Ch. 7:11 also compare Ch. 14:17-24 and Psalm 110:4). How is Christ's role as High Priest different from Levitical priesthood of Aaron? It is different because conferment of high priestly role on Christ is spiritual and not genealogical. It was divinely appointed and not humanly acquired. It was not built on the principle of 'receiving' but on the principle of 'sacrificing'. Christ's once for all sacrifice is the ground for his continued mediation between God and the faithful. Therefore, his high priestly work is eternal.

When the believers are in the presence of God, they realize the enormous sacrifices made by Christ to remove their guilt feelings in order to feel comfortable in the presence of God. As a result, they become recipients of God's blessings. They also realize that this blessing cannot be hidden, but has to be shared with others. Church's understanding of priestly role is modeled mainly on the high priestly role of Christ. The CSI, like all other Churches has also accepted the three fold order of ordained ministry within the Church, namely, Bishop, Presbyters and Deacon. The Constitution is very clear in stating the purpose of this ministry in the following words: 'For the equipment of the whole Church for the fulfillment of its ministry and thus to build up the body of Christ, Christ has given to the Church the gift of the ordained ministry'. (Ch. V, Clause A, page 35) This is further strengthened in the ordination service of Deacons , Presbyters and Bishops. There are two basic elements that are involved in this Ordination service (a) It is God who gives grace and authority for the office and work to which a person is called, and (b) God bestows this grace in answer to the prayers of his Church. Therefore, the ordained ministry is a gift to the Church by God. It also enjoys prayerful support from the faith community. In view of this understanding, the ordained ministry is not just a profession – a means for survival but also a vocation – a commitment to honour the gifts received. The ordained ministry becomes sacred when the concerned persons fulfill the duties entrusted to them by God Himself. What are these duties? It is essentially the duties of a priest modeled on the role of the High priest. There are three basic principles involved in the priestly work.

- To empower, strengthen, console, comfort every individual committed to their charge so that they may have meaningful encounter with the Lord;
- To create and build an atmosphere of harmonious relationship between individuals and the faith community so that they may be able to share and care without any inhibitions; and
- To equip every individual by unraveling the mysteries underlying in the Scriptures and make it possible for them to become 'priests' to their neighbours, co-workers in their secular environment because the Church also believes in the 'priesthood of all believers'.

Therefore, there are three types of priestly roles prevailing in the Church. The first one is high priestly role of mediating a covenant between God and human beings undertaken by Christ, permanently having been appointed by God himself. Secondly, the ordained ministers fulfilling the role of priests of mediating, between God and the faithful. This is a ministry for which some are called and their call is endorsed by the community. There is a third group of priests. They are called to the office of 'Royal Priesthood', being commissioned by God and empowered by the ordained ministers. 'The priesthood of all believers' becomes a reality when the ordained ministers train the faithful appropriately in the spiritual laboratory called the Church to take up their priestly role in the secular world. Conversely, if the faithful are not effective in their priestly role in their secular environment, then the blame should be placed on the ordained ministers for their failure to equip the faithful appropriately and not the other way round. It is this aspect of the failure on the part of ordained ministers in fulfilling their priestly role that Paul criticizes.

The module 'Temple of God', therefore, establishes *ground* for God's mission in this world. It reminds us that God dwells in the midst of people. His mission is to reconcile the world unto Himself. There is no dichotomy between sacred and secular. Secular world is also real and created by God. However, since the world is fallen, in order to reconcile this world, He has sent His Son as mediator of a 'new covenant' between Himself and the world. Christ through His once-for-all sacrifice continues to mediate permanently. In order to further this process of reconciliation God has entrusted priestly role of mediating between God and the faithful to the ordained people whose primary role is to equip the faithful to become priests in the secular world and the role of the faithful is to mediate between God and the secular world. Failure in this process would result in negating the very mission of God in this world. The module provides 'unity in diversity' in its perspective for mission.

The second module 'light of the world' provides the *source* for mission. The Church in its enthusiasm to be involved in mission should never forget that the source is Jesus himself. Apart from this, there is no mission. The job of the Church is to reflect the light originating from Jesus himself. There are two aspects through which the light that originates from Jesus is to be reflected. The one is through the life and witness of the individuals and the second one is through the structures that we adopt for ourselves as an organization so that the light is visible. Both the life and witness of the faithful as well as the structure of the organization should be transparent enough for the light of Jesus to be reflected to the world around. Therefore, the unity in diversity in missions must be accompanied by transparency in life style and structure.

The third module 'salt of the earth' defines the *scope* under which the mission takes place. Like salt, mission is accomplished only to the extent it is put to use. Like salt, the Church is called upon to enhance taste, preserve the perishable from decaying and help in producing better yields. In all the three functions it loses its original form but retains its quality. It is always effective when in minority, loses its worth if administered beyond proportion. Therefore, the Church is called upon to be effective in its utility and not in its hoarding ability.

The three biblical modules discussed above give us a perspective on God's mission in this world. When the Church understands its role, as a privileged community called by God, illuminated by the light originating from Jesus and to utilize the gifts given by God to help people to come closer to God through their appropriate responses, the Church can truly become a partner with God in His efforts of reconciling the world unto Himself.

4. Implementing of Mission Agenda in the CSI

As I was collecting my thoughts for this section, I encountered certain genuine difficulties. These difficulties are not personal, but are those inherent in the system itself affecting the very presentation of the subject in an impartial manner. I decided to put them in a nutshell here so the reader may understand the context before forming an opinion on the subject.

The first difficulty is the diametrically opposite approaches that the missionaries and Indian writers have taken in reporting mission concerns. The missionaries reported to their home board consisting not only of the officials but also the vast number of people supporting the mission work. They were anxious to know how their support helped the transformation process. The reporting was regular and in a specified format published in official communication channels, from the missionaries regular correspondence. The reports are narrative and descriptive and the reflections suggestive. The people whom they served were not their constituency of reporting, but they are the object of reporting. But, when the Church became independent of the missionaries, the reporting became sporadic and not regular. The report was done not by those involved in the ministry and mission, but by those capable of intellectual articulation. The reports became normative and prescriptive and the reflections prospective. As a result, only very few materials are available in the Independent Church which are narrative and descriptive about the mission work of the Church.

The second difficulty is in our understanding of history. It is a well-known dictum that Western understanding of history is linear, and therefore progressive, whereas, the Indian understanding of history is cyclical leading us to believe 'history repeats itself'. But, one can detect at least three different levels of emphasis in understanding history in India within this general framework. One, those coming from Vedic religions or from high castes are proud of their history, so, they would like not only to preserve it but perpetuate it. Look at any matrimonial advertisement seeking alliance, almost invariably there is a mention of the caste of a person seeking alliance from the person of the same caste. The pride, privilege and the superiority of the community is continued by preserving the 'purity of race' through marriage.

The second understanding of history comes from the backward classes. After India attained freedom and particularly since the time of publication of Mandal Commission Report in 1980, there is an upsurge among the backward classes to upgrade themselves by using socio-economic and political tools. They are not high-caste people neither are they socially alienated. This desire on the part of the backward classes, to upgrade their communities in their social standing by using economic, social and political tools, has been described as 'Sanskritisation process' by the eminent sociologist, Mr. M. N. Srinivas of the yesteryears. This process is very effectively used by almost all the backward class communities throughout India now. One example in this regard could be that those communities who were not allowed into the temple earlier are now building temples of their own, but also appointing Brahmin priests in their temples giving respectability of a high caste. The third level of understanding of history comes from the Dalits. These are the people who suffered social alienation in the past and the same social stigma continues even now inspite of the fact that many have achieved educational and economic status. It is precisely for this reason that the Dalit communities who have nothing to be proud of their past nor can they up grade themselves as respectable communities through a process of Sanskritisation would like to escape from their history. Look at the 'Ghar Wapsi programme' those who are re-converted are not given a higher status, but sent back to their original caste group. The Christian Church is no exception to the understanding of history. Therefore, if one wants to grapple with authentic history of the Church, he/she would have to first understand the historical and cultural conditioning of the writer or author of that particular work.

The third difficulty is in our conceptual framework. As noted in earlier chapters the Indian philosophy promotes individual search for authentic spirituality. The Pietism of the early missionaries insisted on individual encounter with Christ. Indian spirituality led to renunciation of the world and the Western pietism taught us importance of 'the world beyond'. As a result, recording of the past events does not seem to be important in our frame of mind. Further, for those coming from oral tradition, recording historical events and activities becomes an unnecessary exercise. For instance, if one were to ask a congregation member of our Church to describe the history of our Church the standard reply would be when the construction of the church building was undertaken and when it was completed. Very rarely, one would get a reply on the people involved in building the community here, what were their compulsions and convictions, what struggles they underwent in building a community of faith, in what way the community of faith relates to the people around. None of these answers would come forth. All these are taken for granted. But in the process, the very history of the Church is lost in memory. In such a situation narrating the congregational involvement in the mission of God in this area becomes difficult, if not impossible.

Finally, I would like to point out another important difficulty. This is in the area of communication within the Church. In line with the democratic principles as mentioned earlier, the Church has adopted three levels of fairly autonomous units within the Church, namely the Synod, the Dioceses and the congregations. Unfortunately, the Church has never thought it fit to work out a meaningful communication system, where in all sections of people could participate. Spirituality is enhanced, when we share with one another our faith concerns. Democracy is enhanced, where there are debates, discussions and exchange of ideas on various issues. Unfortunately, our official channels are used more for dissemination of information than for creating a platform for dissenting people to raise their voices. The Dioceses are so autonomous that there are no communication channels between one with the other. Congregations are caught up so much about their participation that they do not even care to know what is happening in the neighbouring congregations. Further, the multi-lingual nature of some of the Dioceses presents an added difficulty in communicating with one another. As a result the life, ministry and mission of the Church as a whole is neglected in its apathy towards establishing proper communication channels. The result is negativism has occupied prime space in print, electronic and social media over against the positive involvement of the Church in God's mission.

Being aware of these difficulties, I decided to approach the subject in question from a different perspective. My experience as a Church Worker, my visits to all the Dioceses as a leader and my perception of mission activities undertaken by various Dioceses as presented in the biennial reports submitted to the CSI Synod, became the primary tools for my reflection in this section. If in the process salient features of some Dioceses do not figure then it is solely due to my ignorance and not because of any prejudices.

In my view, only the cynics would deny that CSI is a Mission focused Church. The critics would like to hide the mission activities of the Church under the garb of internal squabbles. But, the fact is the Church is ever conscious of its responsibility towards mission. Its implementation may be imperfect and inadequate but the intention cannot be denied. The involvement is described here under different typologies and not as actual events except in cases where it is felt necessary to high light certain actions and programmes to indicate a new direction undertaken. We will notice that while mission is only one – i.e. God's mission of reconciling the world unto Himself the practical implication of the same is multi-dimensional depending on the perception of those who are involved in mission and the context of the recipients.

a. Missionary Society Model

This is the original model. Almost all the missionaries who came to India were sponsored by their respective Missionary Societies. The concept behind every Missionary Society was very clear. It was an association of like-minded people committed to the cause of proclamation of the Gospel, coming together under the umbrella of a society for 'prayers, participation and support' the work of proclamation of the Gospel all over the world and to reach the unreached. All the missionary work undertaken in India originates from various missionary societies. They have also developed suitable structures to promote their agenda and appointed committed personnel to implement the agenda. The society raises funds for their activities through the voluntary and sacrificial giving of the people committed to the task. The official Church may or may not have a part in the missionary societies, but all those who support the mission activities through their society are committed Christians believing in the biblical mandate of, 'Go therefore and make disciples of all nations …' (Matt. 28:19) and 'Woe unto me, if I do not preach the Gospel'. (1 Cor. 9:16) Hence, "go or send" is their motto.

This model of Western Church has been copied very successfully by the Indian Church even before the Church Union. It is said that V S Azariah was inspired by the Jaffna Tamil Christians efforts in starting a missionary society worked tirelessly to establish an 'Indian Missionary Society of Tirunelveli' and in later years, he himself became a missionary to Dornakal through this missionary society. Subsequently, 'National Missionary Society' was established in 1905. Now, there are a number of Missionary Societies established throughout India, both big and small. The motto of these societies is to reach the unreached. The support should come from within India and the mission activities both at the grass-roots level and at the managerial level should be administered by Indians. It is beyond dispute that many Christians belonging to different congregations are the backbone of these societies. It is because of their participation that different missionary societies are able to send hundreds and thousands of missionaries to live and work among different communities throughout India to make the presence of Christ felt in their lives. This could genuinely be described as 'peoples movement' in the sense that ordinary congregation members are involved in 'praying, participating and supporting' these mission agenda initiated by missionary societies who are not directly under the established Church. Proclamation of the Gospel is the primary activity, but of late missionary societies are realizing that proclamation alone is not sufficient it has to be accompanied by some liberative actions.

b. Diocesan Model

When the Union took place all the Dioceses being 'mindful of its missionary calling' have decided to keep 'missions' as their primary focus. They established 'Mission Boards' through which the Mission work could be undertaken. The principles behind the Diocesan Mission organization is exactly the same as that of 'Missionary Society Model', except that the organization comes under the administrative control of the Diocese, and therefore, accountable to various committees. Like the mission work under missionary society model, the Dioceses also identify mission fields, station missionaries, supervise the work through designated persons, obtain periodic reports and circulate the same among the members of the congregations. The finances for the mission work is raised from within the Diocese, by organizing Mission Sundays, Mission Festivals, special efforts, Jathras and revival meetings. Some Dioceses have mission fields within their own territorial jurisdiction, some outside their own jurisdictions and some in both. Some support a large number of missionaries and some a small number but the most important point is the Dioceses are conscious of their responsibility towards mission. Dioceses like, East Kerala, Madhya Kerala, South Kerala, Kanyakumari, Thoothukodi-Nazareth, Tirunelveli have mission fields outside their jurisdiction. The Dioceses like Trichy-Tanjore, Coimbatore, Madras, Vellore, Karnataka Central, Karnataka Southern, Karnataka Northern, Krishna-Godavari, Dornakal and Medak Dioceses have mission fields within their jurisdiction. But, we also see a shift in approach to missions undertaken by the Dioceses in that it is not only the presentation of the Gospel but also some socio-economic activities accompanying it, such as starting of crèches, tailoring classes for women, night schools etc. Therefore, in many places a wholisitic approach to mission is employed. The relief and rehabilitation work undertaken by the affected Dioceses during the time of Tsunami is an example in this direction. Many Dioceses have also entered into new frontiers in mission. Some examples are:

- Mission to sea farers undertaken by Tirunelveli and South Karnataka Dioceses
- Mission to transgenders initiated by the Madras Diocese
- Mission to promote ecological concerns began by the Madhya Kerala Diocese
- Mission to the street children - Makkala Ashraya Kendra for Boys and New Life Centre for Girls, Certificate Course in Computer Training in collaboration with NIIT and also Community College in various skills for young people in KGF when the gold mines were closed in Karnataka Central Diocese.

Thus, the Dioceses are conscious of their role in mission.

c. Women's Fellowship Model

Women are always in the forefront of Missionary work. The Church of South India recognized the role of women in mission work and formed Women Fellowship as an independent body, having their own Constitution beginning from the Pastoral level to the Diocesan and Synod levels. Women Fellowships organize their own programmes and activities, raise their own finances and manage their own organizations. In order to recognize their ministry and mission activities as part of the whole Church, the President and General Secretary of the Women's Fellowship have been made members of the CSI Synod. The work that the Women Fellowships are involved, among the women and children, are plenty in all Diocesan jurisdictions as well as at the Synod level. Each congregation is involved in various activities through the Women's Fellowships.

d. Institutional Model

This is also an inherited model. Missionaries along with their preaching have also started imparting education and organizing health care centre. The purpose of educational institution was not only to impart knowledge, but also to imbibe character. Through college education, the missionaries wanted students to rationally think and follow truth. When they introduced primary education in the villages it was not only to give opportunity to people who did not have access to education, but also to inculcate social awareness by allowing different caste children to study together. Bible teaching was an essential component of education but over the years, the government intervened in the educational policy and removed bible teaching from the syllabus. Character building receded to the background.

These institutions came under the administrative control of the Church when the Union took place and suddenly the Church felt the burden of missions. The main focus of the leaders was to make the pastoral ministry self- supporting. With the interference of the government in terms of syllabus, salary structure of the staff and the examination patterns, the Church was not in a position to organize increased financial requirement to run vast number of educational institutions. Hence, they appointed a Study Committee to decide the future of educational institutions. The Mysore Diocese appointed a Commission in the year 1955, 'to make a review of all schools in the Diocese'. On the basis of the report of the Commission the following decisions were taken:

i. Schools to be closed.
ii. Schools to get grant-in-aid.
iii. Schools to be retained.

As a result, the Convener of the 'Elementary Education Standing Committee' of the Diocese reports to the Diocesan Council of 1957, that 'more than half the number of primary schools in the Diocese had to be handed over to the Government or closed because it was not possible to meet the necessary increase in salaries out of our limited resources'. With this an instrument which brought about social transformation in the villages also suffered very badly, resulting in the ineffectiveness of mission. I am sure other Dioceses have similar stories to tell.

Today, we have three types of educational institutions. The first, grant-in-aid type in which the salaries of the staff are met by the Government, but the Management remains with the Diocese. The second type of educational institutions where the staff receive a paltry sum from the Management and the infrastructural facilities are abysmally low and the third type are private institutions, wherein the Management collects the necessary fees from the students. These institutions are flush with money leading to all sorts of speculations. The Church is yet to study the effectiveness of mission through these institutions.

Similarly, the medical mission was started by the missionaries out of deep compassion for the sick and the dying. Every institution has a story behind its mission. The compassion and care extended by the mission is incomparable. As a result, the institutions grew beyond all expectations. Today, we have large institutions, some are autonomous and some with in the Diocese, but the sad part is a number of dispensaries and primary health care centres which catered to the needs of villages have been closed. However, the institutional mission continues.

e. Non-Governmental Organizational Model (NGO)

The Missionary Model, the Diocesan Model and the Institutional Model, all stem from the basic understanding that for the society to be transformed, individuals need to be transformed first. It is only the transformed individuals who can influence the society to change. But, individuals cannot be transformed unless they are spiritually motivated. It is this dependence on God's mercy which empowers individuals to commit themselves to work for the transformation of society. But, true spirituality also demands socio-economic needs to be addressed and this can be met only through a gradual and sustained effort. Hence, Institutional Model is necessary along with spiritual formation. This is the conviction with which all the above three models function.

There are a few individual Christians, who realized that individuals, though willing, are caught up in the rigid structures that we create for ourselves. The structures become so formidable that it will not allow individuals to extricate themselves. Therefore, any structure that de-humanizes human beings' needs to be broken to liberate individuals from its clutches. Therefore, justice to all which is divinely ordained can be achieved only if the stranglehold of these structures are removed and a humane structure where everyone can express their opinion freely and every one participates in public discourse willingly is introduced. With this conviction, a few individuals formed organizations of like-minded people, registered these organizations with the Government authorities as NGO's. They take up issues affecting the people organize and educate them of their rights and make the concerned people themselves to agitate before appropriate authorities, providing ideological, infra-structural and financial support from behind. Their methodology of organizing is issue based, and hence not religion based. Affected people from all religions are participants. Structures which do not provide solutions to the issues raised are the targets. But, since the structures are managed and controlled, be they at the Government or the Church level by the leaders, they become the targets of these dharnas, protests and agitations. Establishing a just society is their primary goal in their mission activities.

Establishing a just society is not alien to Christian Mission. The Church needs to appreciate their commitment, only the method of implementation is different. The first one aims at inner transformation but in the second, it is collective transformation. For the first one, the support comes from the Christians themselves, whereas for the second, since the methodology is political, and the Christian congregations are traditionally apolitical, the NGO's are not able to raise funds from within the Church and hence they have made foreign donor agencies as their support base. They are not answerable to the official church but in fact, majority of these organizations are critical of the church. But, in the eyes of the Government, in as much as the promoters of the NGO's are Christians - they are Christian NGO's.

f. Individual Model

Personal encounter with Christ affects the life-style of vast majority of Christians. They apply those spiritual values to their personal and family life. They try to live in harmony with the neighbours. But above all, they try to help the people in need as much as possible. They do it quietly and never make it public. They do not call it as a mission, but they do it as their Christian commitment. I will give only one or two examples to highlight such an involvement by the congregation members:

Recently I had a very pleasant but humbling experience. After the Christmas celebrations I met Mr. Norman's family, who always occupy the seats one row ahead of the pew that I normally occupy in the Church and enquired as to how their Christmas celebration was? They replied: 'Bishop, we spent the whole day with the children in the Blind School. We sang, prayed, played and ate with them. The joy in their faces brought tears to our eyes. This was our Christmas.' The family met all the expenses incurred for that day. What a true celebration of Christmas I thought!

My wife tells me that a small time businessman for the last several years has been making two sets of clothes for all children in Makkala Ashraya Kendra at the time of Christmas. The quality of the material is exactly the same as the quality that he would buy for his own children. Another businessman used to purchase shoes for the children to be used for Church services as well as different sets of shoes to be used while going to School. This he continued for many years. We both are personally aware of the number of congregation members who are helping children get proper education by supporting them financially for their fees, uniforms and books or helping people to cover their medical bills. None of them announce their good deeds to others for they believe in the biblical dictum 'do not let your left hand know what your right hand is doing'. (Matt. 6:3) I am sure, there are hundreds and thousands of ordinary Christians who put into practice their Christian commitment. Involvement in mission, however small and insignificant it may be, has been one of the ancient and effective methods in becoming partners with God in His mission.

g. Congregational Model

The Constitution of the Church of South India accords prime importance to the local congregations. It says, 'In the purpose of God every local group of the faithful, organized for Christian life and worship as a congregation or pastorate within the fellowship of the Diocese, represents in that place the same one, holy, Catholic and Apostolic Church.' Further 'every congregation shall, with its pastor be responsible for watching over its members, ... and for the proclaiming of the Gospel to those outside the Church.' (Ch. II, Clause 9, p.12) Therefore, the Constitution lays down two important functions to each congregation – they are unity and mission. It represents the whole church locally. It reaches out to those outside the Church in fulfilling God's mission. We are familiar with individuals in God's mission, Dioceses in God's mission, Institutions in God's mission but sufficient importance has not been given to congregational role in mission.

The decade of 1980, saw a pedagogical shift in the thinking process of the church and affirmed the congregational participation in mission. This is what happened. In one of the Executive meetings of the CSI Synod, a question was raised as to in what way the constitutional mandate of making congregations as mission agents could be brought about? The question was discussed threadbare and many suggestions were given. Then Bishop Victor Prem Sagar, the Deputy Moderator, suggested that the whole Executive be divided into sub groups and entrusting to them a specific issue to discuss and come up with a report to be presented at the meeting the next day. I remember, as a representative of Karnataka Central Diocese, sitting for hours on end in my hotel room working on the preliminary draft for our group. The report of all the Sub Committees were consolidated and Bishop Victor Prem Sagar was asked to take all the recommendations and put it in a theological perspective, which resulted in the production of the document 'Vision for Equipping the Local Congregations in Mission' (VELCOM). Bishop Victor Prem Sagar, when he became the Moderator of the Church in 1988, gave further push to this concept through his addresses, seminars, conference and production of Bible Study materials.

The document envisages four steps:

i. Agape

It simply means the starting point for any congregation to be involved in mission is spirituality of individuals and congregation. It begins with one's love for God, community and to the world and in particular the neighbourhood of the congregation.

ii. Agenda

The congregation as a whole discusses issues prevailing in the neighbourhood and lists them in order of priority.

iii. Analysis

Then an analysis is made to the root cause of those problems and issues. In this process the congregation may take the help of experts in socio-economic, cultural and political field to understand the issues in a scientific manner.

iv. Action

Then the congregation will draw out an action programme based on their biblical understanding relevant to the situation. In implementing, they may also enlist the support and co-operation of the members of the neighbourhood.

The new initiative was accepted by the whole church because theological and biblical perspectives were put in context. Further, the whole Executive Committee of the CSI Synod accepted this new initiative whole heartedly, and sent the same to the Dioceses for study and action. The Communication Department of the CSI Synod was entrusted with the responsibility of implementation and publication. Unfortunately, though the Director of the Communication Department and the reports submitted by the Dioceses to the Synod in subsequent years, state that VELCOM is enthusiastically implemented, there is not a single instance of practical illustration in their reports to demonstrate as to how the concept is working at the congregation level. Hence, in order to help the reader to understand that it is not only possible, but also desirable that the congregations be involved in mission, I have decided to narrate a few instances from my own experience.

Even, before this document was published the Karnataka Central Diocese through their visionary leaders have been emphasizing the congregational role in mission. The Mysore Diocese and subsequently the Karnataka Central Diocese had been blessed with visionary leaders as Bishops. It is pertinent to note their views on Mission. Bishop N. C. Sargant in his Presidential Address to the Diocesan Council called for the exchange of pulpits between different linguistic groups in order to strengthen the fellowship between different congregations worshipping in different languages.

For Bishop Gill, spiritual renewal was the focus. For this to happen, he believed that the life of the congregations must be strengthened. In his own words: 'What is the Church? It is the people of God. It is the congregations. It is where the real Christian witness and presence can be seen … The real evangelist is the member in the congregation and the congregation together'. He reiterated this missive in the year 1979, under the theme, 'Developing congregations for mission'. He states: 'During the last biennium, we have been growing in the conviction that the local congregation should be given more importance'.

After Bishop Gill left the Diocese, and there was no Bishop in the Diocese, the Moderator Solomon Doraiswamy who presided over the Diocesan Council 1981, had this to say: 'Bishop Gill emphasized in his last message the importance of the local congregation. I could very well picture the status of the local congregation and the important role the congregations play in the absence of the Bishop. But, for this life of the local congregations this Diocese would have faced one of the most damages, that could easily happen to any Diocese when the real leadership at the Centre was missing, namely, the Bishop'.

Bishop C. D. Jathanna, while talking about the dynamic creative alternative for mission has this to say in 1991 'Before embarking ourselves to fulfill the mission of God we have to prepare our congregations in their spiritual development. It is absolutely necessary to form several Bible Study groups in the congregations for deeper sense of commitment'. With this conviction he started a project called 'Gubbi Mission' in the Diocese. Gubbi is a small town in the old Mysore State where Methodist Missionaries started their work.

My first address to the Diocesan Council in 1997 was on 'Congregations as missionary communities'. I took as an example the story of a migrant community in Tumkur, which started as worship centre with 5 families and grew to be one of the large congregations in Tumkur. All my seven addresses to the Diocesan Council had some aspects of the congregational life in each of them. Let me now narrate a few instances of congregational involvement in mission in the Karnataka Central Diocese.

1. The first example is from my village. It was in the latter half of the 1960's. I was studying in a College in Mysore. There was a severe drought throughout Mysore District. People irrespective of castes were struggling hard to survive. It was then the Sister who was posted to my village, Hadya, who took the initiative to arrange for relief work. Sister Victoria organized 'Food for Work' through CASA. Since, all were suffering, she organized de-silting of tanks in our village and the surrounding villages. After this work, she took up converting bullock cart roads into wider and motorable roads. It is amazing how she was able to persuade the land owners on either side of the road to give up a portion of their land to widen the road. Whether she worked through the Panchayat leaders or Government revenue officials, I do not know. All I know is that all the land owners had given up a portion of their land for road widening work. In terms of the work, since all were struggling for survival, Sister Victoria asked each family irrespective of their caste background to send one person for work every day for 5 days a week. I had then returned home for the summer holidays. Since I was the only college student, Sister asked me whether I would volunteer and visit the spot where the work was going on and maintain an attendance register, which I readily agreed. On Saturdays, it was the job of the congregation to distribute the wheat, sugar and oil in an orderly fashion on the basis of the attendance register maintained. This work was carried on for nearly 2 months. Sister also organized drilling of borewells in all the villages for different communities through

EFICOR. The village people considered Sister Victoria as God's representative to save them from hunger and thirst. For this noble gesture the Government of Karnataka conferred Rajyotsava Award on Sister Victoria the following year.

2. The first Indian Presbyter to St. Mark's Cathedral was Rev. Harry Daniel, a powerful preacher, a pastor with concern for his people and a leader committed to mission. He used to advise his congregation members 'to hold the Bible in one hand and the newspaper in the other hand', implying our reading of the Bible should be relevant to the day to day life situations. He motivated the congregation to be involved in mission. Three such projects are mentioned here. Firstly, the Urban and Rural Mission with Mr. Paul Shiromani, a deeply committed Christian as its head. His job was to work with communities and with people in organizations related to industry. That was the time when Bangalore was becoming an industrial centre with large establishments like HAL, HMT, BEL, NGEF and others coming up. The mission team from St. Mark's worked as mediators between Management and the Union. The team, gradually realized that industrialization needs to be understood in the context of urban poor. This led Mr. Paul Shiromani to leave St. Mark's premises and move near Tilaknagar Slum in Bangalore initiating 'Tilaknagar Association for People's Development'. He formed a core group consisting of himself, the local pastor, a lay leader of the community and two Catholic nuns. They supported activities dealing with problems of health and education of children. In all their work their main purpose was to ensure that the local community takes responsibility for their own lives and that of the community with a hope for a better future.

The second mission project initiated by St. Mark's Cathedral was 'Rag Picker's Project'. The project envisaged organizing, helping, training and equipping the rag-pickers to fight for themselves for a better future. This again was headed by a committed lay person, by name Alex Devasundaram who worked passionately among rag-pickers and enlightened the congregation members of the causes that led to such a situation and the structural changes necessary to improve the living conditions of the people concerned.

The third mission project undertaken was to share the proceeds of the Harvest Festival with non-Christian organizations, who are involved in humanitarian work. From that time till today, the entire proceeds amounting to Rs. 18–20 lakhs every year, have been shared with three to four organizations. Only for the last two years the entire proceeds have been given to the Karnataka Central Diocesan Mission Fields.

3. After the return of the Scottish Regiment the membership in St. Andrew's Church dwindled over the years. In the decade of 1960, when the last missionary pastor returned, the Officers of the Diocese were in a dilemma whether to close down the worship service or to continue with a very small number of the faithful. Then Bishop Sargant invited Rev. R. G. Heri from Mangalore to revive a dying congregation. He gathered mainly people from the Basel Mission background and built up the congregation. But his successor Rev. S. A. Salins who was known for his pastoral concerns was able to attract people from all denominational background and started the worship service in English and Kannada. Rev. S. A. Salins motivated the congregation to be involved in mission. He started a primary school in Someshwara Slum, right in the centre of Bangalore. Congregation members and particularly Pastorate Committee members took keen interest in this project by appointing the staff and providing infrastructural facilities and subsequent Presbyters continued with the work. Space is a constraint in the slum, so the school building was strengthened which was constructed earlier over the drain that passes through the slum, covering it with cement concrete was inaugurated by the Moderator of the CSI, Ryder Devapriyam. In 2011 additional classrooms and staff room were added as a first and second floor of the earlier building and they invited me as the Moderator to inaugurate the building. Today, the School has got classes up to 7th Standard with seven staff members and 275 children, while the government schools nearby are nearly empty. Today, St. Andrew's is one of the leading congregations in the Diocese.
4. As mentioned in the Preface, the Kothanur CSI Church has only 11 years of history but has many programmes and activities to its credit. The Bible Study programme initiated by Rev. Dexter Maben continues weekly even today in 8 different centres. The Bagalur Mission initiated by Rev. Dexter Maben continues where in a missionary is posted, a crèche is run and medical awareness along with clinical facilities are conducted. The mission to Transgender initiated by Rev. Nirmala Vasanthakumar has borne fruit in that some have accepted the Lordship of Christ and the congregation continues to support this mission.

Many more examples can be narrated but the purpose of the above examples is only to demonstrate that mission through congregations is possible. We also note from the above examples that the congregations become missionary congregations if the pastoral ministry is effective and lay leaders are committed. So, visionary and supportive leadership at the centre, effective pastoral care and unwavering commitment of the lay leaders are the necessary ingredients to make a congregation a missionary congregation.

From the description of the above mission models we can arrive at the conclusion that CSI is a mission focused Church. Each model lays stress on some aspects of mission. No one is perfect, but it should be taken as an honest effort in implementing mission. Missionary society model, gives importance to proclamation of the gospel. Its primary focus is to invite people to have personal encounter with Christ. The Diocesan model continues with the primary focus of the misssionary society model but adds socio-economic developmental activities into proclamation. The institutional model attempts at transforming individuals, i.e. the purpose of educational mission is not only to impart knowledge but also character building. The purpose of medical mission is to make the sick person whole mentally, physically and spiritually through the compassionate service of medical personnel. NGO model attempts at the structural changes in order to make society a better place to live in. Individual model attempts at transformation of individuals through the sacrificial services offered by Christians. Congregational model attempts at transformation of communities they serve. So, there are multiple methods employed in mission. So, mission is one, but methodologies employed are many.

What is the purpose of this mission? Is it not to convert people to Christianity? one might ask. Conversions have taken place in the past. They are taking place even now. Likewise, re-conversions by the name 'Ghar Wapsi' have taken place in the past and they are taking place even now, so different people have different convictions on the subject 'conversion'. Instead of entering into a debate on the subject, I would like to put forward my conviction by way of narrating two incidents.

Sometime after the Australian missionary Graham Staines and his two sons were burnt alive on January 23, 1999 in Manoharpur in Orissa, the then Prime Minister, Shri. Atal Bihari Vajpayee and the Home Minister, Shri. L. K. Advani visited Bangalore on some official business and they were staying in Raj Bhavan. All the Christian denominational heads including the Archbishop of the Roman Catholic Church went to meet the Prime Minister as a delegation. The group asked me to be the spokesperson. The Prime Minister listened to us very patiently without making any comments.

At the end, he asked us to meet the Home Minister who was staying in the next building. We explained to the Home Minister about the incident and sought protection for the Christian minority. Suddenly he told me, Bishop, if a person gets converted to Christianity in Bangalore we believe it is because of his/her conviction, but if a group of illiterate people in the remote corner of Dange District of Gujarat are converted to Christianity then we conclude it is not because of their conviction but due to coercion of various kinds. What would you say?, he asked. In reply, I told the Home Minister, 'Sir, Christian Church will never give up propagating the Gospel for two reasons, one, it is a mandate given by our Lord and every Christian and every Christian Church must fulfill this mandate. Secondly, it is a fundamental right given to us by the Constitution. No one can take away this right. We proclaim the Gospel. It is our duty, but the response is left to the person who hears the Gospel. It is the Holy Spirit who gives vision to accept the new way of life. So, conversion is a matter between the person who responds to the Gospel and God. But Sir, what happened to 5000 years of civilization which preaches and practices tolerance?' The Home Minister changed the subject.

The second instance is from the very first year of my pastoral ministry. I was posted to Shaffer Memorial Church in Bangalore. It was an educated congregation and interested in Church's ministry and mission. A prominent member approached me to talk about Christian faith to one Mr. T. R. Mahalingam who was interested in knowing about Christ. Mr. T. R. Mahalingam was an acclaimed flautist known all over India and abroad. He lived in Sadashivanagar, which is at the northern end of Bangalore and at that time, I lived in Gandhibazar, which is located in the southern part of Bangalore. Every Monday morning, I would go on my cycle to his house. We decided to study St. John's Gospel as it would be more appropriate for a mystic like him. Mr. T. R. Mahalingam was a keen learner asking questions and contributing from Indian philosophy. The whole session used to be interactive and dialogical. This went on for about a year. One day, he asked me to baptize him. I asked him to come to Shaffer Memorial Church and the baptism will take place during the Worship Service. At this suggestion, he was taken aback. He said, 'Pastor, if I take baptism publicly then what will happen to my reputation and social standing? Why don't you baptize me here at home?' I told him one can be a secret follower of Christ, but to be a part of the Church, one has to make a public confession of faith. So, I advised him to continue to follow Christ secretly.

Chapter 9

CSI: A Church at the crossroads

The pilgrim church is on the move. On the way it meets with several challenges, such as natural calamities, attack of the wild beasts, threat of robbers etc. But, people learn to face the challenges as a group. They establish better relationship with one another in the process and help one another resulting in the formation of a community. The pilgrimage is in an unexplored territory. So, they should be alert and cautious at all times. They may reach a stage where they are confronted with three or four different routes. The pilgrims would be at a loss to choose the right route without a sign-post or a proper guide. Politicization of religion, commercialization of service institutions and criminalization of the innocents are the attractive routes which allow some to grab power, wealth and popularity instantly and unethically. The rest would be confused as to which road to pursue. But, if we remove the last 's' from the word 'crossroads' which represents 'self' and turn small 'c' representing 'centre' to capital 'C' representing Christ, that is if we remove 'self centredness and make Christ the centre of our lives the word then becomes *Crossroad*, which means the road leading to the Cross. So the Christian pilgrims, need no reason to be confused if they follow the way of the Cross. Pictorially, we can imagine the Cross to represent four different concerns. The top end of the Cross representing God, moving in to the world. One end of the horizontal plank represents individuals moving to have personal encounter with Christ. The other end represents the Christian community moving to have collective experience of Christ. These three namely God's presence, individuals and the community meet at the centre. In their movement from the centre there is no confusion, for there is only one way left, and that is to the other end of the vertical plank which represents the world. Individuals and the community need to go with the presence of God to the world. Therefore, the way of the Cross is the only way for Christian pilgrims in their journey. The spiritual experience we have as Christians, will be complete, only when God draws the whole world unto Himself. In other words, only when the entire world responds to the presence of God in their midst then the Mission is complete. The Christian Church is a partner with God in this process.

To be at the centre of the Cross means that individuals and the community need to be illumined by the light of Christ as we have noticed in the second mission module. This light needs to be reflected to the world. What does this mean? It means 'to set our house in order so that the world can see light in our house. It also means Gospel should be made relevant to the people in their own context. The way of the Cross demands qualities of love and sacrifice from the pilgrims. Love means: respecting others in spite of differences in their faith, culture and practices. It means: expressing solidarity with the weak, suffering and oppressed. Sacrifice means: giving and not accumulating. It means: undergoing suffering for the well-being of others. In this context, celebration of Christian festivals must acquire new meaning for us. The celebration of Christmas, God becoming man for the sake of humanity, must inspire us to dedicate ourselves to take the presence of God to the world. Maundy Thursday must become a day of remembrance, (Ex.12:21-27) a day in which we trace our past history to the period of oppression. Good Friday should be the day of surrender remembering the supreme sacrifice made by our Lord. Easter should become a day of rejoicing – rejoicing in the liberation brought by our Lord from bondage. Harvest Festival should be a day of not only Thanksgiving, but also a day of confession as in Deut. Chapter 26. We should be able to make a confession on that day saying our 'ancestors were in bondage not in a foreign land but in our own land. They could not worship God like others; they were not allowed to walk in the public path; they could not drink from the wells used by others; they could not share the meals with others. They were treated harshly; they were afflicted them; imposed hard labour on them … When our forefathers cried unto the Lord, He heard their cries and liberated them from oppression. Today as liberated people we celebrate this Harvest Festival and offer our gifts to be used for liberating work of people, who are under oppressed conditions'. This should be the way we celebrate our festivals.

Based on the analysis of the context and the exposition of the scriptural texts, I venture to suggest the following steps to the Christian community in general and the CSI in particular, as a possible way of continuing our participation in the mission of God.

1. Rejoicing in the Past

a. Rejoicing in our Spiritual Heritage

We need to be proud of the wholistic spirituality that we have received from the past. We are recipients of spirituality from three streams - the individual spirituality from the Vedic spirituality, the community spirituality from the Dalit religion and the combination of both from the western Christianity. The western Christianity has added one more dimension into this spirituality, namely, spirituality for others. Therefore, the Christian Church is practicing individual spirituality, community spirituality and spirituality for others which we have termed as 'spirituality for engagement' in the earlier chapters. All the three levels of spirituality are necessary for a Christian. We have received three approaches for spirituality from the Indian philosophy. They are: Gnana Marga, Bhakti Marga and Karma Marga – we as Christians though not acknowledged openly, practice all the three Margas in our spiritual quest. Reading the Bible and interpreting the same in context is Gnana Marga, surrendering ourselves to God through worship, prayer, meditation and singing are ways of expressing our Bhakti – our life style, our actions and particularly, our actions in selfless service constitute Karma Marga. We have also received spirituality, which deals with three dimensions of life namely, 'Life beyond, life in the world and life for others'. So, we need to be proud of this tradition. Our spirituality is not just our own efforts but also is inherited of which we need to be proud of and rejoice in it.

b. Rejoicing in our History

The membership of CSI is drawn from Vedic religion, non-Vedic religion described as backward classes and Dalit and tribal religion. As mentioned in the previous chapter, the members from Vedic religion are proud of their history and they preserve and perpetuate their history. Let me illustrate this point. During the years 1988 – 1989, the Diocese and the Synod sent me for higher studies to Candler School of Theology of Emory University in Atlanta, Georgia, USA. My relative who was staying in Calgary, Canada invited me to spend Christmas holidays with his family. To celebrate that event, he invited his friends for a dinner party. During the course of casual conversation, one gentleman from Kerala asked me as to how many generations I can trace my history. I replied four. Then he replied that he can trace his history to sixty four generations. At that time it looked as an inane remark, but, on reflection it was meant to establish his caste hierarchy over against mine.

Backward classes, as described in the previous chapter, through a process of Sanskritisation are upgrading their history to gain respectability. So, they retain their community feeling rather than emphasizing on the oppressive historical past. Let me illustrate this point. When I was a Pastor in St. Andrew's Church, every Sunday after the service, one person used to come to me asking me to find a bridegroom for his daughter. He would narrate the profile of his daughter and at the end always would add that the groom should be from South. I told him that I was not gifted in that area but even then he would persist his enquiry every Sunday. One day it struck me as to why he adds that last condition every time. Since I did not understand this strange addition, I asked my Church Secretary, Mr. Chellappa as to what the meaning was. He smiled and told me, 'Pastor, groom from South refers to the caste of the groom'. For the first time in my life, I was made to understand that the flames of communal undertones have not been extinguished even in the faith community.

The Dalit Christians irrespective of which communities they come from, have scant respect for their history, for there is nothing to be proud of in their history except the recollection of sufferings, oppression, humiliation and exploitation of their ancestors. So, they try to escape from such memory by neglecting it. On the other hand, the recollection of such a history can inspire those of us, who come from such background to commit ourselves to help those in oppressed conditions to be liberated. One of the very strong point of Israelites is their sense of history. They are not ashamed to confess that their ancestors were under bondage. Such a confession has brought community together as one. Likewise, Christians from Dalit communities should develop a sense of pride in their history.

When we say that we have to develop a sense of pride in our history, it does not mean the history of the castes that we come from. It is not the caste history that we need to be proud of. It is the history of how God liberated our ancestors from bondage. It is a salvation history that we need to celebrate. Liberation is same for everyone whether from high caste or backward class or Dalit caste, for it was brought about by God, only conditions in which people lived were different. The freedom that our forefathers and mothers enjoyed in Christ was more important for them than the call given to them by powerful people to return to their original caste groups. So, they continued with their faith in Christ and enjoyed the fellowship of the new community called the Church. They denounced the caste which was the basis of oppression and enjoyed table fellowship offered by Christ with other believers irrespective of their caste background. Participation in table fellowship was the ultimate symbol of their liberation from bondage. This is the history we need to remember and celebrate.

2. Removing the Barriers

Indian civilization dates back to 5000 years, so we have inherited several good things from this ancient civilization. We have also inherited certain practices which are not conducive to common good. Only two such practices are mentioned here.

a. Hierarchical Structure

It is an undisputed fact that Indian society is hierarchically organized. It is structured as a pyramid. It applies not only in the social realm, but also to economic and political realms also. Socially, it is organized on the basis of castes. Brahmins on top, Kshatriyas below Brahmins, Vysyas below Kshatriyas, Shudras below Vysyas and Dalits far below Shudras as a separate entity who are not even within the pyramid structure. Economically, the rich who are usually from Brahmin class are on top, the upper middle class are from other high castes, the lower middle class from backward communities and the other caste groups form the poor class. In terms of political control, the Brahmins control spiritual power, the Kshatriyas control political power, Vysyas control economic power, Shudras are servant class and the Dalits are slaves. In terms of the modern day democratic set up the ruling class is mostly from high caste, the bureaucracy is from high castes and backward classes with a sprinkling of representatives from Dalit communities and the rest common people.

Protestant Church in India from the beginning insisted on denouncing this hierarchical structure based on caste. They insisted that the converts should denounce caste before baptism. For the basic faith of Christianity proclaims 'there is no longer Jew or Greek, there is no longer slave or free, there is no longer male and female; for all of you are one in Christ Jesus'. But unfortunately the caste feelings have crept into the Church through the back door. It is perpetuated mostly through marriage alliances. It is not visible because it is the hierarchical mindset of people that sustains such a practice in the Church.

b. Hierarchical Thinking

The consequence of the above situation results in our thinking process as well. Those in authority whether at the Synod level or the Diocesan level or even at the congregational level think that they are chosen, hence the members should not only listen to them, but also obey them implicitly. But, Jesus has given a definition of leadership. He says, 'You know that among the Gentiles those whom they recognize as rulers lord it over them and their great ones are tyrants over them. But, it is not so among you; but whoever wishes to become great among you must be your servant and whoever wishes to be first among you must be slave of all.'(Mk.10:42-44). So hierarchical thinking is not Christian. It is in service that the leaders would find their authority.

Therefore perpetuation of caste mentality and hierarchical thinking is unscriptural and creates a barrier which needs to be broken for effective participation in God's mission.

c. Compartmentalization

Generally speaking, majority of Christians truly search for authentic spirituality whether educated or illiterate, rich or poor, people do have this urge for spirituality. They follow all the basic requirements in search of this spirituality. They attend the Church services regularly, read the Bible earnestly and pray to God daily. But, when it comes to its application in day to day life situations many would find it difficult. For the temptations and challenges in secular life are real and burdensome. Hence, consciously or unconsciously we compartmentalize between spirituality and secular life. We stay in one entering into the other only occasionally or when required. We must know that our faith is tested only in our day to day life situations. It is only our spiritual strength that can overcome all temptations and challenges. Hence, we need to break the unnatural barrier that we create for ourselves between spirituality and secular life.

3. Responding to Challenges

There is no Church on earth which is not facing challenges. Likewise, CSI also has number of challenges confronting it. The major challenge is to maintain *unity in diversity*. When the union took place, our leaders' main concern was to unite all the four denominations and yet retain their salient features. For instance, celebration of Eucharist in worship service as emphasized by the Anglican Church; the importance of Biblical preaching as found in the Reformed tradition, the role of lay preachers in building up of the congregation and particularly in the rural context as promoted by the Methodist Church and the lay participation in worship and administration as practiced by the Congregational Church could not be neglected by the Union Negotiators. All these elements were necessary for the common growth, they realized. Hence, they brought out a common liturgy incorporating all the essential elements from the Uniting Churches. The purpose was to unite all the denominations and yet give room for expression of different emphases. So, unity in diversity began at the Worship Service itself.

Today we see the majority of the congregations using the CSI liturgy while in some Dioceses a few congregations use CSI liturgy occasionally preferring to use their traditional liturgy more frequently. The combination of tradition with modern is visible to a perceptive eye in a cosmopolitan city like Bangalore. The worship service begins with a procession led by a cross bearer in St. Mark's Cathedral which is from Anglican background. The worship service in St. Andrew's Church begins with procession, but with Bible in front. This Church is from a Reformed tradition. There is no procession in Hudson Memorial Church which also encourages lay preaching. This Church is from Methodist background. Lay participation is very strong and lay leadership is prominent in Rice Memorial Church which is from the Congregational background. Further, the Church with Episcopalian background uses fermented wine and one chalice for Holy Communion, whereas, the non-Episcopalian background churches use grape juice and individual cups for the Holy Communion. The Churches which are established after the formation of CSI use either of these depending on the decision of their respective Committees. All of them use CSI liturgy, thus one can see unity in diversity being practiced in Worship Service in the CSI. Today to a large extent the denominational barrier has been broken in CSI.

The second challenge within this larger concern for unity in diversity is *integration*. The membership of CSI is not drawn from one homogenous community but from diverse communities. It is a historical fact that we have come from different communities. It cannot be denied. But, it is also a fact that we have been liberated from bondage – bondage of being tied to one's own caste background. When we worship we do not distinguish one from another on the basis of one's background. This unity is particularly demonstrated when we come to the Lord's Table. However, sometimes these traits of being tied to our old affiliations come out in the open. I have witnessed this in marriage alliances, appointments to the Church

Institutions and elections to the Pastorate level, Diocesan level and even at the CSI Synod level. These traits affect the very unity of the Church. Once, one prominent Bishop, when he came to our Diocese remarked referring to some people who hailed from his Diocese and settled in Bangalore saying, that they are 'my people'. I had to correct him saying, 'Bishop, they were once your people, but now they are my people'. This mentality is destructive for unity. It seems that we are united spiritually but divided socially. The challenge for the Church is to integrate people coming from diverse background. The unity in diversity demands integration of all sections of people into one.

Further, integration must include language groups. The CSI is found in all the four southern States of India, speaking four different languages. We worship in our mother tongue, be it in cities or villages. There are a few congregations, where worship service is conducted in Hindi for the benefit of people coming from North India. A small percentage of people prefer to worship in English. There are a few Dioceses where multiple languages are used in worship. This is the strength of CSI – people worshipping in a language that they are familiar with. But, this strength is also our weakness. There is no programme to integrate people speaking different languages. This lack of understanding and co-ordination between different language groups might turn into 'communal vote banks' at the time of elections, if not addressed. Hence, integration of different language groups remains a challenge for the CSI.

Unity in diversity also demands *inclusiveness.* The Church consists of men, women, youth and children. All must feel comfortable in the worship service. All their spiritual needs should be met. It is only through active participation that all the above categories of people not only feel comfortable, but are also spiritually nurtured. The CSI liturgy gives enough scope to include activities for all the categories of people such as physical activity for children, praise and worship for youth, personal testimony for men and women etc. A good pastor encourages people to come up with innovative programmes and increases their participation in the worship service. Where there is lively worship there is better fellowship and creates interest among people to participate in all the activities of the church. The congregation should not become mere spectators, neither should the pastor become the mono actor. Inclusiveness of different categories of people in worship is a requirement to maintain unity in diversity in the Church.

It is not only in the Worship Service, but even in administrative activities women and youth should be included. The CSI has demonstrated its progressive outlook by including the following clause in its Constitution, while forming Committees: 'In all such Committees at least 25% of the total membership (excluding Officers of the Council) shall be youth under the age of 35 years and 25% shall be women'. (CSI Constitution Ch.VIII, Clause 10, page 74) The Constitution, in removing constitutional barrier to ordain women to the Presbyterate, has opened the door for women in ordained ministry as well. Now many Dioceses have both men and women on the roll of ordained ministries, though some are yet to catch up with this inclusive understanding of this ministry. So, the CSI has made it mandatory to include women and youth in all the Committees beginning from the Pastorate level to the CSI Synod level which is a good progress. But two concerns emerge in the implementation of the above clause. The first one is that even though 50% of the membership in all the Committees consist of youth and women when it comes to the leadership positions in majority of the cases it is always men who are preferred. Leadership position is denied to youth and women either by design or by default. The second concern is that in many cases youth and women are chosen not for their talents but merely as supporters of powerful persons or invisible dominant party-for we do not have party system in electoral process. In such a situation, the youth and women chosen to Committees are mere spectators in the Committees and not as active participants. Both the above concerns need to be addressed adequately so that the voice of youth and women are heard in policy making bodies.

Unity in diversity calls for *accommodation.* A democratic church functions differently from that of traditional church, where authority is derived from tradition or even from monolithic Church, where authority is derived from hierarchy. The core principle of democracy is participation of all people. Even though the Committees and leadership are chosen through an electoral process, all their decisions automatically become subject of discussion and debate among different sections of society. Likewise, in the Church also, all decisions taken by the leadership and the governance of the organization becomes a subject matter among congregation members. It is particularly so in CSI because it upholds the principle of participation of laity in governance. (Ch. IV, Clause 4, page 32) While the majority of people choose to remain silent, a tiny minority at the Pastorate level, Diocesan level and at the Synod level choses to voice their concerns publicly. As the days go by, these voices of concern are turned into voices of 'dissent'. In order to ensure that their voices are heard this tiny minority resort to legal remedies filing both civil and criminal cases, print their articles in print media and appear in electronic media and also send out messages through social media. We need to recognize that presently those who are involved in such acts are not only fighting for what they claim to be 'just cause', but in the process they are destroying the very image of the leaders and much more so of the Church. Many a time, their intentions may not be honest, otherwise how can some people who had enjoyed leadership positions in the Church and its institutions suddenly find fault with the Church? Does that mean that in their time the Church and its institutions were perfect and now they are corrupt? Or how can people with meager financial resources fight expensive legal battles against the Church in the Courts? However, the Church needs to take note of the justice concerns that these people are raising and address them sincerely and honestly. Further, we need to understand that 'dissent voice' is a necessary outcome of democratic system. The Church having adopted democratic form of government cannot escape from reality. We need to create an appropriate forum to hear and address the concerns of people who raise dissenting voices. Fighting a legal battle is expensive and time consuming. The Church needs to learn to accommodate the dissenting voices within its structure itself.

The CSI is facing one more serious challenge – a challenge of *incorporation*. It is a challenge to incorporate the village Christian congregations into the mainstream. We may recollect that villages were the cradle of Protestant Christianity. Village people themselves became carriers of the Gospel to the neighbours. Missionaries, who were critical in the initial stages, later extended pastoral care by training and appointing local leaders as Evangelists and Bible Women. Pastoral care was available within the context of the village congregations themselves. Further, missionaries opened Primary Schools and Dispensaries to serve not only Christians but the entire population. So, the spiritual nurture went hand in hand with social empowerment activities. Over the years, the educated moved from villages to cities in search of jobs and economic freedom. Service institutions in the villages are either closed down or in a dying stage. The pastors posted to villages prefer to stay in urban centres and occasionally visit the village congregations following the model of visiting professors. As a result, the village congregations, which were once bubbling with enthusiasm to participate in God's mission are now left to care for themselves. It is to the credit of village Christians, that they continue with their unwavering faith in Christ.

The members who migrated from villages have become part of city congregations. The difference between village and urban congregations is glaring. The village congregations are poor, uneducated, having no status in life, whereas urban congregations are economically strong, consisting of people, who have occupied important positions in Church and Society and therefore, are influential. As a result, the urban congregations come to the forefront in Christian activities relegating the village congregations to the background. It is this gap that needs to be bridged. The Church has an enormous responsibility of strengthening village congregations by providing adequate pastoral care through innovative programmes. Then the village congregations and the urban congregations together can become effective instruments for the cause of the Mission of God.

4. Re-Assessing the Structure

The Union Negotiators had two major concerns in accepting a governing structure for the United Church. The first concern was to find a structure which brings unity while retaining the salient feature of the uniting churches. The second one was to find a structure which demonstrates our Indianness. To satisfy the first concern, they adopted three levels of governance, namely, the Synod, the Diocese and the congregation. To satisfy the second concern they adopted the democratic pattern of governance. It must be said to the credit of union negotiators that the combination of two concerns did yield some good results. It brought unity among the different denominations. It allowed participation of lay members in the formation of government. Unity in diversity became the basic theme of the CSI. However, as the days went by some lacunae in the structure could be noticed. While it is a great principle to affirm three levels of administration, they cannot function effectively, without a properly defined powers and functions and a system to assess the effectiveness and introduce corrective measures periodically.

Secondly, while democratic system is the best form of government the Church has adopted, only a part of democratic form of governance in accepting electoral system is in practise. The other requirements such as effective body for re-dressal of grievances and a platform to discuss and debate the dissenting voice is not established. Further, with the intervention of the secular government in all the corporate activities of the society including the Church, the principle of unity in diversity is put to severe test. There are rules and regulations stipulating conditions for admission, collection of fees, pattern of syllabi, system of administration in our educational activities, imposed by the government. There are rules stipulating the running of the Hospitals and medical institutions. There are rules for receiving and rendering accounts from foreign sources. There are rules for accounting system and submission of accounts to government bodies. In all these the government stipulates a uniform system to be followed. For instance, as pointed out earlier, the CSITA is registered under Company's Act. The Company's Act demands that all activities of the Company should be brought under one umbrella, follow one system in accounting and in maintaining and submission of accounts. This principle of uniformity comes in direct confrontation with the principle of unity in diversity at times. In order to rectify such a situation a suitable structure of governance needs to be implemented. This calls for a thorough assessment of the existing structures, which may lead to constitutional amendments. We need to remind ourselves that constitution should be dynamic and not static. Amendments in piecemeal can only be cosmetic in nature, but does not touch the heart of the problem. Therefore, a review of Constitution taking into consideration mission in its context should be taken up seriously.

5. Re-Focussing on Mission

That the CSI is a mission focused Church is undeniable. The Church is involved in mission through the medium of different models mentioned above. We have also noted that the mission is only singular, i.e. God reconciling the world unto Himself. Implementing this mission is multi-dimensional depending on the perception of those who are involved in mission and the context of the recipients. However, the Church needs to guard itself against the proliferation of mission activities which might end up in losing focus on mission itself. Hence, the Church needs to constantly ask itself the question in what way our involvement enhances the process of God's mission. It involves a process of 'reflection and action'. Our action should be based on our reflection. Reflection involves understanding the biblical testimony in the right perspective and being mindful of historical response, i.e. the testimony of our forefathers and mothers in their own context. Action involves innovative programmes suitable to the context and not a blind repetition of the programmes implemented in the past. In order to have a clear understanding of mission in context, let us re-capitulate briefly what we have stated earlier.

For Jesus fulfilling the will of God was mission of God. He implemented the mission by preaching, teaching and healing. Involvement in mission also meant for Jesus expressing solidarity with the marginalized and the poor. To fulfill God's mission Jesus took the way of the Cross, that is, to sacrifice his life on the Cross in order to draw people closer to God.

In the texts that we have looked into, for Paul effective mission can take place only when there is unity in the Church. In fact, for Paul unity is mission – but unity cannot be achieved if the Church is not involved in equipping the saints. Equipping the saints is the primary requisite for a Church to be united in mission.

The early missionaries inspite of their pietistic background, were also receptive to the context in which people lived but they never compromised on individual commitment to Christ. They used different methods in different contexts. To the educated, they used the rational way of presenting the Gospel, i.e. Gnana Marga. To the illiterates, they told biblical stories using the existing art forms and urging them to surrender to Christ, i.e. Bhakti Marga. To the sick and the dying they showed compassion, to the children they gave opportunity to be educated by opening schools. Through the educational institutions, they also gave opportunity for the children to interact with children of high caste background, and thereby overcome caste prejudices. This is Karma Marga.

Through the mass movements our ancestors have taught us that mission is not limited to individuals alone but it extends to communities as well and particularly to the communities under oppression. They demonstrated that community spirituality is equally important along with individual spirituality to be involved in mission of God.

While the early missionaries treated Hinduism with disdain, the intellectuals of the Christian community began to treat it with respect. Some began to reflect on some Christian concepts using concepts found in Hinduism, while others began to unravel how Christ is already at work in Hinduism and called for a dialogical approach in mission.

As mentioned earlier, for the union negotiators, denominationalism has its roots in western Christianity. It was not suitable to Indian situation, they realized. Unity among the denominations was the basic requirement for mission. Further the structure should be suitable for Indian context. Therefore, for the union negotiators the United Church rooted in Indian soil was a basic requirement for mission.

From the above descriptions, it is obvious that while mission of God is one, the methodologies differ from context to context. Mission should be understood as multi-dimensional in context. Understanding the context is equally important to evolve an effective strategy and action oriented programme in mission. The context today is entirely different from that of missionary era. At that time, there was no conceptual unity in Hinduism, their unity was limited only to caste structure. The introduction of Christianity, and particularly aggressive evangelism adopted by the missionaries as well as movement of groups of people to Christianity, has altered the mindset of Hindu adherents. It prompted thinking Hindus to start reform movements by deleting some evil practices. Secondly, the introduction of Christianity has made intellectuals among the Hindu community to raise the conscience among its adherents resulting in Renaissance of Hinduism all over India. Thirdly, a section of the people also formed Hindu militant groups. The basic purpose of the first was to reform Hinduism by looking inwards. The basic purpose of the second is to instill pride of their religion among Hindu practioners. The basic purpose of the third group is to protect Hinduism from the onslaughts of the 'outsiders' who 'defile' the society of Hinduism. Today, we have progressive Hindus who have given up a number of practices which are not suitable to modern way of life. We also have a large number of Hindus who are proud of their religion. We also have a few organizations who are wedded to the Hindutva ideology and go to any extent of 'protecting' Hinduism from the perceived 'threat from alien religions', namely, Christianity and Islam. We can call this process as consolidation of Hinduism.

The relationship between religion and politics has also changed drastically from the period of missionaries. We noted earlier that the East India Company was against missionaries. This meant separation of State and religion. The British Empire adopted a policy of 'neutrality'. It meant neither promoting nor assisting any religion or religious activities. On the basis of this policy of neutrality, the British Empire, consisting of Christians, removed teaching of the Bible in all educational institutions. On the whole, the policy of separation of State and Religion was very much prevalent. But today's context is entirely different. Religion and Politics intermingle with each other. As we have observed earlier, Hinduism operates at different levels such as philosophy, practical observance, social structure and culture. All these make inroads into public domain in some form or the other; some of which are absorbed by the State. Conversely, the State also passes legislations and makes rules and regulations which are in the domain of religion. As a result, we see politicization of religion in India today. The process of politicization of religion begins at the very beginning of the electoral system. The politicians capture religious heads or community heads of caste groups at the time of elections. Religious groups and caste groups are considered as vote banks by politicians. In turn, they try to bring legislations, favouring the groups which support the politicians. Party tickets are issued based on the community's strength of the candidate in the constituency. Study of Hindu religious texts is introduced in the syllabi at various levels of educational institutions. Re-writing of history, based on the cultural past glory is emphasized. Legislations based on the religious convictions of the powers that be, are introduced affecting the daily lives of people in terms of what to eat, how to dress, how to behave in public places, and to implement this there are fringe elements who are being supported tacitly by the powers that be. In short, the situation is no longer separation of State and Religion. It is the politicization of religion that is prevalent in today's India.

Thirdly, the context of the Dalits has also changed considerably. The Constitution has removed certain social disabilities with which the Dalits were suffering. They now can worship in a temple, use the public roads and wells, have access to public services. Further, by way of 'affirmative action' their education and employment are ensured. They even have reservation in political representation based on the proportion of their communities. Even though caste prejudices continue, the Dalits seem to have been included in the cultural milieu of cultural nationalism.

Fourthly, the context in which the Church is called to be involved in mission is different from that of missionary era. Missionaries preached the Gospel with the sole purpose of converting people to Christianity. Today, the Supreme Court has passed a judgement to the effect that the right to propagate does not include right to convert. Further, many States have introduced Freedom of Religion Bill, restricting the Christian missionary activities. It should be mentioned to the credit of Christian Church, that in spite of prevalence of so many bills so far, not a single person hase been convicted for converting people using 'force, inducement or fraudulent means'. Missionaries started educational and medical institutions, but the State has imposed a number of conditions in running and administering these institutions. Further, the Christians from Dalit background are denied all the benefits accruing for scheduled caste people which to say the least is discriminatory.

It is in this context, that the church has been called upon to involve in mission of God. From the above description, we can conclude that the methodology of implementing mission differs from context to context. A strategy adopted in one context may not be suitable to the other. Therefore, it requires a collective effort. Mission is not a sporadic action, but, a carefully drawn out reflection-action process and particularly if we want to see congregations as mission agents. We need a visionary leader at the centre supported by the concerned elected body, who not only provide a vision for mission, but also able to understand the context in which each congregation is placed. We need presbyters and local leaders who are capable of capturing the vision for mission and translate it into local context. In particular, the Presbyters and local leaders must act as catalysts in discovering the hidden talents among the congregation members and encourage them to use it for the common good. Thirdly, the job of the Presbyter, in co-operation with the other leaders, is to equip the congregation members by using innovative and participatory method of worship by giving them wholistic biblical teaching as well as making the gospel relevant to the context. A congregation can effectively involve in mission, only if there is harmonious relationship among members and there is co-operation and co-ordination between one to the other. Above all, the programme that is envisaged for a community must ensure that the recipient community feels that their human dignity is held intact, and that they only experience Christ's love through the action of the Christian community. Therefore, the mission has to be *with* the people and not *for* the people to be effective.

6. Returning to Basics

Among the many things, that the early church as a community were involved, three of their activities stand out. They are: Worship, study of the Bible and equipping of saints. These three activities sustained and encouraged them in their spiritual journey. There is no doubt that the present day church is continuing these activities, but we need to strengthen them.

a. Worship

The early Church took the central act of Jewish faith, namely, worship and made it as a central act of Christian faith. From the time the Christian faith began to spread after the Pentecost, worship became a central act of the new community. The very first converts were involved in 'apostles teaching, fellowship, breaking of the bread and prayers. (Acts 2:42) They spent their time together in the temple, (vs. 46) praising God and having the goodwill of the people. (vs. 47)

True worship achieves three things. Firstly, it brings us face to face with God and we are in the presence of God. We begin to wonder, filled with awe about the attributes of God so we adore Him. We realize what we are and all that we have, has come from God, so we thank Him. We realize our sinful nature in the presence of the Almighty God, so we confess our sins. We know that God will fulfill all our needs, so we bring our supplications before Him. We also become aware of our responsibility towards others, so we bring intercessory prayers before God. Secondly, true worship achieves fellowship among the believers. Worship not only is a link to God, but is also a basis to achieve fellowship among believers. It makes us to open ourselves to others; understand others and share our God given gifts with others. This act makes others to open themselves to us, resulting in establishing deeper fellowship between one another. Thirdly, it prepares us to go into the world in confidence and involve in transforming activities in the world. Every worship service must be like a Transfiguration experience for the disciples where they experienced the true bliss of God's presence (Mk. 9:2-8). The purpose was that they should come down and face the challenges of the world to make the human beings truly human.

The CSI liturgy has all the necessary elements such as, adoration, thanksgiving, confession, supplication and intercession. Thereby, it is a wholistic order of service. It also gives room for silence for individuals to reflect and meditate. Further, there is scope for extempore prayers as well. Thus, CSI liturgy is a well- balanced liturgy. However, constant use will bring in familiarity and the familiarity may lose the essence. When that happens it becomes a ritual and not a spontaneous response to God's goodness. It also loses creativity. We need to guard against such situations. Another aspect of CSI liturgy is that it is a combination of Eastern and Western spirituality. The West insists on order; whereas the East insists on surrender. For the Western mind, God is a God of order. But, for the Eastern mind it is Bhakti that matters. Therefore, liturgy expresses order whereas silent meditation, singing lyrics, extempore prayers represents the eastern Bhakti. How much importance we give to our eastern inputs in worship is a matter of debate depending on the tradition that we follow and the language that we use.

The fact that we emphasize on order as well as Bhakti has made one forget celebratory aspect of worship. This was brought home to me with my experience as a member of the Executive Committee of the World Alliance of Reformed Churches. The Executive Committee used to meet once a year in different parts of the world. I invited the WARC on behalf of the CSI to hold its meetings in Bangalore in 2001. For the inaugural worship which was held in St. Mark's Cathedral a new liturgy prepared by some of our pastors was used. At the end of the service I asked the General

Secretary, Rev. Dr. Setri Nyomi from Ghana with whom I had a good rapport as to what his experience of the liturgy was? He replied, it was good, but there is no celebration in your liturgy. I did not understand the import of his comment till I went to the General Assembly of WARC in 2004. One day, all the delegates were taken on a 'pilgrimage tour' to a place about 200 kms away from Accra. This is on the coast of Ghana, adjacent to the sea was a hill and on top of the hill there was a fort, inside the fort a huge area used as barracks for soldiers. Inside the barracks there was a quadrangle in the centre which was open to the sky. At the far end there was a dungeon, which was directly connected to the sea. The first floor above this quadrangle had rooms for Officers with a chapel at the centre. We were told that the army would go around and plunder the villages confiscating their animals for their food, capturing able bodied men to be shipped as slaves to different parts of the world and young women were brought and kept inside the barracks. They would be paraded naked in the quadrangle. The Officer from the first floor would choose a particular young lady and ask the sentries to bring her up to his room. After using her, the Officer would ask the sentries to throw her into the dungeon. As we heard the story, almost all of us were in tears. When we returned, the Organisers had arranged a 'thanksgiving service' in which the delegates from Netherlands began to confess for the sins of their ancestors with tears in their eyes. All the delegates were very quiet the incident still reverberating in their minds. Then suddenly a few African delegates came to the centre accompanied by drums and singing and dancing. Their exuberance was such that all the delegates including those from Netherlands joined the singing and dancing. The General Secretary then explained that 'experience of the historical past should not make us bitter. On the other hand, it should lead us to celebration – celebrating the mighty hand of God in liberating our ancestors from a life of slavery'.

I know that I could not introduce dance in worship service as it is not our culture but I asked my pastors to introduce 'praise and worship' in our churches wherever possible so that there is a semblance of celebration in our worship service. I am glad that some of the Churches in the Diocese have incorporated this in their worship service allowing young people to lead the congregation using instruments which are not traditionally used in our worship services. True worship literally lifts us up to a higher plane to experience the goodness of God, establishes fellowship among believers and prepares us for God's work in the world. This is the true Bhakti Marga.

b. Study of the Bible

Protestant Churches from the beginning have attached importance to the knowledge of scripture in its original language. Desiderius Erasmus of Rotterdam was the first one to publish Greek New Testament in the year 1516, which was made available to scholars. This gave them opportunity to study New Testament in its original language. Similarly, Reuchlin of Germany acquired the knowledge of Hebrew from a Jew and made available the Old Testament in Hebrew. The knowledge of the Bible in its original language led to criticism of the prevailing practices of the Church. Later, when the scriptures were translated into various European languages, even the ordinary people had the privilege of reading the Bible in their own language. This had a tremendous effect on the life of the Church which led the Reformers to declare 'scripture alone' as one of the cardinal principles of the Reformation movement. In England, Henry VIII ordered in 1538, that a copy of the Bible in English be placed in every parish church. This became the basis on which the King James Version published in 1611 became the authorized version and was accepted. We also noticed that the missionaries who came to India were the products of Pietistic movement which again emphasized on the primacy of scriptures. So, it is no wonder that the Protestant Churches in India have also adopted 'scripture alone' as one of the cardinal principles of their Church. The knowledge of Scripture among the CSI members is quite high and particularly among women and youth. Some read it book by book in their daily devotions and some others following 'daily readings' given out either by the Church or by one of the Christian agencies.

Reading the scriptures is different from studying the scriptures. Mere reading may lead one to come to a conclusion which may or may not be the original intention of the passage. Sometimes, it may also lead to ultra-fundamentalist position which is detrimental to the person concerned as well as to the society at large. Mere reading may also lead to 'knowledge' without the 'substance'. The Bible has to be studied to understand its true meaning. We should not be under the impression that studying the scriptures is only for the scholars and theological students and not for congregation members who are not equipped to study in such a rigorous and disciplined manner. On the other hand, it is more important for the congregation members who encounters day to day challenges in the world to understand the true meaning of the scripture so that with those spiritual values they can face the challenges boldly.

That the message of the Bible is for every human being in all seasons and everywhere is undeniable, for it deals with how God has been acting in history to save humanity; His decisive act in sending his son to the world; how God empowers his Church to become His partners in his re-creative and redemptive work. It also deals with how human beings have been responding to God at different times in history and the call given by God to them to turn to Him. In this way, the Bible deals with salvation history. But, the Bible was originally written to meet the needs of different people in different situations. The different books of the Bible have been written over a period of 1000 years. So, we need to understand the text in its own context in order to make it relevant to our context. Let me illustrate this point.

All the four Gospels are the accounts of the life, ministry, death and resurrection of Jesus Christ. But, each one was written to cater to the specific needs of that time. Mark was the earliest Gospel written in a context when there was no Christian literature available in writing. For Mark, narration of Jesus' activities on earth beginning with his baptism was important, so it does not carry infancy narratives or resurrection events – only an announcement that 'he had been raised', if we take the majority scholars opinion that the real ending of Mark is 16:8. Matthew traces the geneology to Abraham because he wanted to present Jesus, the Messiah was son of David who was from Abrahamic descent. This was because Matthew was writing to people of Jewish background. Luke traces the geneology to Adam because he was passionate about Jesus' graciousness towards the outcastes, the poor, women and Samaritans. Luke links Jesus' geneology to Adam and not just to Abraham. John was writing to a cosmopolitan community with philosophical bent of mind, so he traces the incarnation to the beginning of creation itself stating that the word which was with God became incarnate in the world. The purpose of the passage becomes clearer if it is understood in its own context.

Let us take another example. St. Paul's phrase 'justification by faith' and 'faith without works is dead' by St. James may appear contradictory to one another. In fact, Martin Luther called Letter of St. James as a 'right strawy epistle' but if we understand both the concepts in its own context the meaning of both becomes clear. St. Paul was writing to first generation Christians who needed encouragement to grow in faith, so Paul emphasizes the role of faith in the life of believers. But, St. James was writing to the second generation Christians who in the name of faith neglected the right conduct, so James had to remind them that right response to the Gospel is through their works. Understood in their own context then Paul and James are not really in conflict. Paul would definitely agree that the good works are the necessary fruits of good faith and James would not hesitate to say the basis of good works is deep faith in the Lord.

The third example is the controversy between Jewish Christians and Gentile Christians in the early Church that made the two stalwarts namely, Peter and Paul taking opposite sides which ultimately resulted in the Jerusalem Council. (See Acts 15 and Gal. 2). The controversy was imposition of Jewish Christian practice of circumcision upon Gentile Christians. But, deep within it was a controversy of the two communities integrating with one another. God had to teach Peter through a vision in Acts 10, that He does not distinguish between human beings and He reconciles both to Himself. Do the people who perpetuate casteism in the Church have anything to say against this word of God?

The above mentioned examples demonstrate the fact that if the Bible is understood in its own context, the meaning of the word, a verse in the passage or a book in the Bible becomes clear. But, understanding the Bible in its own context is not sufficient. That understanding has to be transmitted to our context. When the meaning of the Biblical text is unraveled in its own context and applied to our own context, diligently and faithfully, then it becomes Word of God for us. Therefore, study of the Bible is necessary for our spiritual growth and for participation in the ministry and mission effectively. This is the true Gnana Marga.

Let me illustrate how a good Bible Study group can influence one's own thinking. Exposure to local Christian life prior to the actual meetings of the Executive Committee was a practice in WARC. In the year 2000, when the Executive Meeting of the WARC met in Indonesia, all the delegates were sent to different parts of Indonesia. I was sent to Maden, a hill station, and a devoted Christian Doctor's family welcomed me to their home. The lady of house was kind enough to take me and show me the different activities conducted by the Church. One evening, after dinner she took me to a Bible Study group. The group met in a shoe shop owned by a Christian. There were about 30-35 people young and old, men and women present in the study group. All of us sat on the floor and at around 8 p.m. the Bible Study started. The Bible Study was in Gharo language and my host was kind enough to sit next to me and translate the proceedings in English for me. I could see three things in everyone's hand – a Bible, a book containing Bible Study notes published by the Church and a scribbling pad with a pen in which each one had scribbled their thoughts.

The meeting was moderated by a young teenage girl. The participation in the discussion was extremely good, the chairperson carefully prompting the silent listeners to give their opinion. At some stage in the discussion, one person asked for the exact translation of a particular word in the Bible. After discussion, they realized that they did not have the exact word in their language which conveys the true meaning of the Biblical word.

Then I shared my own experience in a situation like that with them. In the year 1983, I was asked to be the Co-ordinator of translation of the New Testament which was to be brought out jointly by the Bible Society of India and the Roman Catholic Church. The Roman Catholic Kannada Christians did not have their own version of the New Testament then. We were correcting the translation by an individual in the committee. The draft on that day was on Romans. When it came to the word 'righteousness' as it applied to human beings, we checked the word used in all the four Dravidian languages. We found that all the four languages used a word which indicates 'the one who has conquered sin' but the Bible is emphatic that no one is sinless except Jesus Christ. We struggled hard to find a suitable word but ultimately had to give up and 'paraphrased' to bring out the original meaning. When I shared this experience with them they were so thrilled and said that they would communicate this outcome to those who prepared the official notes for them. The Bible Study went beyond midnight and no one grumbled. This Bible Study has remained fresh in my mind for the lessons that it taught me –

- Preparation for the Bible Study – the leadership of the Church involved in preparing the Bible Study material
- Availability of the material for all
- Individual members' study and preparation
- Participation of the members in discussion
- Encouragement of the young people in asking them to take up leadership even when elders were present.
- The desire to understand the true meaning of the Bible.
- The willingness to apply the same in their day to day context.

History confirms that study of the Scriptures had revolutionary effect at the time of Reformation. It motivated the Christians of the West to bring Gospel to our land. The Church should now take the study of the Bible seriously in order to remain relevant in God's mission.

c. Equipping the Saints

Worship connects us emotionally to God and the community. Study of the Bible in its own context provides us rational basis for our faith. But, this faith has to be applied in our day to day life. Every job in the world, be it big or small, reputed or menial, requires certain skills. Skills are imparted through training, either through institutional training or training on the job. It is the same in the case of application of our faith into our daily life. But, life situations differ from individual to individual, community to community, society to society. So, 'one size fits all' policy will not be useful in different situations in life. All that can be done is to impart skills which can be used by individuals and community in their own contexts. Preparing the individuals and the faith community and imparting necessary skill is called equipping the saints.

In the formative stages of Protestant Christianity in India we had three centres to impart Christian education. Firstly, the family – every Christian family used to begin the day with family prayers and end the day with family prayers, particularly mothers used to teach the children Christian values and influence their behavior and conduct. The joint family system was another added advantage in shaping the behavior of all the members of the family. Modern nuclear family system in an urban setting has brought many changes in our family life. Both husband and wife are working and they leave home at different times and return at different times and so time available for family is very limited and as a result, Christian education at home becomes a casuality among other things.

Secondly, Christian educational institutions were the centres imparting Christian education. Study of the Bible was compulsory in all Schools. In fact from the reports of my alma mater, I notice that most of the prizes in Bible examination used to be bagged by students of other faiths. But, with the Government stipulation that Schools cannot teach scriptures, this centre of learning is also closed.

That leaves only the third centre, namely, the Church for imparting Christian education. In fact, we must appreciate the vision of our forefathers and mothers in creating a conducive atmosphere in the Church by establishing various wings such as Sunday School, Youth Group, Women's Group, Men's Group, Professional Fellowship, Teacher's Fellowship, Medical Personnel Fellowship wherein faith is applied in their own context. Each Diocese has a Committee or Department to deal with these issues. Similarly, the CSI Synod also has established different departments to help the Church in organizing training programmes for various interest groups in the Diocese. But with all its good intentions the Church has failed to provide a sustainable and long lasting Christian education programme for all and particularly for the congregations. The purpose of Christian education is two-fold. One, to prepare and instill skills in the individuals, to face the challenges of the world with Christian values. Two, to prepare and instill skills for the congregations to be involved in secular life. For instance, how can a Christian lead a life worthy of calling in a context, where clear discrimination is made in the work place simply because he/she professes Christian faith? That is never discussed in our Christian education programme. Or what it means to be involved in mission in a context of Supreme Court ruling, 'propagation does not include conversion' or Hindu fundamentalists involving in 'Ghar Wapsi' programme is never debated in our Christian education programme. Equipping the saints means preparing and providing skills for people to face the challenges in the world with a Christian perspective and devise concrete action plans suitable to the context. Each action should be relevant to the context and it should be based on Christian faith. This involves 'reflection-action-reflection' process. This is Karma Marga. The Bhakti Marga which involves emotions (heart), the Gnana Marga which involves reason (mind) leads to Karma Marga that is planned actions. Therefore, our surrendering to God, our study of the Scripture and our life style and actions are all integrally connected to one another and not separate from each other.

Let me illustrate from my experience how good initiatives will see their end if a proper planning is not made to sustain them for the future. I served in Tumkur Area from 1976 to 1983. During this time, I was also elected as Area Chairman. Tumkur Area which is the only area which covers a radius of about 100 kms from Tumkur. It is a rural area. People were poor and contribution to the Church was minimal. The Diocese did not help the Area financially as well. As an Area Chairman, first I began to have Presbyters Fellowship once a month. To cover the expenses each Pastor would contribute Rs. 20/- towards the travel pool and each time one pastor would host the lunch as part of his/her contribution. The fellowship really became strong and we began to discuss various progrmmes necessary for the development of the area. One such was a Sunday School Teachers' Training programme. We thought of innovative programmes. The plan was to bring all the Sunday School Teachers together on one weekend every month and impart teaching involving a child psychologist, a craft teacher, a counselor, a pastor etc. They would learn from them on Saturday and Sunday of that week-end and implement what they have learnt in their respective Sunday

Schools and return the following month for reflection and further input. This went on for six months. Realizing the importance of training, the churches and the individuals in the congregation contributed towards the expenses. The result was phenomenal. In my own church earlier there were only 30 children attending Sunday School. At the end of six months we had 250 children. The Teachers were extremely happy about what they learnt and all the congregations in the area were appreciative of the programme. After a few years, the initial enthusiasm died down and the Sunday School went back to its old style. It is because we failed to think of training as a continuous process.

The second example is from the CSI Synod. After every Synod the Executive sets up various committees and commissions. Usually each Bishop is asked to chair a particular committee or commission. I was asked to be the Chairman of the Christian Education Department for three terms, Rev. B. D. Prasada Rao who has now become the Bishop of Rayalaseema Diocese was the Director. The Committee envisaged writing of a syllabus for different age groups for Sunday Schools throughout the CSI. The Director identified talented Pastors and lay-people from various Dioceses and completed their work which was approved by the Committee. Along with the syllabus they brought out Teachers' Guide Book and Children's Work Book. All these were translated into four Southern languages. The Director convened the meeting of the Directors of Christian Education from each Diocese and explained the salient features of the new syllabus. The books were sent to the Dioceses. Some used it and a majority of the congregations did not. It was a visionary project but we failed to 'train the trainers'.

The above two examples depict that equipping the saints should be a continuous process. It should be innovative and contextual. We should also train required personnel to continue the initiative. There should be an appraisal system so that mistakes can be rectified. Such a process of equipping would definitely yield good results in the long run.

Conclusion

Hans Conzelmann in his book, *The Theology of St. Luke*, presents the salvation history according to Luke in three stages:

1. The period of Israel (Lk. 16:16).
2. The period of Jesus' ministry (Lk. 4:16ff and Acts 10:38) which he calls as centre of history.
3. The period of the Church beginning from Ascension till Parousia - Coming of the Lord.

The three epoches are interrelated. The Church owes its existence to the person of Jesus Christ and to his salvific action which is timeless and yet historical. Therefore, the period of Jesus is at the centre of salvation history. In the words of Conzelmann: 'The Church understands her present existence by recognizing that period (period of Jesus) as the authentic manifestation of salvation and thereby is enabled to understand not only her present, but also her future existence. And on the other hand, she comes to understand the nature of her Lord by looking at his historical existence'. (page 14). The salvation history begins with election of Israel as God's people, which is the beginning of the period of Israel. The period of Jesus' ministry begins with the announcement of God's mission being accomplished in his person (Luke 4:16ff). The period of the Church begins with the Ascension of Jesus as recorded in Luke 24:50-53 and Acts 1:6ff. This period continues till the coming of the Lord, 'which does not represent a stage within the course of salvation history, but the end of it'.

In this sense, the Church is often been described as New Israel - a newly chosen community, a community chosen to continue the work of Jesus on earth, for which they were empowered with the gift of the Holy Spirit. The Church, therefore, is a new Israel not for its merit nor for its genealogical superiority not even for its theological purity. It is chosen because its members have had the personal encounter with the Lord and the community is empowered with the gift of the Lord. It is purely out of His grace that God has chosen the Church to continue the work of Jesus on this earth. Therefore, the Church is a privileged community entrusted with the responsibility of God's mission in this world. The CSI is proud to be part of this chosen community.

The CSI is also blessed in many other ways which need to be recognized. Firstly, being an Indian Church it has imbibed in itself certain qualities from Indian spirituality. Individual spirituality of the Vedic religions, the community spirituality of the Dalit religions are embedded in our innermost being. The three approaches to spirituality namely, Bhakti Marga, Gnana Marga and Karma Marga together make up the true Christian spirituality. We should not be shy of acknowledging inheritance we have received from Indian spirituality just as we are not afraid of disowning some of the Hindu religious practices which are not conducive to our understanding and practice of spirituality.

Secondly, the CSI has received a lot of blessings from the missionaries who worked in our areas. Their commitment to Christ, their personal sacrifice for the mission work, their willingness to confront the political authorities of the time in the interest of justice for the under privileged should remain an inspiration for the present generation. More than that the faith that we have received, the congregations that they have built up and the Christian values that they have imparted have become foundational structure on which the emerging Church could be built.

The Christian faith that the Church received from the Western Missionaries also emphasized on individual spirituality and community spirituality. So, the Eastern and Western spirituality merged together in the Indian Church. The Western spirituality added one more dimension in the form of spirituality for others. Thus, the Protestant Church in India has inherited both Indian and Western Spirituality. The Indian Church, therefore, has become recipient of three dimensions of spirituality, namely, individual spirituality, community spirituality and spirituality for others which we have described as spiritualty for engagement.

Thirdly, the CSI is enjoying the fruits of the labour of Union Negotiators. Their vision for the United but a national Church was unwavering in the midst of manifold hurdles. Their efforts in achieving denominational unity led them on the path of convergence and not abolition, comprehension and not absorption, by retaining the salient features of each denomination. As a result, CSI has become a United Church with unity in diversity as its primary goal. The Union Negotiators also worked hard to establish a national church. For this purpose, they promoted three cardinal principles for the emerging Church, namely, self-governing, self-supporting and self-propagating Church. These have remained cardinal principles till today. Apart from this, the union negotiators have also left behind for us as a legacy of certain value systems. They are: the value of perseverance in the midst of frustrations; the value of accommodating points of view of others without sacrificing their own position; and the value of tolerating the dissenting voice by allowing free debate and discussion. These should remain model for the present day church.

Therefore, the CSI is a blessed Church. First and foremost it has the proud privilege of receiving divine call to continue Jesus' ministry and mission in Southern India. Secondly, it has inherited Indian spirituality. Thirdly, it has become recipient of heritage from Western spirituality. Fourthly, it enjoys the fruits of the labour of the union negotiators in receiving a united and national church as a gift.

The corporate life of CSI, her ministry to the faithful and her mission activities to the people around ever since its inauguration till today must be assessed in the light of the blessings that we as a corporate body have received. The CSI has transmitted several blessings into practical reality, but failed in many. Some of its strengths are noted here:

Firstly, the emphasis on individual spirituality, historically as well as existentially, has made the individual Christians to realize the importance of their commitment to Christ. Various wings of the Church beginning from the Sunday School and even the sermons reiterate the necessity for individual surrender to God. The emphasis is not on correct doctrine, but on Christ centred life - this has been the strength of CSI for the last seventy years of its existence.

Secondly, the love for the Church and the desire to belong to a faith community is quite strong among the members. The choice of membership in a particular congregation is not parish based neither is it pastor centric. People choose to belong to a particular congregation for various reasons, such as proximity to their residence, the language of worship, membership of their relatives, sentimental reasons etc. When once they become members of a particular congregation, they participate willingly, contribute liberally, build up fellowships freely. At times, they may be disappointed with the lack of pastoral care, or quality of leadership. In such cases, some may go in search of better spiritual atmosphere, but very rarely it would end up in change of membership. This is one of the reasons why the CSI Churches are always full and overflowing during the worship services.

Thirdly, with the emphasis on congregation of the faithful as one of the necessary elements in the life of the Church, the congregations are fairly free to decide the direction in which they should move with regard to ministry and mission. This strength could be particularly seen in the congregational life of the Dioceses which were devoid of episcopal leadership for some period of time.

Fourthly, the vision of the union negotiators in having a national church which is self-governing, self-supporting and self-propagating has been realized to a great extent. The Church is completely 'free from any control, legal or otherwise of any Church of society external to itself'. (Constitution, p. 26) The Church decides its policies and programmes and no external bodies can impose any of their policies and programmes on the CSI. A cursory glance at the recent consolidated statement of accounts submitted by the Hon. Treasurer to the CSI Synod and when compared with that of accounts of the formative years of CSI would reveal to what extent the Church has become self-supporting. Only for specific programmes such as child care, training programmes and programmes for environmental concerns, some Dioceses are receiving foreign funds which is a small percentage when compared to the finances raised locally. In this regard, it must be stated that the CSI congregations are 'giving congregations' contributing liberally for ministry and mission. The contributions from the people of God can be broadly categorized under the headings 'ministry, church construction and mission activities'. It must also be acknowledged that their contributions for Church construction and mission activities are more than their contributions to Church's ministry. The individual contributions to mission activities are made either through the Church or directly to mission organizations in which case the concerned organization accounts for the same and not the Church. It has been the policy of the Church from the beginning that no foreign personnel or foreign funds would be utilized for the purpose of mission work. So, no charges can be made against the Church seriously for using either the foreign personnel or foreign money for mission work. Mission work is carried out by Indians with the support from Indian Christians.

Fifthly, the vision of union negotiators in having a church which is united yet diverse in practice has become a reality now. Unity in diversity can be seen in almost every aspect of the Church's life. As pointed out earlier, even though we have a common liturgy, churches are allowed to have liturgical practice suitable to them. Even in terms of administrative practices there are differences. Till recently, the Constitution has allowed each Diocese to hold Diocesan Councils according to their earlier patterns. As a result, some were having Diocesan Councils once in two years, some once in three years and others once in four years. I understand a Constitutional amendment has been made recently which has not been circulated yet, prescribing that all the Diocesan Councils should meet once in three years. As a consequence, even the Synod would meet once in three years instead of two years. Unity in diversity is a major achievement in the CSI.

The Church of the present as well as the Church of the future, both depend on the understanding of the salvation achieved by Jesus of history. By implication, the Church of the present has an obligation to leave a legacy for the Church of the future, an uninterrupted salvation history. In order to achieve this, the Church of the present needs to assess its life, ministry and mission.

During the 1970's a new management principle called 'Management by objectives' became popular all over the world. It is being put into practice in almost all the important companies all over the world. The basic principles involved in Management by Objectives are as follows:

- Objective of the organization should be developed involving all the people in the organization at different levels.
- Each Manager should develop objectives and integrate them with other Managers and the whole Company.
- There should be periodic appraisal of performance.
- Line of authority should be clearly defined.

The idea of management by objectives was first promoted by Peter Drucker in his book '*The Practice of Management*' published in 1954. Drucker outlines a number of priorities for management. He points out that Managers are often caught up with 'the activity trap' that they often forget their original objectives. This seems to be true of the Church as well. We are either caught up with our day to day activities that we seldom stop to assess our activities in the light of original objective. Or the Church is caught up with the internal squabbles so much that it leaves no time and space to think of the purpose of our existence itself. Hence, in the following few pages we will make an attempt to assess the present day church in the light of the original objective for the sake of leaving an appropriate legacy for the future. The missionaries left behind a legacy of the 'mission focused church', the union negotiators entrusted to us a legacy of 'united church for mission' – what are we leaving for the future? – a hierarchical church? or a quarrelling church? or a church which is engaged in mission of God? If the last option is the right answer then we need to have some 'course correction' in the life, ministry and organization of the Church.

1. Objective

The objective is only one – that is 'God reconciling the world unto Himself'. This is a divine mandate. In order to achieve this goal, God has acted decisively in the person of Jesus Christ, who sacrificed his life on the Cross to bring human beings closer to God. But, God raised him from the dead and is now seated on the right hand of God. The Mission of God needs to be continued in this world even after Jesus' earthly ministry. For this purpose, God has chosen the Church as His instrument of carrying on His mission. The Church, therefore, has a privilege to participate in God's mission. The Church should never forget this call and privilege given by God to her. The objective, therefore, is to be involved in the mission of God which is given and not acquired.

In order to implement God's mission, Jesus used 'preaching, teaching and healing' as his methodology. Missionaries also used the same methodology, but their strategy of implementation differed from context to context. The Church, therefore, has fourfold responsibility:

- To be conscious of God's mission at all times.
- To understand the wholistic nature of mission as revealed in the Scriptures.
- To understand the socio-political-religious-cultural context of the nation and the communities the Church wishes to serve.
- To equip the congregations to become mission agents in their own context.

2. Mission Agents

That the whole Church needs to be mission focused is not disputed. However, we have to recognize that different responsibilities are entrusted to different people in the Church, all for the purpose of preparing and supporting the local Christian communities to become effective mission agents. In other words, to make each congregation to become a 'basic ecclesial community' engaged in mission. Basic ecclesial community is one where congregation members worship God spiritedly, share and care without hesitation with each other in the community willingly. A community engaged in mission is one where the congregation identifies the needy area or people, understand their problems and their aspirations, express solidarity with the people whom they are serving and plan and implement a suitable action programme along with the people concerned.

3. Role of the Leaders

a. A. Presbyters

To equip the congregations to become mission agents is the responsibility of the leaders, particularly of the pastors. A theologically trained person as a leader of the congregation, is a blessing the Church has inherited from the past. The purpose is to lead and guide the congregation. In this sense, a congregation is different from a business organization. The motive of a business organization is to make profit, whereas the motive of a congregation is service. A business organization recruits qualified and skilled people to achieve its goal, whereas, the congregation members are not professionally trained. Their only qualification is commitment to Christ, love for the Church and willingness to be involved in mission. Therefore, the task of the leader in the Church is not the control and management of the subordinates to ensure production of quality material – rather it is to train and equip the congregation members to become effective instruments of God. A pastor's role is varied. He/she leads the congregation members to have a meaningful encounter with Christ through innovative worship service. He/she unravels the mysteries underlying in the scripture by way of a scientific exposition of the text. He/she explains the complex but ever changing socio-political-economic and religious context of the people and the nation in a language that people can understand. Further, a pastor is effective only if he/she has personal rapport with the congregation members through pastoral visits. He/she has to become a guide, a friend, a counselor, depending on the situation. But, pastor is not a super human being to carry out all these tasks. Hence, he/she should build up a team ministry. In this sense, a pastor is not a Manager which seems to be the trend these days rather a pastor is a spiritual guide to the members of the congregation.

Only then his/her ministry in the congregation will be effective and he/she is able to equip the congregation in the required direction.

b. Bishops

A Presbyter can be effective in his/her ministry only if he/she is convinced of the support and encouragement from the Bishop. Working for people and with people brings the greatest satisfaction for the pastor. However, working with people of different temperaments and views also presents challenges. In such a situation, Pastors can only look for understanding, support and encouragement from the Bishop. It is often said that the Bishop is 'the pastor of pastors'. Pastors become Bishop's congregation. To look after the well-being of the pastors, to support them and encourage the pastors in their ministry is the primary responsibility of the Bishop. Hence, the Bishop should make himself available for pastors in discussing and guiding them in their ministry.

4. Structural Reforms

The objective of the Church is clear. The mission agents are identified. The role of the Presbyters and Bishops in equipping the congregation is noted. However, all these need to be supported by an organizational structure which promotes mission activities. As mentioned earlier, the organizational structure adopted by CSI is the most suitable structure for our context. It has incorporated salient features of the uniting churches into its structure. It has representation of Bishops, Presbyters and lay-people in the decision making bodies. It has scope for the participation of women and youth in these bodies. It is an independent church, whose decisions are subject to itself and not bound by external bodies outside of itself. It is a national church proving that our patriotism can never be questioned by fringe elements in society.

However, if mission of God is our objective, congregations are mission agents, presbyters are mission trainers and bishops are mission enablers, then there is need for structural reforms in our organization. Based on the discussions found in the earlier chapters, without going into the details a few areas that need reforms are pointed out here below:

- Powers and functions of various officers at different levels must be defined and accountability fixed whether appointed or elected or nominated to those offices.

- A suitable platform should be created within the church at different levels to listen, discuss, debate and find solution of the dissenting voices in the Church.
- One of the primary tasks of the Diocese and the Synod should be to promote unity in diversity not only in terms of spiritual unity but it should cover caste integration, cultural cohesion and class co-ordination.
- The unity in diversity in terms of property, financial and personnel administration should also take into consideration the demands of uniformity, accountability and transparency and suitable solution found.
- The mission objective should be stated clearly, mission agents identified and the role of Presbyters as Trainers and Bishops as Enablers identified, in the Constitution. Further, the Constitution should also state the role of the Diocese as mission organizers by promoting missions through congregations and the Synod as Mission Co-ordinator by publishing the work of the congregations through their official channels so that the whole Church is informed of the work done in local congregations and learn from one another.

Those of us who have accepted the Lordship of Jesus Christ are called upon to follow the way of the Cross in our spiritual journey. It is not an easy path. At times, it appears as though the demands of the Cross are difficult to fulfill. It demands that we as individual believers must surrender ourselves totally to Christ. This means removing 'self' from the centre and put 'Christ' at the centre of our lives. It requires of us to belong to a faith community and grow up by sharing and caring for one another. It also commands us to look beyond ourselves to serve the people around us. In this process, we face many temptations and hurdles due to our sinful nature and socio-cultural, economic and political pressures. Many a time, we yield to these temptations and pressures, either knowingly or unknowingly. However, we also need to recognize that we have rich spiritual treasures made available to us through inheritance, heritage, salvation history of our forefathers and mothers, and the exemplary life-style of thousands of ordinary but faithful members of the Church. When we draw spiritual resources from these treasures, then the way of the Cross becomes easy and blessed, both for us and the people whom we serve, because we are not journeying alone but we are journeying with God Himself. We are in the presence of God, enjoying the fellowship with God and human beings and remaining in the domain of God, being partners with God in His act of reconciling the world unto Himself.

The Church of South India has been a source of blessing for many, both within and outside the Church inspite of its manifold failure. It can continue its role of a blessing even in the days to come, provided individual members commit themselves completely to Christ, the congregations, the Dioceses and the Synod understand their role in God's Mission and the leaders at all levels promote reforms within the Church and motivate people for 'Spiritual Engagement' with the people around. It is my sincere prayer that God may continue to use the Church of South India and its people for His Mission in the world.